Inventory Optimization

Inventory management is a very tedious task faced by all the organizations in any sector of the economy. It makes decisions for policies, activities and procedures in order to make sure that the right amount of each item is held in stock at any time. Many industries suffer from indiscipline in ordering and production mismatch. Providing best policy to control such mismatch would be invaluable to them.

The primary objective of this book series is to explore various effective methods for inventory control and management using optimization techniques. The series will facilitate many potential authors to become the editors or author in this book series. The series focuses on an aspect of Operations Research which does not get the importance it deserves. Most researchers working on inventory management are publishing under different topics like decision making, computational techniques and optimization techniques, production engineering etc. The series will provide the much needed platform for them to publish and reach the correct audience.

Some of the areas that the series aims to cover are:

- Inventory optimization
- Inventory management models
- Retail inventory management
- Supply chain optimization
- Logistics management
- Reverse logistics and closed-loop supply chains
- Green supply chain
- Supply chain management
- Management and control of production and logistics systems
- Datamining techniques
- Bigdata analysis in inventory management
- Artificial intelligence
- Internet of things
- Operations and logistics management
- Production and inventory management
- Artificial intelligence and expert system
- Marketing, modelling and simulation
- Information technology

This book series will publish volumes of books which will be edited and reviewed by the reputed researcher of inventory optimization area. The beginner and experienced researchers both can publish their innovative research work in the form of edited chapters in the books of this series by getting in touch with the contact person. Practitioners and industrialist can share their real time experience bolstered with case studies. The objective is to provide a platform to the practitioners, educators, researchers and industrialist to publish their valuable work in the area of inventory optimization.

This series will be beneficial for practitioners, educators and researchers. It will also be helpful for retailers/managers for improving business functions and making more accurate and realistic decisions.

More information about this series at http://www.springer.com/series/16688

Nita H. Shah · Mandeep Mittal
Editors

Soft Computing in Inventory Management

Springer

Editors
Nita H. Shah
Department of Mathematics
University of Gujarat
Ahmedabad, Gujarat, India

Mandeep Mittal
Department of Mathematics
Amity Institute of Applied Sciences
Amity University
Noida, Uttar Pradesh, India

ISSN 2730-9347 ISSN 2730-9355 (electronic)
Inventory Optimization
ISBN 978-981-16-2155-0 ISBN 978-981-16-2156-7 (eBook)
https://doi.org/10.1007/978-981-16-2156-7

This Springer imprint is published by the registered company Springer Nature Singapore Pte Ltd.
The registered company address is: 152 Beach Road, #21-01/04 Gateway East, Singapore 189721, Singapore

Contents

Editors and Contributors

About the Editors

Prof. Nita H. Shah heads the Department of Mathematics in Gujarat University, India. She is a post-doctoral visiting research fellow of University of New Brunswick, Canada. Professor Nita's research interests include inventory modeling in supply chain, robotic modeling, mathematical modeling of infectious diseases, image processing, dynamical systems and its applications etc. She has completed 3-UGC sponsored projects. She has published 13 monograph, five textbooks, and 475+ peer-reviewed research papers. Her five edited books have been published by international publishers such as Springer. She has guided 28 Ph.D. students and 15 M.Phil. students till now. She has travelled in USA, Singapore, Canada, South Africa, Malaysia, and Indonesia for lectures and visiting faculty posts. She was Vice-President of Operational Research Society of India, and council member of Indian Mathematical Society.

Dr. Mandeep Mittal started his career in the education industry in 2000 with Amity Group. Currently, he is working as Head and Associate Professor in the Department of Mathematics, Amity Institute of Applied Sciences, Amity University Uttar Pradesh, Noida. He earned his post-doctorate from Hanyang University, South Korea, in 2016, Ph.D. (2012) from the University of Delhi, India, and post-graduation in Applied Mathematics from IIT Roorkee, India (2000). He has published more than 70 research papers in international journals and proceedings papers in international conferences. He has co-edited five research books with international publishers such as Springer. Awarded the Best Faculty Award by the Amity School of Engineering and Technology, New Delhi for the year 2016–2017, he has so far guided four Ph.D. scholars, and four students working with him in the area of Inventory Control and Management. He also served as Dean of Students Activities at Amity School of Engineering and Technology, Delhi, for nine years, and worked as Head, Department of Mathematics in the same institute for a year. He is a member of editorial boards of *Revista Investigacion Operacional*, *Journal of Control and Systems Engineering*, and *Journal of Advances in Management Sciences and Information Systems.*

Contributors

Aastha Department of Mathematics and Statistics, Banasthali Vidyapith, Banasthali, India

Mohammed Abid SRM Institute of Science and Technology, Ghaziabad, Uttar Pradesh, India

Olufemi Adetunji Department of Industrial and Systems Engineering, University of Pretoria, Pretoria, South Africa

Navin Ahlawat Department of Computer Science, SRM Institute of Science and Technology, Ghaziabad, Uttar Pradesh, India

Rafid Alrikabi Department of Industrial and Systems Engineering, University of Pretoria, Pretoria, South Africa

Tripti Chakrabarti Department of Applied Mathematics, University of Calcutta, Kolkata, India;
Basic Science, Techno India University, Kolkata, India

Urmila Chaudhari Government Polytechnic Dahod, Dahod, Gujarat, India

Vinti Dhaka Department of Mathematics and Statistics, Banasthali Vidyapith, Banasthali, India

Mrudul Y. Jani Department of Applied Sciences, Faculty of Engineering and Technology, Parul University, Vadodara, Gujarat, India

Mahesh Kumar Jayaswal Department of Mathematics and Statistics, Banasthali Vidyapith, Banasthali, Rajasthan, India

Aditi Khanna Department of Operational Research, University of Delhi, Delhi, India

Navneet Kumar Lamba Department of Mathematics, S.L.P.M., Mandhal, R.T.M. Nagpur University, Nagpur, India

Poonam Mishra Department of Mathematics, School of Technology, Pandit Deendayal Petroleum University, Gandhinagar, Gujarat, India

Mandeep Mittal Amity Institute of Applied Sciences, Amity University Uttar Pradesh (AUUP), Noida, Uttar Pradesh, India

Monika K. Naik Vadodara, Gujarat, India

Sarla Pareek Department of Mathematics and Statistics, Banasthali Vidyapith, Banasthali, India

Milan B. Patel Department of Mathematics, Gujarat University, Ahmedabad, Gujarat, India

Nita H. Shah Department of Mathematics, Gujarat University, Ahmedabad, Gujarat, India

Azharuddin Shaikh Institute of Management, Nirma University, Ahmedabad, India

Srabani Shee Department of Applied Mathematics, University of Calcutta, Kolkata, India

Farah Siddiqui Department of Operational Research, University of Delhi, Delhi, India

Anupam Swami Department of Mathematics, Government Post Graduate College, Sambhal, Uttar Pradesh, India

Isha Talati Department of Engineering and Physical Sciences, Institute of Advanced Research, Koba Institutional Area, Gandhinagar, India

Venkata S. S. Yadavalli Department of Industrial and Systems Engineering, University of Pretoria, Pretoria, South Africa

Ajay Singh Yadav Department of Mathematics, SRM Institute of Science and Technology, Ghaziabad, Uttar Pradesh, India

Rita Yadav Department of Mathematics and Statistics, Banasthali Vidyapith, Banasthali, Rajasthan, India

Shikha Yadav Department of Operational Research, University of Delhi, Delhi, India

Retailer's Optimal Ordering Policy Under Supplier Credits When Demand is Fuzzy and Cloud Fuzzy

Nita H. Shah and Milan B. Patel

Abstract This paper deals with retailer's optimal ordering inventory model under fuzzy and cloud fuzzy environment. In this study, crisp model is considered first and then by assuming demand rate as triangular fuzzy number and cloud triangular fuzzy number the model is formulated and solved. Extension of Yager's ranking index is utilized for defuzzification in cloud fuzzy model. The objective of the present work is to minimize the total inventory cost and to compare the results obtained by the existing crisp model. With the help of numerical examples for different cases under different environments, optimal solutions are compared and analysed by performing sensitivity analysis. For better visualization of results, graphical representation of solutions is given.

Keywords Inventory · Fuzzy demand · Cloud fuzzy demand · Deterioration · Delay in payments

1 Introduction

Among many of the factors affecting the performance of a business firm, management of inventory system is considered to be one of the most important aspects, as it directly affects the profit of the firm and the satisfaction of customers. From a small retailer shopkeeper to large industries always keep on applying new business tactics in order to attract new customers and to increase sales of their products. Out of these many business tactics, an idea implemented by many such suppliers is to provide a cash discount or grace period (i.e. trade credit period) to their customers in order to pay for the consignment. In such cases, it becomes indispensable for the retailer to make a balance between the situation of stock-out and the situation of overstocking. This study aims at modelling such phenomenon under uncertain demand rate and to provide retailers an optimal ordering policy when supplier offers some trade credit period.

N. H. Shah (✉) · M. B. Patel
Department of Mathematics, Gujarat University, Ahmedabad, Gujarat 380009, India

N. H. Shah and M. Mittal (eds.), *Soft Computing in Inventory Management*, Inventory Optimization, https://doi.org/10.1007/978-981-16-2156-7_1

After the pioneering work of Harris (1913) of developing economic order quantity (EOQ) model, many researchers have devoted their efforts towards modelling the inventory system. Haley and Higgins (1973) introduced a trade credit policy of an inventory system having constant demand. Goyal (1985) firstly extended an EOQ model by allowing permissible delay in payments. For more literature in the field of trade credit policy under the crisp environment, one may refer to the works of Shah (1993), Aggarwal and Jaggi (1995), Liao et al. (2000), Chang and Teng (2004), Teng (2009), Shah and Cardenas-Barron (2015), Giri and Sharma (2016), and Mahata et al. (2020).

Since the decision-making process involves human thoughts and reasoning, it always has some imprecision in it. Fuzzy set theory introduced by Zadeh (1965) is the most powerful tool to express uncertainties. The above-mentioned inventory research papers were formulated by assuming the parameters to be crisp. However, to make these models more realistic and applicable, one needs to incorporate the fuzzy set theory. Park (1987) extended an EOQ model under fuzzy sense. Since then, many researchers have contributed significantly in developing inventory modelling under fuzzy sense. Following are some of the research papers related to this study.

Mahata and Goswami (2007) developed an EOQ model for deteriorating item by allowing delay in payments in fuzzy sense. The paper also generalizes the previous publications in this direction. Ouyang et al. (2010) worked on an optimal inventory policy by considering rate of interest earned, rate of interest charged and deterioration rate as triangular fuzzy number. Mahata and Mahata (2011) studied an inventory model for a retailer under two-level trade credit in fuzzy sense. Shah et al. (2012) established a fuzzy EOQ model by allowing demand rate, ordering cost and selling price as fuzzy quantities. They have used centre of gravity method for defuzzification. Jaggi et al. (2014) gave an inventory model in which they have used trapezoidal fuzzy numbers to represent uncertainty in some parameters. Bag and Chakraborty (2014) worked on a fuzzy inventory model with bi-level trade credit policy. Sujatha and Parvathi (2015) discussed an inventory model for variable deteriorating items with time-dependent Weibull demand rate by allowing shortages. Majumder et al. (2015) studied an economic production quantity (EPQ) model under partial trade credit by incorporating crisp as well as fuzzy demand rate. Das et al. (2015) developed an integrated inventory model for supplier and retailer with fuzzy credit period. Yadav et al. (2015) studied retailer's inventory model by discussing the effects of the inflation rate, deterioration rate and delay in payment on total profit of the inventory. Shukla and Suthar (2016) worked on fuzzy economic ordering policy to minimize total cost by taking into account the items having uncertain maximum lifetime. Huang et al. (2019) developed a vendor–buyer ordering policy of perishable items under crisp and fuzzy environment.

The concept of fuzzy number utilized in the above-mentioned papers dealing with fuzzy inventory modelling assumes fuzziness to be constant forever which may not be the case in real scenario. Decision-maker can make better decision over time as he gains experiences from the previous consignments. Owing to this idea, the concept of cloud fuzzy number is introduced recently by De and Beg (2016) and applied by some researchers in order to make the inventory models more realistic. De and Mahata

(2016) introduced the concept of cloudy fuzzy number and formulated an inventory model with backorder. Berman et al. (2017) formulated a backordered inventory model with inflation under cloudy fuzzy environment. Karmakar et al. (2018) worked on extension of classical EOQ model under cloudy fuzzy demand rate. De and Mahata (2019a) studied cloudy fuzzy EOQ model for imperfect quality items. Further, De and Mahata (2019b) developed EOQ model under fuzzy monsoon demand. Maiti (2019) utilized the concept of cloudy fuzzy number and studied economic production lot-size model with fixed set-up cost with cloudy fuzzy demand rate.

The present study is an attempt to extend Chang and Teng (2004) model under fuzzy and cloud fuzzy demand rate. To study the model under fuzzy environment, demand rate is assumed to be triangular fuzzy number. For the extension of model under cloud fuzzy environment, cloud triangular fuzzy number is employed. For defuzzification in fuzzy environment, the researchers have used Yager's ranking index method (1981).

2 Notations and Assumptions

Following notations and assumptions are considered while formulating mathematical models.

2.1 Notations

h	holding cost (in \$/unit/year)
c	purchase cost (in \$/unit)
s	sales price (in \$/unit)
A	ordering cost (in \$/order)
θ	rate of deterioration $0 \leq \theta < 1$
r	rate at which cash discount is given $0 < r < 1$
Ic	rate at which interest is charged (in %/year)
Ie	rate at which interest is earned (in %/year)
M_1	1st credit limit for retailer
M_2	2nd credit limit for retailer
T	cycle length (in year)
R	demand rate per year
$\overline{R}$	fuzzy demand rate per year
$\widetilde{R}$	cloud fuzzy demand rate per year
Q	order quantity

(continued)

(continued)

h	holding cost (in \$/unit/year)
$\overline{Q}$	fuzzy order quantity
$\widetilde{Q}$	cloud fuzzy order quantity
K	total inventory cost (in \$/year)
$\overline{K}$	total fuzzy inventory cost (in \$/year)
$\widetilde{K}$	total cloud fuzzy inventory cost (in \$/year)

2.2 *Assumptions*

(i) Rate of deterioration is considered to be constant. Further, no replenishment or repair of deteriorated items occurs during planning horizon.
(ii) Retailer has two choices for payment. Either pay at credit limit M_1 with discounted price $(1-r)c$ with $0 < r < 1$ or pay at credit limit M_2 without any discount. $(M_1 < M_2)$
(iii) Up to the credit period (i.e. M_1 or M_2), the amount generated by sales is deposited in an interest earning account. At the end of this period, retailer pays the amount generated in the account to supplier. If this amount is not sufficient to settle payment, the retailer starts paying off the remaining amount whenever he has money generated by sales.
(iv) Shortages are not permitted.
(v) Demand rate for crisp model is constant.
(vi) For fuzzy and cloud fuzzy model, demand is not precise and characterized by triangular fuzzy number $\overline{R} = (R_1, R_2, R_3)$ and cloud triangular fuzzy number $\widetilde{R} = \left(R_2\left(1 - \frac{\beta}{1+t}\right), R_2, R_2\left(1 + \frac{\gamma}{1+t}\right)\right)$, respectively.
(vii) Planning horizon is infinite.

3 Preliminary Concepts

3.1 *Triangular Fuzzy Number (TFN)*

A triangular fuzzy number (TFN) defined on the set of real numbers $\mathbb{R}$ can be expressed as $\overline{R} = (R_1, R_2, R_3)$. Its membership function can be defined as

$$f(\overline{R}) = \begin{cases} \frac{x-R_1}{R_2-R_1}, & R_1 \le x \le R_2 \\ \frac{x-R_3}{R_2-R_3}, & R_2 \le x \le R_3 \\ 0, & \text{otherwise} \end{cases} \tag{1}$$

3.2 α- Cut of TFN

α- cut of TFN $\overline{R} = (R_1, R_2, R_3)$ is a crisp set $\alpha_{\overline{R}} = [L_\alpha, R_\alpha]$, where $L_\alpha = R_1 - \alpha(R_1 - R_2)$ is known as left α- cut and $R_\alpha = R_3 - \alpha(R_3 - R_2)$ is known as right α- cut $(0 \leq \alpha \leq 1)$.

3.3 Cloud Triangular Fuzzy Number (CTFN)

A triangular fuzzy number is known as cloud triangular fuzzy number (CTFN) if the set converge to a crisp number as time tends to infinity.

$$\widetilde{R} = \left(R_2\left(1 - \frac{\beta}{1+t}\right), R_2, R_2\left(1 + \frac{\gamma}{1+t}\right)\right) \tag{2}$$

where $\beta, \gamma \in (0, 1)$ and $t > 0$. From Eq. (2), it can be seen that as $t \to \infty$, $\widetilde{R} \to \{R_2\}$.

Membership function of CTFN can be defined as follows:

$$g(\widetilde{R}, t) = \begin{cases} \frac{x - R_2\left(1 - \frac{\beta}{1+t}\right)}{\frac{\beta R_2}{1+t}}, & R_2\left(1 - \frac{\beta}{1+t}\right) \leq x \leq R_2 \\ \frac{R_2\left(1 + \frac{\gamma}{1+t}\right) - x}{\frac{\gamma R_2}{1+t}}, & R_2 \leq x \leq R_2\left(1 + \frac{\gamma}{1+t}\right) \\ 0, & \text{otherwise} \end{cases} \tag{3}$$

3.4 Left and Right α- cut of CTFN

Left and right α- cut of CTFN can be expressed as

$$L_{\alpha,t} = R_2\left(1 - \frac{\beta}{1+t}\right) + \frac{\alpha\beta}{1+t}R_2 \quad \& \quad R_{\alpha,t} = R_2\left(1 + \frac{\gamma}{1+t}\right) - \frac{\alpha\gamma}{1+t}R_2 \tag{4}$$

respectively.

3.5 Yager's Ranking Index Method (1981)

According to Yager's ranking index method, defuzzification for a TFN can be given by

$$YRI(\overline{R}) = \frac{1}{2}\int_{0}^{1} (L_\alpha + R_\alpha)\, d\alpha \tag{5}$$

where L_α and R_α are left and right α- cut of TFN, respectively. By substituting the value of L_α and R_α, Eq. (5) reduces to

$$YRI(\overline{R}) = \frac{1}{4}(R_1 + 2R_2 + R_3) \tag{6}$$

3.6 Yager's Ranking Index Method for CTFN

It is an extension of Yager's ranking index method for TFN given by De and Mahata (2017). By this method, defuzzification of CTFN can be given by

$$YRI(\widetilde{R}) = \frac{1}{2T}\int_{\alpha=0}^{\alpha=1}\int_{t=0}^{t=T} (L_{\alpha,t} + R_{\alpha,t})\, d\alpha\, dt \tag{7}$$

Substituting the value of left and right α- cut of CTFN from Eqs. (4) and (7) reduces to

$$YRI(\widetilde{R}) = R_2\left(1 - \frac{(\beta-\gamma)}{4}\frac{\log(1+T)}{T}\right) \tag{8}$$

4 Mathematical Modelling

As per the model given by Chang and Teng (2004), total inventory cost for different cases under crisp environment is as follows:

Case A: $T \geq M_1$

$$\begin{aligned} K_A(T) = {} & \frac{A}{T} + \frac{R[h + c\theta(1-r)]}{\theta^2 T}\left(\theta T + \frac{\theta^2 T^2}{2}\right) - \frac{hR}{\theta} - \frac{sIeR}{2T}M_1^2 \\ & + \frac{IcR}{2sT}\left[\frac{c(1-r)}{\theta}\left(\theta T + \frac{\theta^2 T^2}{2}\right) - sM_1\left(1 + \frac{IeM_1}{2}\right)\right]^2 \end{aligned} \tag{9}$$

Case B: $T < M_1$

$$K_B(T) = \frac{A}{T} + \frac{R[h + c\theta(1-r)]}{\theta^2 T}\left(\theta T + \frac{\theta^2 T^2}{2}\right) - \frac{hR}{\theta} - sIeR\left(M_1 - \frac{T}{2}\right) \tag{10}$$

Case C: $T \geq M_2$

$$K_C(T) = \frac{A}{T} + \frac{R(h + c\theta)}{\theta^2 T}\left(\theta T + \frac{\theta^2 T^2}{2}\right) - \frac{hR}{\theta} - \frac{sIeR}{2T}M_2^2 + \frac{IcR}{2sT}\left[\frac{c}{\theta}\left(\theta T + \frac{\theta^2 T^2}{2}\right) - sM_2\left(1 + \frac{IeM_2}{2}\right)\right]^2 \tag{11}$$

Case D: $T < M_2$

$$K_D(T) = \frac{A}{T} + \frac{R(h + c\theta)}{\theta^2 T}\left(\theta T + \frac{\theta^2 T^2}{2}\right) - \frac{hR}{\theta} - sIeR\left(M_2 - \frac{T}{2}\right) \tag{12}$$

Order quantity can be expressed as

$$Q = \frac{R}{\theta}\left(e^{\theta T} - 1\right) \tag{13}$$

4.1 Formulation of Fuzzy Mathematical Model

In order to extend Chang and Teng (2004) model under fuzzy environment, demand is assumed to be triangular fuzzy number $\overline{R} = (R_1, R_2, R_3)$. Fuzzifying the expression given in Eq. (9), the problem under fuzzy environment for Case A reduces to

$$\text{Minimize } \overline{K_A}(T) = \frac{A}{T} + \frac{\overline{R}[h + c\theta(1-r)]}{\theta^2 T}\left(\theta T + \frac{\theta^2 T^2}{2}\right) - \frac{h\overline{R}}{\theta} - \frac{sIe\overline{R}}{2T}M_1^2 + \frac{Ic\overline{R}}{2sT}\left[\frac{c(1-r)}{\theta}\left(\theta T + \frac{\theta^2 T^2}{2}\right) - sM_1\left(1 + \frac{IeM_1}{2}\right)\right]^2 \tag{14}$$

$$\text{with respect to } \overline{Q} = \frac{\overline{R}}{\theta}\left(e^{\theta T} - 1\right) \tag{15}$$

With the help of Eq. (1), membership function for fuzzy objective function and fuzzy order quantity can be expressed as follows:

(i) Membership function for total fuzzy inventory cost:

$$f_1(K) = \begin{cases} \frac{K-K_1}{K_2-K_1}, & K_1 \le K \le K_2 \\ \frac{K-K_3}{K_2-K_3}, & K_2 \le K \le K_3 \\ 0, & \text{otherwise} \end{cases} \tag{16}$$

where K_i for $i = 1, 2, 3$ can be obtained by replacing R with R_i in fuzzy inventory cost function.

(ii) Membership function for fuzzy order quantity:

$$f_2(Q) = \begin{cases} \frac{Q-Q_1}{Q_2-Q_1}, & Q_1 \le Q \le Q_2 \\ \frac{Q-Q_3}{Q_2-Q_3}, & Q_2 \le Q \le Q_3 \\ 0, & \text{otherwise} \end{cases} \tag{17}$$

where $Q_i = \frac{R_i}{\theta}(e^{\theta T} - 1)$ for $i = 1, 2, 3$.

Other cases can be formulated under fuzzy environment similarly.

By applying Yager's ranking index method for TFN (see Sect. 1.3.5), defuzzified value of total fuzzy inventory cost and fuzzy order quantity for each case is obtained. Defuzzified value of total fuzzy inventory cost for Case A, Case B, Case C and Case D is

$$I(\overline{K_A}) = \frac{A}{T} + (R_1 + 2R_2 + R_3)\left\{ \begin{array}{l} \frac{1}{4\theta^2}\left[(h + c\theta(1-r))\left(\theta + \frac{1}{2}\theta^2 T\right)\right] - \frac{h}{4\theta} - \frac{sIeM_1^2}{8T} \\ + \frac{Ic}{8sT}\left[c(1-r)\left(T + \frac{1}{2}\theta T^2\right) - sM_1\left(1 + \frac{IeM_1}{2}\right)\right]^2 \end{array} \right\} \tag{18}$$

$$I(\overline{K_B}) = \frac{A}{T} + (R_1 + 2R_2 + R_3)\left\{ \begin{array}{c} \frac{1}{4\theta^2}\left[(h + c\theta(1-r))\left(\theta + \frac{1}{2}\theta^2 T\right)\right] - \frac{h}{4\theta} \\ - \frac{sIe}{4}\left(M_1 - \frac{T}{2}\right) \end{array} \right\} \tag{19}$$

$$I(\overline{K_C}) = \frac{A}{T} + (R_1 + 2R_2 + R_3)\left\{ \begin{array}{l} \frac{1}{4\theta^2}\left[(h + c\theta)\left(\theta + \frac{1}{2}\theta^2 T\right)\right] - \frac{h}{4\theta} - \frac{sIeM_2^2}{8T} \\ + \frac{Ic}{8sT}\left[c\left(T + \frac{1}{2}\theta T^2\right) - sM_2\left(1 + \frac{IeM_2}{2}\right)\right]^2 \end{array} \right\} \tag{20}$$

$$I(\overline{K_D}) = \frac{A}{T} + (R_1 + 2R_2 + R_3)\left\{ \frac{1}{4\theta^2}\left[(h + c\theta)\left(\theta + \frac{1}{2}\theta^2 T\right)\right] - \frac{h}{4\theta} - \frac{sIe}{4}\left(M_2 - \frac{T}{2}\right) \right\} \tag{21}$$

respectively.

Defuzzified value of fuzzy order quantity can be represented as

$$I(\overline{Q}) = \frac{1}{4\theta}(R_1 + 2R_2 + R_3)\left(e^{\theta T} - 1\right) \tag{22}$$

4.2 Formulation of Cloud Fuzzy Mathematical Model

Fuzzifying the expression given in Eq. (9), the problem under cloud fuzzy environment is given by

$$\text{Minimize } \widetilde{K}_A(T) = \frac{A}{T} + \frac{\widetilde{R}[h + c\theta(1-r)]}{\theta^2 T}\left(\theta T + \frac{\theta^2 T^2}{2}\right) - \frac{h\widetilde{R}}{\theta} - \frac{sIe\widetilde{R}}{2T}M_1^2 + \frac{Ic\widetilde{R}}{2sT}\left[\frac{c(1-r)}{\theta}\left(\theta T + \frac{\theta^2 T^2}{2}\right) - sM_1\left(1 + \frac{IeM_1}{2}\right)\right]^2 \tag{23}$$

$$\text{with respect } to \quad \widetilde{Q} = \frac{\widetilde{R}}{\theta}\left(e^{\theta T} - 1\right) \tag{24}$$

With the help of Eq. (3), membership function for cloud fuzzy objective function and cloud fuzzy order quantity can be expressed as follows:

(i) Membership function for total cloud fuzzy inventory cost:

$$g_1(K, T) = \begin{cases} \frac{K-K_1}{K_2-K_1}, & K_1 \le K \le K_2 \\ \frac{K-K_3}{K_2-K_3}, & K_2 \le K \le K_3 \\ 0, & \text{otherwise} \end{cases} \tag{25}$$

where K_1, K_2, K_3 can be obtained by replacing $\widetilde{R}$ with $R_2\left(1 - \frac{\beta}{1+t}\right)$, R_2 & $R_2\left(1 + \frac{\gamma}{1+t}\right)$,respectively, in Eq. 23.

(ii) Membership function for cloud fuzzy order quantity:

$$g_2(Q, T) = \begin{cases} \frac{Q-Q_1}{Q_2-Q_1}, & Q_1 \le Q \le Q_2 \\ \frac{Q-Q_3}{Q_2-Q_3}, & Q_2 \le Q \le Q_3 \\ 0, & \text{otherwise} \end{cases} \tag{26}$$

where $Q_1 = \frac{1}{\theta}R_2\left(1 - \frac{\beta}{1+T}\right)\left(e^{\theta T} - 1\right)$, $Q_2 = \frac{R_2}{\theta}\left(e^{\theta T} - 1\right)$ & $Q_3 = \frac{1}{\theta}R_2\left(1 + \frac{\gamma}{1+T}\right)\left(e^{\theta T} - 1\right)$

Defuzzified value of cloud fuzzy total inventory cost and cloud fuzzy order quantity as per extension of Yager's ranking index method can be derived using the following equation.

$$I\left(\widetilde{K}\right) = \frac{1}{T}\int_{t=0}^{t=T} \frac{1}{4}(K_1 + 2K_2 + K_3)\,dt \tag{27}$$

where the value of $\frac{1}{4}(K_1 + 2K_2 + K_3)$ for different cases is as follows:

For Case A:

$$\frac{1}{4}(K_1+2K_2+K_3)=\frac{A}{T}+\left(4-\frac{(\beta-\gamma)}{1+T}\right)\left\{\begin{array}{l}\frac{1}{4\theta^2}\left[R_2(h+c\theta(1-r))\left(\theta+\frac{1}{2}\theta^2T\right)\right]\\+\frac{IcR_2}{8sT}\left[c(1-r)\left(T+\frac{1}{2}\theta T^2\right)-sM_1\left(1+\frac{IeM_1}{2}\right)\right]^2\\-\frac{hR_2}{4\theta}-\frac{sIeR_2M_1^2}{8T}\end{array}\right\} \tag{28}$$

For Case B:

$$\frac{1}{4}(K_1+2K_2+K_3)=\frac{A}{T}+\left(4-\frac{(\beta-\gamma)}{1+T}\right)\left\{\begin{array}{l}\frac{R_2}{4\theta^2}\left[(h+c\theta(1-r))\left(\theta+\frac{1}{2}\theta^2T\right)\right]-\frac{hR_2}{4\theta}\\-\frac{sIeR_2}{4}\left(M_1-\frac{T}{2}\right)\end{array}\right\} \tag{29}$$

For Case C:

$$\frac{1}{4}(K_1+2K_2+K_3)=\frac{A}{T}+\left(4-\frac{(\beta-\gamma)}{1+T}\right)\left\{\begin{array}{l}\frac{R_2}{4\theta^2}\left[(h+c\theta)\left(\theta+\frac{1}{2}\theta^2T\right)\right]-\frac{hR_2}{4\theta}-\frac{sIeR_2M_2^2}{8T}\\+\frac{R_2Ic}{8sT}\left[c\left(T+\frac{1}{2}\theta T^2\right)-sM_2\left(1+\frac{IeM_2}{2}\right)\right]^2\end{array}\right\} \tag{30}$$

For Case D:

$$\frac{1}{4}(K_1+2K_2+K_3)=\frac{A}{T}+\left(4-\frac{(\beta-\gamma)}{T}\right)\left\{\begin{array}{l}\frac{R_2}{4\theta^2}\left[(h+c\theta)\left(\theta+\frac{1}{2}\theta^2T\right)\right]-\frac{hR_2}{4\theta}\\-\frac{sR_2Ie}{4}\left(M_2-\frac{T}{2}\right)\end{array}\right\} \tag{31}$$

Defuzzified value of cloud fuzzy order quantity by using extension of Yager's ranking index method can be expressed by

$$I(\widetilde{Q})=\frac{R_c}{\theta}\left(e^{\theta T}-1\right)\text{ where, }R_c=R_2\left(1-\frac{(\beta-\gamma)\log(1+T)}{4T}\right) \tag{32}$$

5 Numerical Analysis and Proof of Convexity

Along with the proof of convexity in all four cases under fuzzy and cloud fuzzy environment, this section consists of numerical examples in all four cases in order to compare the results obtained in Chang and Teng model with the fuzzy and cloud fuzzy model derived in the present study.

Example 1: (for Case A) Let us consider the value of various parameters for crisp, fuzzy and cloud fuzzy environment as follows: $R = 1000$ units/year, $h = \$\,3$/unit/year, $A = \$\,10$/order, $Ic = 9\%$/year, $Ie = 3\%$/year, $c = \$\,20$/unit,

$s = \$30$/unit, $r = 0.02$, $\theta = 0.03$, $M_1 = 30/365$ years. For fuzzy model, consider $R_1 = 950$, $R_2 = 1000$, $R_3 = 1040$, and for cloud fuzzy model, let $\beta = 0.20$, $\gamma = 0.14$.

Example 2: (for Case B) Consider $R = 1000$ units/year, $h = \$3$/unit/year, $A = \$10$/order, $Ie = 3\%$/year, $c = \$20$/unit, $s = \$30$/unit, $r = 0.02$, $\theta = 0.03$, $M_1 = 30/365$ years. For fuzzy model, consider $R_1 = 950, R_2 = 1000$, $R_3 = 1040$, and for cloud fuzzy model, let $\beta = 0.95$, $\gamma = 0.10$.

Example 3: (for Case C) Consider $R = 1000$ units/year, $h = \$4$/unit/year, $A = \$25$/order, $Ic = 9\%$/year, $Ie = 6\%$/year, $c = \$30$/unit, $s = \$45$/unit, $r = 0.02$, $\theta = 0.03$, $M_1 = 20/365$ years, $M_2 = 30/365$ years. For fuzzy model, consider $R_1 = 950$, $R_2 = 1000$, $R_3 = 1040$, and for cloud fuzzy model, let $\beta = 0.14$, $\gamma = 0.15$.

Example 4: (for Case D) Consider $R = 1000$ units/year, $h = \$6$/unit/year, $A = \$10$/order, $Ie = 6\%$/year, $c = \$20$/unit, $s = \$30$/unit, $r = 0.02$, $\theta = 0.03$, $M_2 = 30/365$ years. For fuzzy model, consider $R_1 = 950$, $R_2 = 1000$, $R_3 = 1040$, and for cloud fuzzy model, let $\beta = 0.18\gamma = 0.14$.

Using the method explained in Sects. 1.4.1 and 1.4.2 for fuzzy and cloud fuzzy model, respectively, the values of decision variables are obtained under different environments for Example 1, Example 2, Example 3 and Example 4 and results are shown in Table 1. Also, the comparison between all cases under a different environment is graphically represented in Fig. 1.

Proof of convexity of total inventory cost function for fuzzy and cloud fuzzy model for Case A, Case B, Case C and Case D is shown in Figs. 2, 3, 4, 5, respectively.

Table 1 Optimal solutions for all cases under different environments

Case	Environment	Cycle time T (in year)	Order quantity Q	Total cost K (in \$)
A ($T \geq M_1$)	Crisp	0.08241	82.51	19,845.49
	Fuzzy	0.08247	82.37	19,796.18
	Cloud fuzzy	0.19573	195.14	19,751.01
B ($T < M_1$)	Crisp	0.0667	66.82	19,825.62
	Fuzzy	0.0668	66.73	19,776.43
	Cloud fuzzy	0.0820	74.91	15,961.41
C ($T \geq M_2$)	Crisp	0.0940	94.15	30,407.54
	Fuzzy	0.0941	94.42	30,332.19
	Cloud fuzzy	0.5328	537.17	30,322.53
D ($T < M_2$)	Crisp	0.0487	48.83	20,261.93
	Fuzzy	0.0488	48.76	20,211.79
	Cloud fuzzy	0.0812	80.96	20,129.51

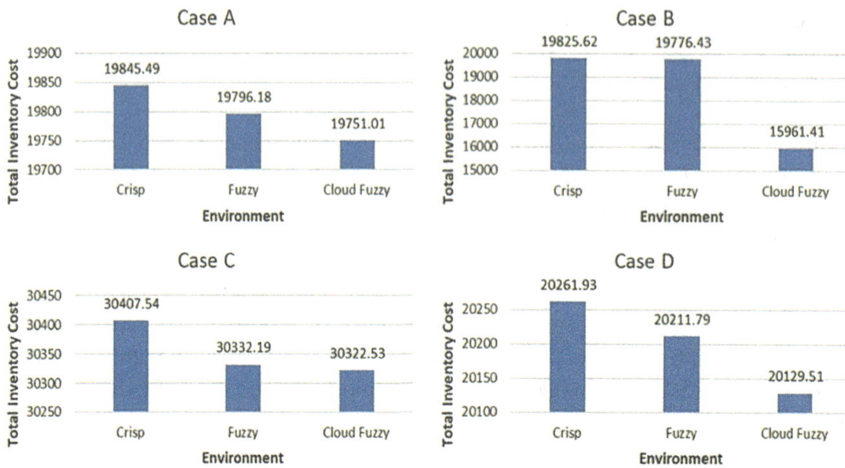

Fig. 1 Total inventory cost of all cases under different environments

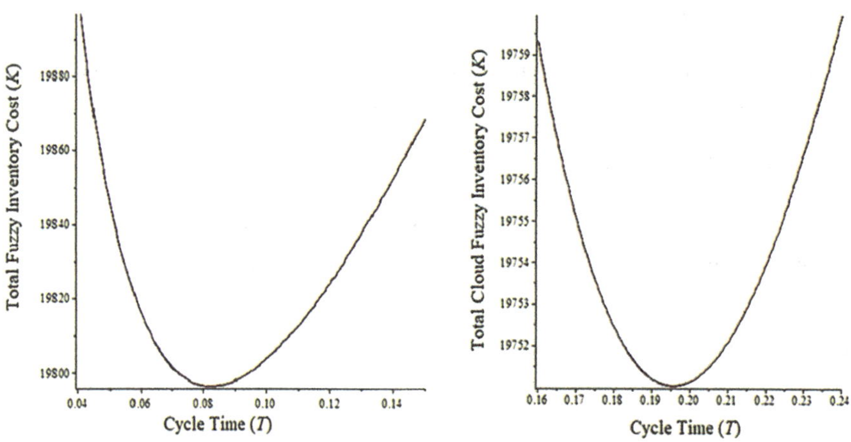

Fig. 2 Convexity of objective function of Case A under fuzzy and cloud fuzzy environment

6 Sensitivity Analysis

To figure out the most critical inventory parameters in fuzzy and cloud fuzzy model, sensitivity analysis is performed by changing one inventory parameter by −20%, −10%, 10% and 20% while keeping other parameters unchanged.

Sensitivity analysis for Case A as shown in Figs. 6 and 7 reveals that holding cost and order cost are highly sensitive parameters under both environments. It can also be observed from the graphs that increase in selling price also increases the total inventory cost significantly, while the period of cash discount has negligible effect on the total inventory cost. Increase of deterioration rate increases the total cost. Further,

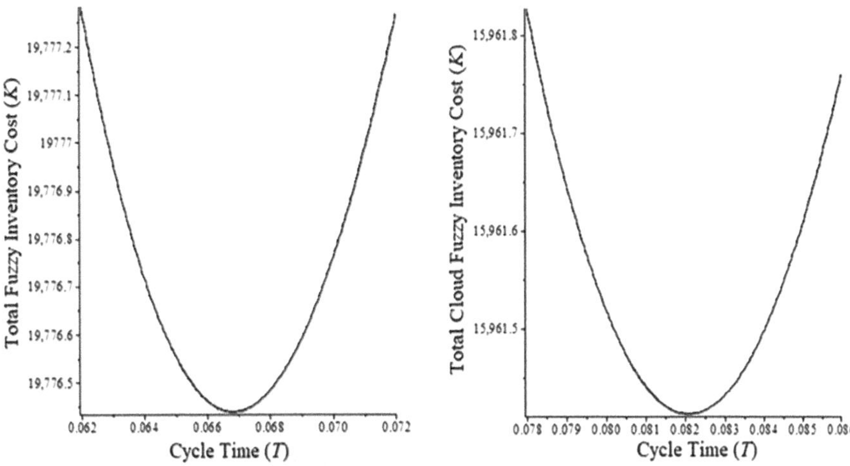

Fig. 3 Convexity of objective function of Case B under fuzzy and cloud fuzzy environment

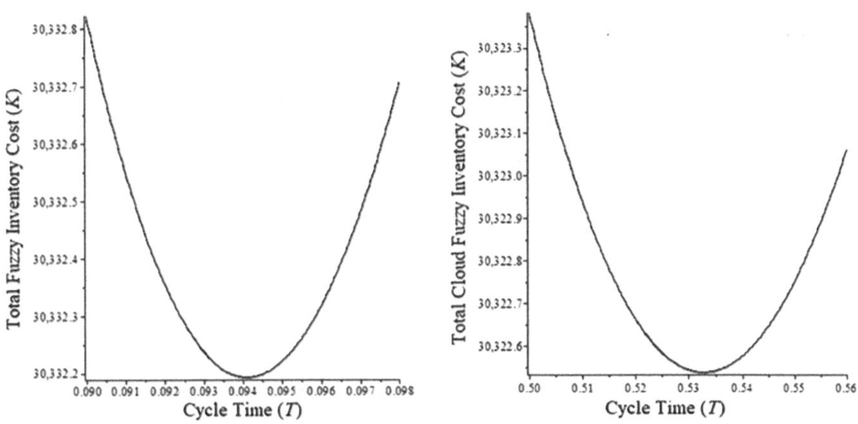

Fig. 4 Convexity of objective function of Case C under fuzzy and cloud fuzzy environment

increase in interest earned results in to lower inventory cost. Under both fuzzy and cloud fuzzy environments, increase in interest charged increases the total inventory cost, which suggests retailer to make the payment as early as possible in order to minimize the total inventory cost. The sensitivity analysis also concludes that cloud fuzzy parameters β and γ are highly sensitive to the inventory cost. Further, it can be clearly concluded from the graph that the behaviour of all the inventory parameters is same under both the environments.

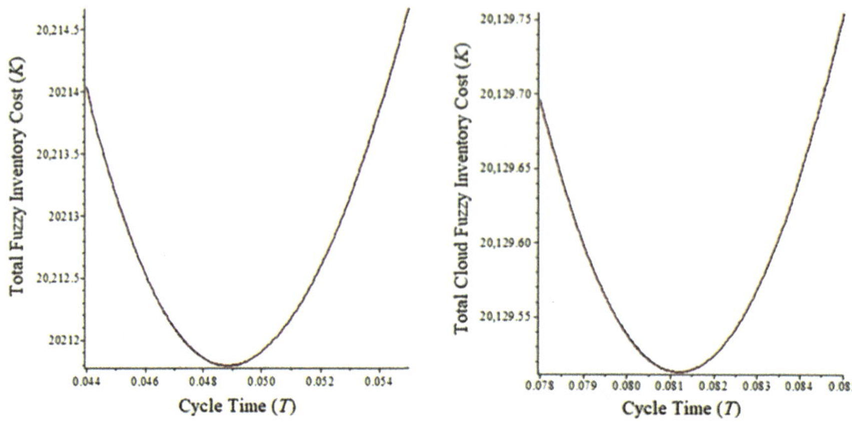

Fig. 5 Convexity of objective function of Case D under fuzzy and cloud fuzzy environment

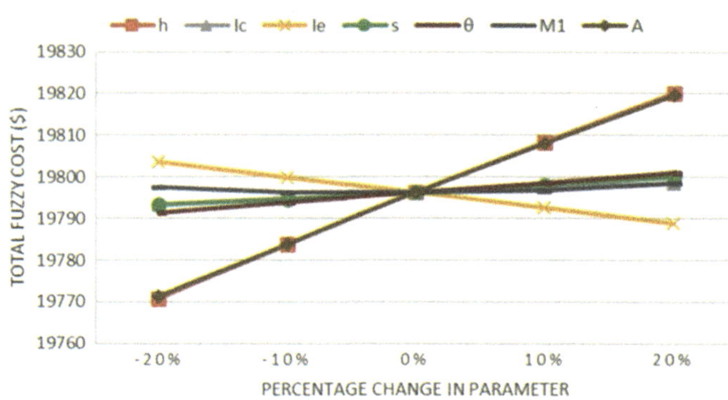

Fig. 6 Sensitivity analysis for Case A under fuzzy environment

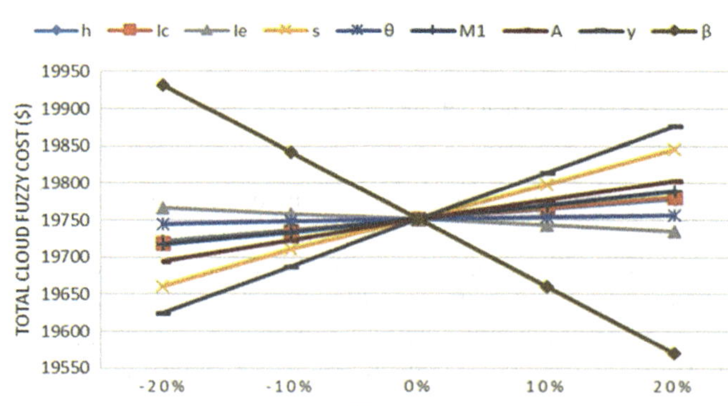

Fig. 7 Sensitivity analysis for Case A under cloud fuzzy environment

7 Conclusion and Future Scope

This paper has extended the Chang and Teng (2004) model over fuzzy and cloud fuzzy environments. Cloud fuzzy is the newly introduced concept in modelling inventory problems. Demand was characterized by triangular fuzzy number and cloud triangular fuzzy number. Throughout the study, it has been observed that the results obtained under uncertain environments are much economic than in the crisp model. The present study proved the superiority of cloud fuzzy model over crisp and fuzzy model. Yager's ranking index was used for defuzzification. Choosing the best case for retailer mainly depends upon three parameters: interest earned, interest charged and cycle time of the inventory. In order to minimize the total inventory cost, retailer should carefully select the time of payment by observing the interest earned, interest charged and cycle time. Numerical example and sensitivity analysis were carried out, and changes in solutions under different environments were analysed. The study has the scope of extension by assuming more than one parameter as fuzzy and cloud fuzzy numbers.

Acknowledgements The authors thank DST-FIST file # MSI-097 for the technical support to the department.

References

Aggarwal, S. P., & Jaggi, C. K. (1995). Ordering policies of deteriorating items under permissible delay in payments. *The Journal of the Operational Research Society, 46*(5), 658–662.

Bag, S., & Chakraborty, D. (2014). Fuzzy EOQ model under bi-level trade credit policy. *Annals of Fuzzy Mathematics and Informatics, 7*(4), 607–617.

Barman, H., Pervin, M., Roy, S. K., & Weber, G. W. (2017). Back-ordered inventory model with inflation in a cloudy-fuzzy environment. *Journal of Industrial and Management Optimization.* https://doi.org/10.3934/jimo.2020052

Chang, C. T., & Teng, J. T. (2004). Retailer's optimal ordering policy under supplier credits. *Mathematical Methods of Operations Research, 60*(3), 471–483.

Das, B. C., Das, B., & Mondal, S. K. (2015). Multi-item integrated inventory model with fuzzy credit period and fuzzy space constraints. In *Proceedings of International Conference on Frontiers in Mathematics* (pp. 44–50). Guwahati, Assam

De, S. K., & Beg, I. (2016). Triangular dense fuzzy sets and new defuzzification methods. *Journal of Intelligent & Fuzzy Systems, 31*(1), 469–477.

De, S. K., & Mahata, G. C. (2016). Decision of a fuzzy inventory with fuzzy backorder model under cloudy fuzzy demand rate. *International Journal of Applied and Computational Mathematics, 3*(3), 2593–2609.

De, S. K., & Mahata, G. C. (2019). A cloudy fuzzy economic order quantity model for imperfect-quality items with allowable proportionate discounts. *Journal of Industrial Engineerings, 15*(4), 571–583.

De, S. K., & Mahata, G. C. (2019). A comprehensive study of an economic order quantity model under fuzzy monsoon demand. *Sādhanā, 44*(4), 89.

Giri, B. C., & Sharma, S. (2016). Optimal ordering policy for an inventory system with linearly increasing demand and allowable shortages under two levels trade credit financing. *Operations Research, 16*(1), 25–50.

Goyal, S. K. (1985). Economic order quantity under conditions of permissible delay in payments. *The Journal of the Operational Research Society, 36*(4), 335–338.

Haley, C. W., & Higgins, R. C. (1973). Inventory policy and trade credit financing. *Management Science, 20*(4), 464–471.

Harris, F. W. (1913). How many parts to make at once. *Journal: the Magazine of Management, 10*(2), 135–136.

Huang, Y. D., Wee, H. M., Praharsi, Y., & Lo, C. C. (2019). An integrated vendor–buyer replenishment policy for deteriorating items with fuzzy environment and resource constraint. *INFOR: Information Systems and Operational Research, 57*(4), 667–691.

Jaggi, C. K., Sharma, A., & Jain, R. (2014). EOQ Model with permissible delay in payments under fuzzy environment. In M. Tavana (Ed.), *Analytical Approaches to Strategic Decision-Making: Interdisciplinary Considerations* (pp. 281–296). USA: IGI Global.

Karmakar, S., De, S. K., & Goswami, A. (2018). A study of an EOQ model under cloudy fuzzy demand rate. *International Conference on Mathematics and Computing, 834*, 149–163.

Liao, H. C., Tsai, C. H., & Su, C. T. (2000). An inventory model with deteriorating items under inflation when a delay in payment is permissible. *The International Journal of Production Economics, 63*(2), 207–214.

Mahata, G. C., & Goswami, A. (2007). An EOQ model for deteriorating items under trade credit financing in the fuzzy sense. *Production Planning and Control, 18*(8), 681–692.

Mahata, G. C., & Mahata, P. (2011). Analysis of a fuzzy economic order quantity model for deteriorating items under retailer partial trade credit financing in a supply chain. *Mathematical and Computer Modelling, 53*, 1621–1636.

Mahata, P., Mahata, G. C., & De, S. K. (2020). An economic order quantity model under two-level partial trade credit for time varying deteriorating items. *International Journal of Systems Science: Operations & Logistics, 7*(1), 1–17.

Maiti, A. K. (2019). Fuzzy economic production lot-size model under imperfect production process with cloudy fuzzy demand rate. *International Journal of Scientific Research and Management, 4*(3), 111–126.

Majumder, P., Bera, U. K., & Maiti, M. (2015). An EPQ model of deteriorating items under partial trade credit financing and demand declining market in crisp and fuzzy environment. *Procedia Computer Science, 45*, 780–789.

Ouyang, L. Y., Teng, J. T., & Cheng, M. C. (2010). A Fuzzy inventory system with deteriorating items under supplier credits linked to ordering quantity. *Journal of Information Science and Engineering, 26*(1), 231–253.

Park, K. S. (1987). Fuzzy-set theoretic interpretation of economic order quantity. *IEEE Transactions on Systems, Man, and Cybernetics Part B: Cybernetics, 17*(6), 1082–1084.

Shah, N. H. (1993). A lot-size model for exponentially decaying inventory when delay in payments is permissible. *Cahiers Du Centre D'études De Recherche Opérationnelle, 35*(1–2), 115–123.

Shah, N. H., & Cárdenas-Barrón, L. E. (2015). Retailer's decision for ordering and credit policies for deteriorating items when a supplier offers order-linked credit period or cash discount. *Journal of Applied Mathematics and Computing, 259*, 569–578.

Shah, N., Pareek, S., & Sangal, I. (2012). EOQ in fuzzy environment and trade credit. *International Journal of Innovative Computer Science & Engineering, 3*(2), 133–144.

Shukla, K. T., & Suthar, M. S. (2016). A note on optimal ordering policy for deteriorating items with uncertain maximum lifetime. *Cogent Mathematics, 3*(1), 1232899.

Sujatha, J., & Parvathi, P. (2015). Fuzzy inventory model for deteriorating items with Weibull demand and time varying holding cost under trade credit. *Innovative Research in Computer and Communication Engineering, 3*(11), 11110–11123.

Teng, J. T. (2009). Optimal ordering policies for a retailer who offers distinct trade credits to its good and bad credit customers. *The International Journal of Production Economics, 119*(2), 415–423.

Yadav, D., Singh, S. R., & Kumari, R. (2015). Retailer's optimal policy under inflation in fuzzy environment with trade credit. *International Journal of Systems Science, 46*(4), 754–762.
Yager, R. R. (1981). A procedure for ordering fuzzy subsets of the unit interval. *Information Science, 24*(2), 143–161.
Zadeh, L. A. (1965). Fuzzy sets. *Information and Control, 8*(3), 338–353.

An Application of PSO to Study Joint Policies of an Inventory Model with Demand Sensitive to Trade Credit and Selling Price While Deterioration of Item Being Controlled Using Preventive Technique

Poonam Mishra, Azharuddin Shaikh, and Isha Talati

Abstract This article contributes a joint inventory model for single deteriorating item with acceptable delay in payment. Effect of deterioration is considered and it is controlled by making an appropriate investment in preservation technology. The retailer gets credit period from the manufacturer with a deal to share portion of profit during this term and settle the accounts at the end of it. To boost the sales retailer permits credit period to a fraction of customers. To investigate the scenario mathematical model has been developed representing different cases. The corresponding problem is a nonlinear constrained optimization problem which is optimized by deploying Particle Swarm Optimization (PSO) algorithm. The objective is to cleverly decide unit selling price with suitable investment for preventive measures, cycle time and extended credit period; which maximizes the total profit. Lastly, to authenticate the model examples are presented and to examine the inventory parameters sensitivity analysis is carried out.

Keywords Deterioration · Integrated model · Particle swarm optimization · Permissible delay · Preservation technology investment · Profit-sharing contract

MSC 90B05 · 90B85 · 90C26

P. Mishra (✉)
Department of Mathematics, School of Technology, Pandit Deendayal Petroleum University, Raisan, Gandhinagar, Gujarat 382007, India

A. Shaikh
Institute of Management, Nirma University, Sarkhej-Gandhinagar Highway, Ahmedabad 382481, India

I. Talati
Department of Physical Science, Institute of Advance Research, Koba Institutional Area, Gandhinagar, Gujarat 382426, India

N. H. Shah and M. Mittal (eds.), *Soft Computing in Inventory Management*, Inventory Optimization, https://doi.org/10.1007/978-981-16-2156-7_2

1 Introduction

The concept of paying the cost price of an item at its delivery time has now been outdated. In business transaction, offer of permissible credit period for stock purchased acts as a marketing tool for enhancing the sales, because it buys time for clearing accounts. Generally, in market, when the items are procured the account is not immediately settled by retailer; retailer gets some time from the supplier. Nowadays, permissible delay in payment is a common practice among players of supply chain. From supplier's view, offering delay in payment attracts retailer and results increase in sales with reduced holding cost. For retailer, delay in payment reduces the opportunity cost of monetary fund to be invested, while retailer can also make surplus income by investing generated revenue in some interest bearing account during the permitted term. Hence, both supplier and retailer get benefited by implementing permissible delay period. The first Economic Order Quantity (EOQ) model permitting fixed delay period after the products are received is given by Goyal (1985). Afterwards, Aggarwal and Jaggi (1995) proposed inventory model with permissible delay for deteriorating items. For detailed review of permissible delay (trade credit) into inventory models refer Chang et al. (2008) and Soni et al. (2010). Sarkar (2012) discussed an inventory model that allows delay in payments in presence of imperfect production. For demand dependent on selling price and permissible delay period, Giri and Maiti (2013) proposed a model in which retailer takes bank loan to clear the debt. Mishra et al. (2019) determined the best payment option for the retailer along with finding the optimal cycle time.

It is not just that the supplier can avail the benefit by offering permissible credit period, even retailer can improve his sales by extending credit period to the end customers. To demonstrate that retailer also gets benefitted when permissible delay period availed from the supplier is extended to end customer, Huang (2003) proposed an EOQ model. In this model, delay period (N) offered to end customer by retailer was assumed to be less than the credit period (M) received. Later, by easing the assumption $N < M$, Teng and Chang (2009) studied an Economic Production Quantity (EPQ) model. This setup is also termed as two-level trade credit. Few articles using two-level trade credit policy are Min et al. (2010), Kaanodiya and Pachauri (2011), Shah et al. (2014), Shaikh and Mishra (2018). The mentioned articles emphases to reveal optimal strategies either from the supplier or retailer point of view.

There are a number of competitors in supply chain network and to survive in such situation is a difficult task. The motto of every competitor is to enhance the business by different means. In a non-integrated supply chain, members have different motives and this possibly can clash with supply chain's objective. To enhance the productivity of supply chain network, members should unite and make decisions jointly, which can help in fulfilling customers need at lowest inventory cost. The first integrated model to study inventory policies was given by Goyal (1977). Afterwards, Abad and Jaggi (2003) combined the concept of permissible delay and integrated inventory model. Sarmah et al. (2007) gave the idea of sharing profit among the two members during the credit period. Assuming demand as a downstream credit period function, He and Huang (2013) studied a joint inventory model for items deteriorating non-instantaneously. In presence of two-level trade credit, Chung and Cárdenas-Barrón (2013) proposed an easy technique to get optimal solution for an inventory model with demand dependent on displayed units. In presence of permissible delay, Wu et al. (2014) studied replenishment policies for deteriorating items with demand reliant on price and stock. Aggarwal and Tyagi (2014) examined credit and inventory policies with demand related to date terms credit. Shah (2015) formulated an integrated model with an agreement of profit-sharing under two-level trade credit. Mishra and Shaikh (2017a) established an integrated model utilizing two warehouses with demand dependent on displayed units and trade credit liable on order size. Mishra and Shaikh (2017b) also studied ordering and pricing policies in an integrated environment for stock and price sensitive demand.

Another important concern for inventory items is deterioration, it is unavoidable. It plays a substantial role in inventory modelling as utility of item is affected. It occurs for items such as edibles, milk products, clothing, fashion accessories, and medical supplies. To overcome the effect of deterioration preventive steps should be taken. Several researchers have formulated models for controlling deterioration by investing in preservation technology. The first EOQ model including exponential decay was given by Ghare (1963). Hariga (1995) studied an EOQ model incorporating shortages for deteriorating items and demand varying with time. An EOQ model under inflationary conditions for deteriorating items with time-varying demand is given by Jaggi and Mittal (2003). Jaggi and Mittal (2011) also gave an EOQ model in presence of imperfect quality for deteriorating items. In presence of imperfect quality and demand dependent on displayed stock, Shah and Shah (2014) developed an inventory model incorporating the effect of inflation. For preservation of seasonal products, Sarkar et al. (2017) presented an inventory model with stock-dependent demand. Mishra et al. (2017) studied an EOQ model with demand dependent on displayed stock and selling price. An imperfect manufacturing system considering quadratic demand with inflation was given by Shah et al. (2017). Mishra and Shaikh (2017c) studied joint decision policies using preservation technology to control deterioration with quadratic demand sensitive to permissible credit period. Shaikh and Mishra (2019) formulated an inventory model for deteriorating items following price sensitive quadratic demand with suitable investment in preservation technology in an inflationary environment.

Generally, optimal solutions for most of the inventory models are obtained by traditional or gradient-based optimization methods. While employing these methods, one frequently faced limitation is that the traditional approach gets stuck to the local maxima or minima. In addition, these methods are unable to optimize nonlinear constrained complex problems. To overcome such limitations many evolutionary algorithms are used these days to solve real-world problems, Genetic Algorithm and particle swarm optimization (PSO) are two of them. Hence, the use of evolutionary algorithms would be advantageous as there will be less chances of getting stuck at local extrema while using them. For an inventory model with two warehouses and permissible delay, Bhunia and Shaikh (2015) utilized PSO to study optimal policies for deteriorating units. In an inventory model with items deteriorating in nature and demand dependent on marketing strategy and displayed stock, Bhunia et al. (2018) used Genetic Algorithm and PSO to frame optimal strategies. These search techniques are also used in optimizing the Multi-objective function. Garai and Garg (2019) studied multi-objective linear fractional inventory model with possibility and necessity constraints under intuitionistic fuzzy set environment. Shaikh et al. (2020) utilized Multi-objective Genetic Algorithm to allocate order in the list of available suppliers. Mishra et al. (2020) also used Multi-objective Genetic Algorithm to optimize the supply chain network through player selection. Waliv et al. (2020) presented a nonlinear programming approach to solve the stochastic multi-objective inventory model using the uncertain information. The use of heuristic search techniques for obtaining optimal solution has been rarely used by researchers working in the area of inventory management.

Reviewing the available literature, gap for an integrated inventory model under the following condition is observed; (i) the retailer's demand increases with hike in permissible delay period offered to customer and decreases with hike in unit selling price, (ii) retailer gets a fix time slot from the manufacturer with a mutual agreement to share fraction of profit, (iii) items are deteriorating and precautionary measures are taken to control it, (iv) lastly, to determine the optimal value of decision variables the use of PSO algorithm is rarely done by researchers working in the area of inventory management. Hence, these are a few gaps as per our observation and proposed model is an attempt to fill it up.

This chapter is an effort to study the joint policies of manufacturer and retailer by means of an integrated inventory model. The retailer's demand function is assumed as an elevating function of permissible delay period offered to customer, while declining function of unit selling price. Retailer avails fix credit period from the manufacturer with a mutual agreement to share fraction of profit during this period. Inventory items are deteriorating in nature and to control the deterioration process, appropriate amount is to be invested in preservation technology. The aim is to cleverly decide unit selling price with suitable investment for preventive measures, cycle time and credit period to be offered; which maximizes the total profit. The succeeding part of this chapter is arranged in the following manner. The notations used and assumptions made for proposed model is given in Sect. 2. In Sect. 3, the math modelling is done which leads to formulation of objective function. Along with this we present an overview of particle swarm optimization (PSO) algorithm. Then, to authenticate the model and to test the performance of the PSO algorithm, numerical examples are presented in Sect. 5. In Sect. 6, sensitivity analysis of inventory parameters is conducted. Lastly, in Sect. 7 conclusion is presented.

2 Notation and Assumptions

The notations used and assumptions made for proposed model are as follows:

2.1 Notation

Inventory Parameters for Retailer

A_r	Retailer's ordering cost per order
C_r	Retailer's unit purchase cost
h_r	Holding cost per annum
θ	Constant deterioration rate, $0 \leq \theta < 1$
δ	Fraction of profit to be shared with manufacturer during the credit period M; $0 \leq \delta < 1$
I_b	Interest rate on the loan taken from bank
I_e	Interest earned rate by the retailer
γ	Fraction of customer allowed by retailer to avail a trade credit period N
$I_r(t)$	Retailer inventory level at time t
$f(u) = 1 - \frac{1}{1+\mu u}$	Proportion of reduced deterioration of item
π_r	Retailer total profit per unit time

Inventory Parameters for Manufacturer

C_m	Manufacturing cost of item per unit, $C_m < C_r$
A_m	Manufacturer setup cost per lot
h_m	Holding cost per annum
M	Credit period retailer gets from the manufacturer
I_m	Interest rate lost by manufacturer because to offering permissible delay period
$T_m = xT$	Manufacturer time delay to initiate the production, $(0 < x < 1)$
$I_m(t)$	Manufacturer inventory level at time t
π_m	Manufacturer total profit per unit time

Decision Variables

T	Cycle time
N	Credit period offered to end customer by retailer
S	Retailer unit selling price, $S > C_r$
u	Investment in preservation technology

For PSO

r_1, r_2	Random variable which is uniformly lying between [0, 1]
p_size	Size of the population
$c_1 (> 0)$	Cognitive learning rate
$c_2 (> 0)$	Social learning rate
m-gen	Maximum iteration/generation

$x_i^{(k)}$	Velocity of ith particle at kth iteration/generation
$p_i^{(k)}$	Best previous position of ith particle at kth iteration
$p_g^{(k)}$	Position of best particle among all other particle in the population
χ	Constriction factor

Inventory Parameters Relation

$N \leq M$

$S > C_r > C_m$

$0 \leq \theta < 1$

Functions

$D(N, S)$	Retailer's demand rate; $D(N, S) = \alpha - \eta S + \beta N$, where $\alpha > 0$ represents scale demand, $\eta > 0$ signifies price elasticity and $\beta > 0$ is trade credit markup rate
$P(N, S)$	Manufacturer production rate proportionate to retailer's demand rate, $P(N, S) = \lambda \cdot D(N, S),\ \lambda > 1$
$\pi(N, S, T, u)$	Joint total profit of manufacturer and retailer $(\pi_m + \pi_r)$

The aim of the integrated inventory model is stated as:

$$\text{Max} \quad \pi(N, S, T, u)$$

Subject to,

$$N \leq M,$$

$$N, S, T, u \geq 0$$

2.2 Assumptions

1. Inventory system consists of lone manufacturer, lone retailer dealing with single item.
2. The retailer's demand function is assumed as an elevating function of permissible delay period offered to customer, while declining function of unit selling price. Therefore, demand rate is expressed as $D(N, S) = \alpha - \eta S + \beta N$. In this chapter, $D(N, S)$ and D are used interchangeably for notational convenience.
3. Manufacturer's production rate $P(N, S)$ is more than the retailer's demand $D(N, S)$. This indicates manufacturer has adequate production ability to meet retailer's demand.

4. Retailer avails fix credit period (M) from the manufacturer with a mutual agreement to share fraction of profit during this period.
5. When the cycle time exceeds the delay period permitted by manufacturer, retailer is bound to clear the accounts from the spare of his sales revenue. However, retailer does not have adequate fund to settle the accounts. So, to pay the rest of purchase cost at the end of the credit period M retailer avails a bank loan at an interest rate I_b. Later, retailer pays the loan amount to the bank at the end of the cycle time.
6. During the permitted delay period, manufacturer incurs an interest loss at the rate of I_m. Further, retailer earns interest on generated income at the rate of I_e.
7. Only a fraction of customers is provided credit period ($N < M$) by the retailer.
8. The quantity of reduced deterioration rate $f(u)$ is presumed to be continuously increasing and concave function of u (i.e., preservation technology investment), i.e., $f'(u) > 0$ and $f''(u) < 0$. Also $f(0) = 0$, in this model $f(u)$ and f are used interchangeably for notational convenience.
9. Shortages are not allowed. Planning horizon is infinite and lead time is zero.

3 Mathematical Model

3.1 Retailer's Total Profit Per Unit Time

In the proposed model, the following differential equation indicates the status of retailer's inventory level $I_r(t)$ at time t:

$$\frac{dI_r(t)}{dt} + \theta(1-f)I_r(t) = -(\alpha - \eta S + \beta N), \quad 0 \le t \le T \tag{1}$$

with $I_r(0) = Q$ and $I_r(T) = 0$. The solution of (1) using $I_r(T) = 0$ is,

$$I_r(t) = \frac{(\alpha - \eta S + \beta N)}{\theta(1-f)}\left[1 - \exp(\theta(1-f)(T-t))\right] \tag{2}$$

Employing the other condition $I_r(0) = Q$ and (2), optimal order quantity is

$$Q = \frac{(\alpha - \eta S + \beta N)}{\theta(1-f)}\left[1 - \exp(\theta(1-f)(T))\right] \tag{3}$$

Further, costs associated with retailer's total profit are

- Sales revenue generated, $SR_r = S\left[\int_0^T (\alpha - \eta S + \beta N)dt\right]$
- Purchase cost, $PC_r = C_r Q$
- Ordering cost, $OC_r = A_r$
- Investment in preservation technology, $IPT = u$

- Holding cost, $\text{HC}_\text{r} = h_\text{r}\left[\int_0^T I_\text{r}(t)\text{d}t\right]$.

Next, depending on the values of M, N and T, i.e., delay period availed and offered by the retailer and cycle time T. Either of the three situation may arise (i) $N \le M \le T$, (ii) $N \le T \le M$ and (iii) $T \le N \le M$. Further explanation of each scenario is as follows:

Case I: $N \le M \le T$

According to the contract, during the permitted delay period $[0, M]$ retailer is bound to share $\delta\%$ of the profit with the manufacturer. Therefore, the profit shared with manufacturer is, $\text{FP}_1 = \delta(S - C_\text{r})\int_0^M (\alpha - \eta S + \beta N)\text{d}t$ and the remaining of the sales revenue can be utilized to clear the accounts. At the end of the credit period M, retailer avails a bank loan at an interest rate I_b. When the cycle time ends retailer pays the loan amount to the bank. Therefore, interest charged by the bank is,

$$\text{ICB}_\text{r} = I_\text{b}\left[C_\text{r}\int_0^T (\alpha - \eta S + \beta N)\text{d}t - S\int_0^M (\alpha - \eta S + \beta N)\text{d}t + \text{FP}_1\right](T - M) \tag{4}$$

Next, during the cycle time interest earned by the retailer is,

$$\text{IE}_{\text{r}1} = I_\text{e}S\left[\int_0^M ((\alpha - \eta S + \beta N)\cdot t)\text{d}t + \int_0^{T-M} ((\alpha - \eta S + \beta N)\cdot t)\text{d}t\right] \tag{5}$$

Also, opportunity cost bared by retailer for offering partial credit period N is,

$$\text{OL}_{\text{r}1} = \gamma I_\text{e}S\left[\int_0^N ((\alpha - \eta S + \beta N)\cdot t)\text{d}t\right] \tag{6}$$

Hence, retailer's profit per unit time is given by,

$$\pi_{\text{r}1} = \frac{1}{T}(\text{SR}_\text{r} - \text{PC}_\text{r} - \text{OC}_\text{r} - \text{HC}_\text{r} - \text{FP}_1 - \text{ICB}_\text{r} - \text{OL}_{\text{r}1} + \text{IE}_{\text{r}1}) - \text{IPT} \tag{7}$$

Case II: $N \le T \le M$

In this case, the profit shared with manufacturer during permissible delay period is, $\text{FP}_2 = \delta(S - \text{C}_\text{r})\int_0^T (\alpha - \eta S + \beta N)\text{d}t$ and interest earned during the cycle time by the retailer is,

$$\mathrm{IE_{r2}} = I_e S\left[\int_0^T ((\alpha - \eta S + \beta N)\cdot t)\mathrm{d}t + Q(M - T)\right] \tag{8}$$

Also, retailer's opportunity loss during $[0, N]$ is,

$$\mathrm{OL_{r2}} = \gamma I_e S\left[\int_0^N ((\alpha - \eta S + \beta N)\cdot t)\mathrm{d}t\right] \tag{9}$$

Here, the retailer has sufficient fund to settle the accounts, so there is no need of taking loan from the bank. Therefore, retailer's profit per unit time is given by,

$$\pi_{r2} = \frac{1}{T}(\mathrm{SR_r} - \mathrm{PC_r} - \mathrm{OC_r} - \mathrm{HC_r} - \mathrm{FP_2} - \mathrm{OL_{r2}} + \mathrm{IE_{r2}}) - \mathrm{IPT} \tag{10}$$

Case III: $T \leq N \leq M$

Here, the profit shared with manufacturer during permissible delay period is same as in case II, $\mathrm{FP_2} = \delta(S - C_r)\int_0^T (\alpha - \eta S + \beta N)\mathrm{d}t$ and interest earned during the cycle time by the retailer is,

$$\mathrm{IE_{r3}} = I_e S\left[\int_0^T ((\alpha - \eta S + \beta N)\cdot t)\mathrm{d}t + Q(M - T)\right] \tag{11}$$

Also offering credit period to end customer retailer incurs opportunity loss during $[0, N]$ which is given by,

$$\mathrm{OL_{r3}} = \gamma I_e S\left[\int_0^T ((\alpha - \eta S + \beta N)\cdot t)\mathrm{d}t + Q(N - T)\right] \tag{12}$$

For this scenario, the retailer has adequate fund to settle the accounts, so there is no need of taking loan from the bank. Therefore, retailer's profit per unit time is given by,

$$\pi_{r3} = \frac{1}{T}(\mathrm{SR_r} - \mathrm{PC_r} - \mathrm{OC_r} - \mathrm{HC_r} - \mathrm{FP_2} - \mathrm{OL_{r3}} + \mathrm{IE_{r3}}) - \mathrm{IPT} \tag{13}$$

3.2 Manufacturer Total Profit Per Unit Time

In the proposed model, the following differential equation indicates the status of manufacturer inventory level $I_m(t)$ at time t:

$$\frac{dI_m(t)}{dt} = P(N, S) - D(N, S), \quad T_m \le t \le T \tag{14}$$

with $I_m(T) = 0$. The solution of (14) using this condition is,

$$I_m(t) = (\lambda - 1)(\alpha - \eta S + \beta N)(t - T) \tag{15}$$

The manufacturer total profit per unit time consists of setup cost, holding cost, opportunity loss sales revenue and production cost.

- Setup cost, $OC_m = A_m$
- Holding cost, $HC_m = h_m\left[\int_{T_m}^{T} I_m(t)dt\right]$
- Interest loss happened for offering trade credit M to retailer,

$$OL_m = I_m C_r M\left[\int_{T_m}^{T} \lambda \cdot (\alpha - \eta S + \beta N)dt\right] \tag{16}$$

Under the contract, $\delta\%$ of the profit made by the retailer is shared with the manufacturer during the permissible delay period. Thus, the portion of profit availed by manufacturer is given by,

$$FP_m = \begin{cases} FP_{m1} = \delta(S - C_r)\int_0^M (\alpha - \eta S + \beta N)dt, & M \le T \\ FP_{m2} = \delta(S - C_r)\int_0^T (\alpha - \eta S + \beta N)dt, & M > T \end{cases} \tag{17}$$

Therefore, total profit of manufacturer per unit time is given by

$$\pi_{m1} = \frac{1}{T}\left[(C_r - C_m)\int_0^T (\alpha - \eta S + \beta N)dt - OC_m - HC_m - OL_m + FP_{m1}\right], \quad M \le T \tag{18}$$

$$\pi_{m2} = \frac{1}{T}\left[(C_r - C_m)\int_0^T (\alpha - \eta S + \beta N)dt - OC_m - HC_m - OL_m + FP_{m2}\right], \quad M > T \tag{19}$$

3.3 *Joint Profit of Supply Chain*

The joint total profit of integrated supply chain is given by sum of retailer and manufacturer profit, which is a multivariable function of partial trade credit, selling price, cycle time and preservation technology investment. Hence, depending on the cycle time and permissible delay period duration, joint total profit per unit time of supply chain is given by:

$$\pi(N, S, T, u) = \begin{cases} \pi_1(N, S, T, u) = \pi_{r1} + \pi_{m1}, & N \le M \le T \\ \pi_2(N, S, T, u) = \pi_{r2} + \pi_{m2}, & N \le T \le M \\ \pi_3(N, S, T, u) = \pi_{r3} + \pi_{m2}, & T \le N \le M \end{cases} \quad (20)$$

The aim is to maximize joint total profit of the supply chain with partial trade credit, unit selling price, cycle time and preservation technology investment as decision variables.

4 Solution Procedure

Several researchers have effectively employed heuristic search techniques to optimize their difficult problems in various streams of sciences. Few of the well-known techniques are simulated annealing, Genetic Algorithm, ant colony optimization and particle swarm optimization. For this study, we utilize the commonly used particle swarm optimization method for optimizing the objective function formed.

Based on the individual experience and social interaction of the population, Particle swarm optimization (PSO) is a heuristic global search technique. This technique was anticipated by Eberhart and Kennedy (1995a, 1995b). Getting inspiration from the social behaviour of bird gathering or fish schooling, this technique is generally used to optimize challenging problems. PSO algorithm initiates with random set of solutions (also known as particles) flying in the search space. These particles hunt for the optima in each iteration (also known as generation) by following the current optimal solutions. In each iteration, position of all the particles is updated by utilizing two best solutions. One of these best solutions is the personal best position so far attained by the particle and is denoted by $p_i^{(k)}$, while the second one is the present best position so far attained by any of the particle and is denoted by $p_g^{(k)}$.

In every iteration, the velocity and position of ith ($i = 1, 2, \ldots$, p_size) particle is updated by using:

$$v_i^{(k+1)} = wv_i^{(k)} + c_1 r_1\left(p_i^{(k)} - x_i^{(k)}\right) + c_2 r_2\left(p_g^{(k)} - x_i^{(k)}\right) \quad (21)$$

and

$$x_i^{(k+1)} = x_i^{(k)} + v_i^{(k+1)} \quad (22)$$

where k (= 1, 2, ..., m-gen) represents the iterations (generations); w is the inertia weight. The cognitive learning rate $c_1(> 0)$ and social learning rate $c_2(> 0)$ are the responsible acceleration constants for varying the particle velocity in the direction of $p_i^{(k)}$ and $p_g^{(k)}$ respectively.

The updated velocity of ith particle is given by (21) which involves three components. The explanation of each of this component is as follow: (i) particles velocity in previous iteration, (ii) the distance between particle's current and previous best position and (iii) the distance between particle's current and swarm's best position (the optimal position of particle in the swarm). The velocity given by (21) is also restricted by $v_{\max}$ called the maximum velocity of the particle; hence the range of velocity update is $[-v_{\max}, v_{\max}]$. Picking too small value for $v_{\max}$ can result to tiny change in velocity update and particles position at each iteration. As a result, algorithm can take longer time to converge and might face the problem of getting stuck at local extrema. To get rid of these circumstances, Clerc (1999), Clerc and Kennedy (2002) proposed a better rule to update velocity by using a constriction factor χ. Using this factor, the velocity is updated using the following equation,

$$v_i^{(k+1)} = \chi\left[v_i^{(k)} + c_1 r_1\left(p_i^{(k)} - x_i^{(k)}\right) + c_2 r_2\left(p_g^{(k)} - x_i^{(k)}\right)\right] \tag{23}$$

Here the constriction factor χ is expressed as

$$\chi = \frac{2}{\left|2 - \phi - \sqrt{\phi^2 - 4\phi}\right|} \tag{24}$$

where $\phi = c_1 + c_2, \phi > 4$. The constriction factor is a function of c_1 and c_2. Generally, values of c_1 and c_2 is set to 2.05 which results ϕ as 4.1; hence, the constriction coefficient value is 0.729. This algorithm is recognized as constriction coefficient-based PSO.

The search technique of particle swarm optimization is summarized as below:

1. Define the PSO parameters and set bounds for the decision variables.
2. Initialize with a set of particles (solution) from search space with random positions and velocities.
3. Calculate the fitness value of every particle.
4. For each particle, keep track of the location where particle attains its best fitness value.
5. Keep track of the location with the global best fitness.
6. Update the velocity and position of each particle.
7. If the termination criterion is fulfilled, go to next step, else go to step 3.
8. Display the location and fitness score of global best particle.
9. End.

5 Numerical Examples

For PSO parameters we use the subsequent values

p_size = 100, $c_1 = 2.05$, $c_2 = 2.05$ and m-gen = 100.

Example 1: Consider $\alpha = 80, \beta = 0.5, \eta = 0.7, \lambda = 1.5, x = 0.1, C_m = \$8$ per unit, $\delta = 10\%$, $C_r = \$15$ per unit, $A_r = \$15$ per order, $h_r = \$5$ per unit per year, $I_b = 11\%$ per annum, $I_e = 10\%$ per annum, $M = 0.6$ year, $\theta = 30\%$, $\mu = 15\%$, $h_m = \$3$ per unit per year, $\gamma = 0.5$, $I_m = 10\%$ per annum and $A_m = \$20$ per setup.

Here, the maximum profit is $\pi_1 = \$604.57$ for cycle time is $T = 0.8428$ years at unit selling price \$41.59, offering credit period $N = 0.3008$ years to end customers and investing \$10.93 in preservation technology. It represents the scenario $N \leq M \leq T$ and Figs. 1, 2, 3, 4, 5 and 6 represents concavity of the profit function.

Example 2: Let $M = 0.8$ year and values of other inventory parameters as in Example 1. The maximum profit is $\pi_2 = \$609.97$ which comes out for scenario $N \leq T \leq M$ at $T = 0.5622$ years, $S = \$41.19$, $N = 0.2049$ years and $u = \$7.07$.

Example 3: Consider $\beta = 1.57$, $M = 1.2$ year and all other parameters same as in Example 1. The situation $T \leq N \leq M$ yields maximum profit as $\pi_3 = \$623.53$ which comes out at $T = 1.1168$ year, $S = \$43.56$, $N = 1.1849$ year and $u = \$13.98$.

Figure 7 shows the joint and individual profit for all the three examples, which represent all the possible cases. Next, to compare the integrated decision making policy with independent decision making policy we maximize retailer's total profit with same values of inventory parameters as in Example 1 (i.e., retailer is the decision maker). Here the retailer's total profit turns out to be $\pi_{r1} = \$463.46$ for cycle time $T = 0.9574$ year at unit selling price \$44.94, offering credit period $N = 0.2990$ year to end customers and investing \$11.18 in preservation technology. It represents the

Fig. 1 Concavity for T and N. *Source* Own

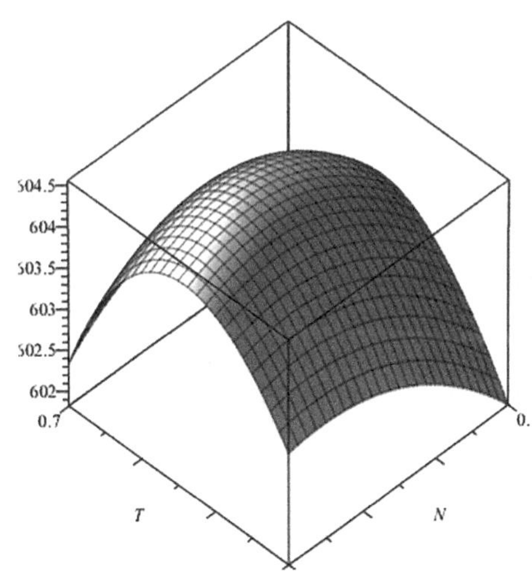

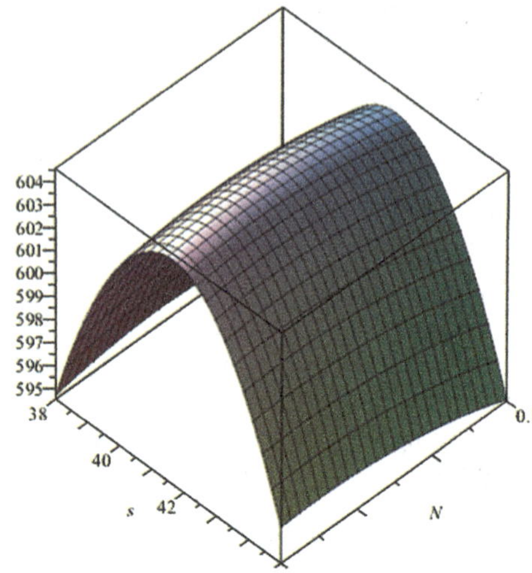

Fig. 2 Concavity for S and N. *Source* Own

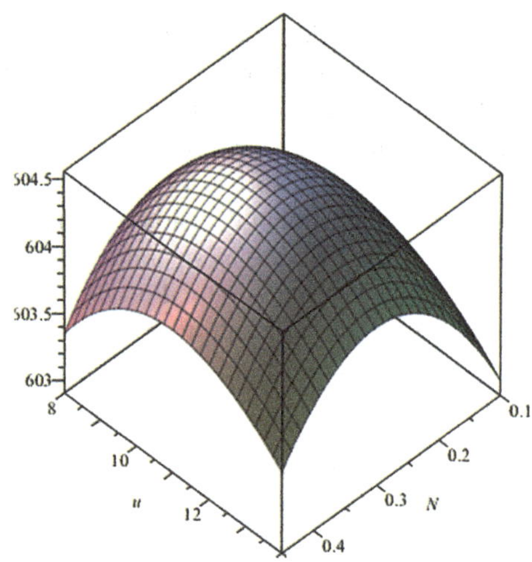

Fig. 3 Concavity for u and N. *Source* Own

scenario $N \leq M \leq T$ and for these values the manufacturer's total profit is \$133.16. Therefore, the joint profit from independent decision making is sum of retailer's profit and manufacturer's profit, which is \$596.62. This represents that decision made in an integrated environment turns out to be more profitable for members of supply chain compared to independent one. The comparison of integrated and independent decision for Examples 2 and 3 is also shown in Table 1.

Fig. 4 Concavity for S and T. *Source* Own

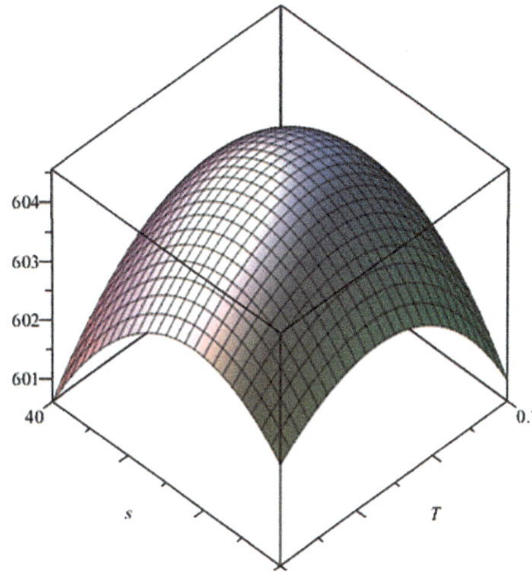

Fig. 5 Concavity for u and T. *Source* Own

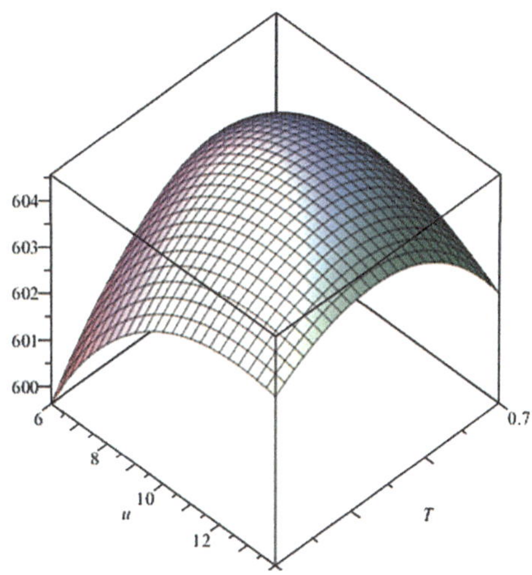

6 Sensitivity Analysis

To study the impact of inventory parameters in decision making, we consider inventory parameter values same as taken in example 1. Next, by changing each parameter once at a time by −20%, −10%, +10% and +20% optimal solution is obtained. The solutions obtained are analysed cautiously and based on it managerial insights are provided as follows.

In Fig. 8, credit period (N) offered to end customer is plotted for variation in inventory parameters. It is being observed that increase in manufacturer's holding cost, setup cost, manufacturing cost, credit period offered to retailer, retailer ordering

Fig. 6 Concavity for u and S. *Source* Own

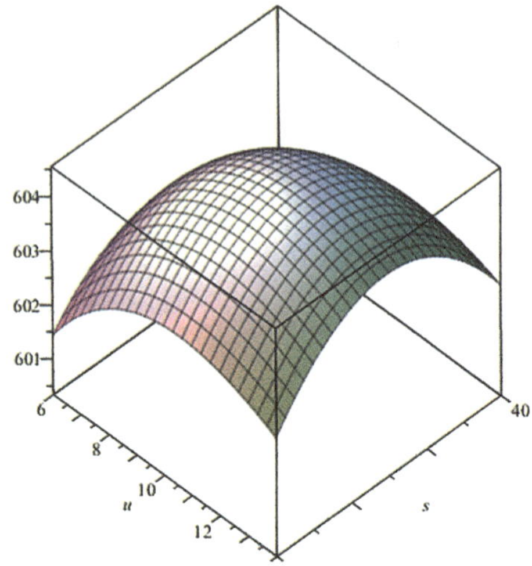

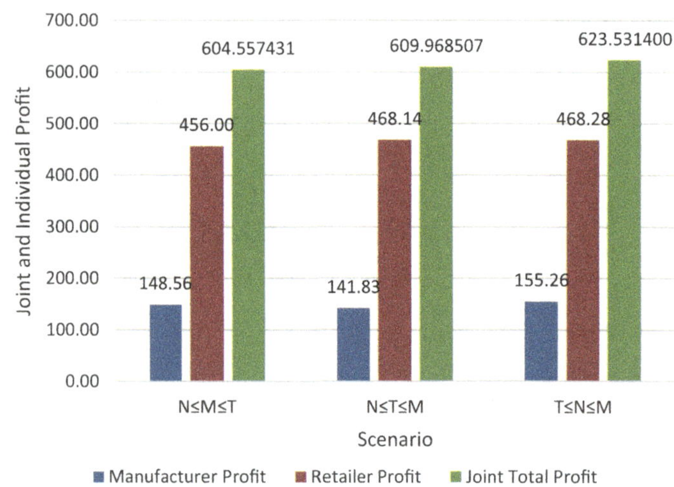

Fig. 7 Joint and individual profit. *Source* Own

cost, preservation rate and interest rate on amount borrowed increases the delay period (N) offered to end customer. Whereas it increases significantly for markup rate for trade credit and λ. Other inventory parameters show a negative impact on credit period (N) offered to end customer; among which scale demand, price elasticity, retailer's holding cost and fraction of customer offered trade credit are highly sensitive.

In Fig. 9, impact of inventory parameters on cycle time is observed. The major observations are; increase in markup for trade credit, manufacturer's holding cost, interest loss rate, credit period offered to end customer, manufacturing cost, retailer ordering cost, preservation rate and interest rate on borrowed amount increases the

Table 1 Comparison of independent and integrated decision

Example	Decision	Unit selling price ($)	Cycle time (year)	Permissible delay period offered to end customer (year)	Preservation technology investment ($)	Joint total profit ($)
1 ($N \leq M \leq T$)	Integrated	$41.59	0.8428	0.3008	10.93	604.57
	Independent	$44.94	0.9574	0.2990	11.18	596.62
2 ($N \leq T \leq M$)	Integrated	$41.19	0.5622	0.2049	7.07	609.97
	Independent	$43.50	0.3506	0.1109	3.24	590.97
3 ($T \leq N \leq M$)	Integrated	$43.56	1.1168	1.1849	13.98	623.53
	Independent	$45.84	0.9084	1.0560	16.08	612.82

Source Own

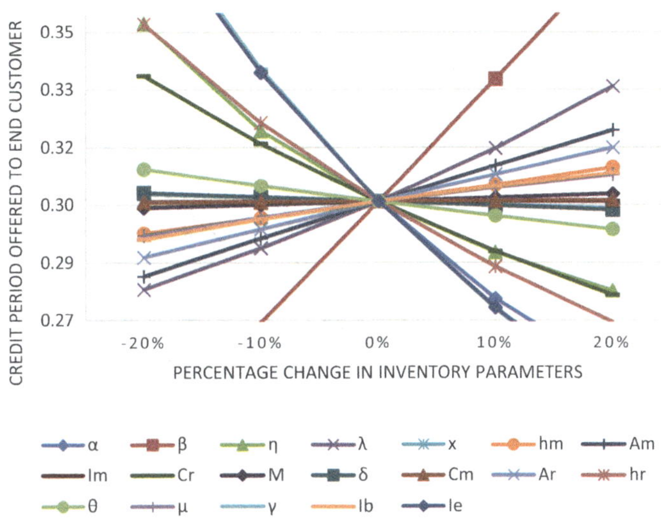

Fig. 8 Variation in credit period offered to end customer (N). *Source* Own

cycle time. Whereas λ and manufacturer setup cost increases cycle time rapidly. Other inventory parameters show negative impact on cycle time among which price elasticity, retailer's unit purchase cost and holding cost are highly sensitive.

In Fig. 10, unit selling price is plotted for variation in inventory parameters. It is being observed that increase in fraction of profit shared with manufacturer, manufacturer's holding cost, preservation rate and fraction of customer offered trade credit decreases the unit selling price. Whereas it decreases significantly for price elasticity. Other inventory parameters show a positive impact on unit selling price; among which scale demand and unit manufacturing cost are highly sensitive.

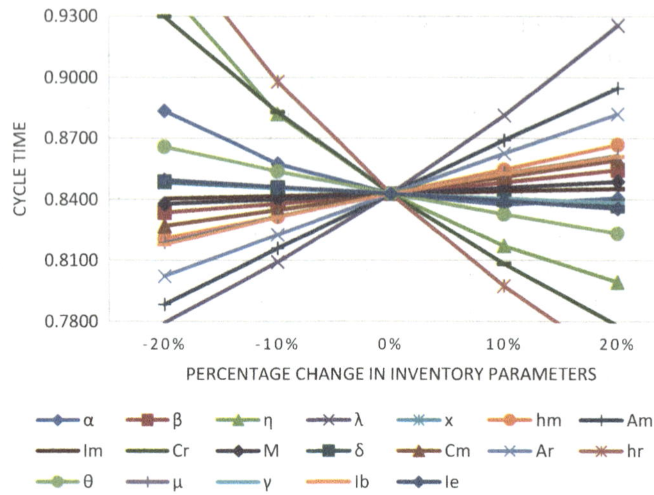

Fig. 9 Variation in cycle time (T). *Source* Own

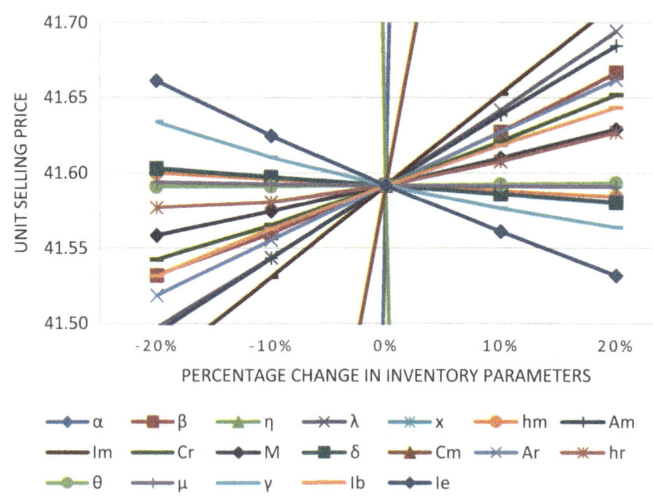

Fig. 10 Variation in unit selling price (S). *Source* Own

In Fig. 11, effect of inventory parameters on preservation technology investment is observed. It shows that scale demand and deterioration rate has a high positive impact on preservation technology investment; while preservation technology investment decreases for increase in price elasticity and retailer holding cost. Effect of other inventory parameters can be seen in the figure.

In Fig. 12, the effect of change in inventory parameters on joint total profit can be seen. The major observations made are; scale demand has a high impact on profit,

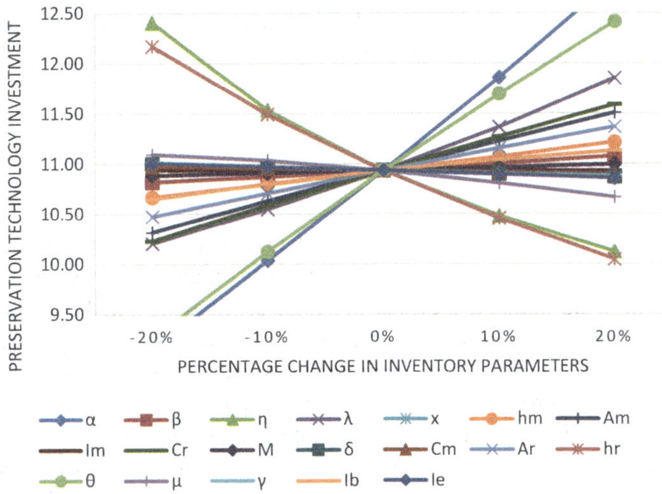

Fig. 11 Variation in preservation technology investment (u). *Source* Own

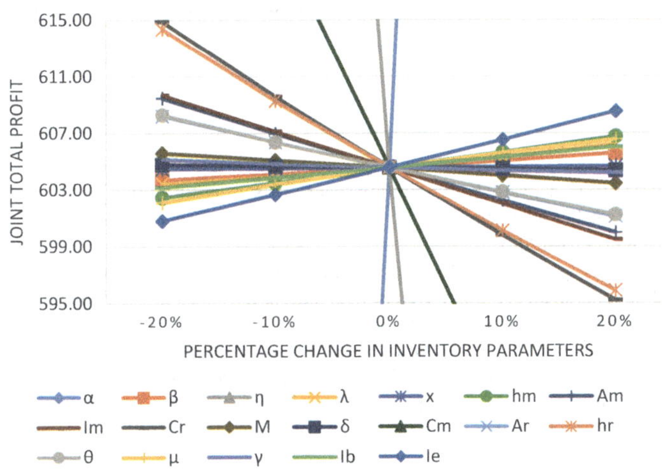

Fig. 12 Variation in joint total profit. *Source* Own

while markup for trade credit, λ, x, manufacturer holding cost, preservation rate, interest rate on borrowed amount and interest earned rate has a positive impact on profit. Whereas the other parameters show a negative impact on profit among which price elasticity, unit manufacturing cost, retailer's unit purchase cost and holding cost are highly sensitive.

On the basis of change in values of inventory parameters and their impact, the manufacturer and retailer can wisely interpret the cause that leads to increase and decrease in the values of decision variables. Hence, they can cleverly tune up the values of decision variables which will lead to favorable outcomes.

7 Conclusion

In this study, we optimize the formulated integrated inventory model using PSO algorithm. While performing the sensitivity analysis, major observations made are; (1) Increase in scale demand elevates the total profit with hiked up selling rate, preservation technology investment and reduces cycle time and credit period offered. (2) Higher deterioration rate leads to more investment in preservation technology resulting decrease in profit. (3) Retailer's holding cost is very negatively sensitive to all decision variable except for selling price, which reduces the profit. For the numerical examples presented, integrated and independent decisions are studied and it has been found that an integrated decision is more fruitful for the supply chain. This model is applicable for variety of items like grains, vegetables, electronic devices, utility vehicle, etc. In addition, this model can be extended by allowing shortages, items possessing fixed lifetime, considering trade credit dependent on order size.

References

Abad, P. L., & Jaggi, C. K. (2003). A joint approach for setting unit price and the length of the credit period for a seller when end demand is price sensitive. *International Journal of Production Economics, 83*(2), 115–122.

Aggarwal, K. K., & Tyagi, A. K. (2014). Optimal inventory and credit policies under two levels of trade credit financing in an inventory system with date-terms credit linked demand. *International Journal of Strategic Decision Sciences (IJSDS), 5*(4), 99–126.

Aggarwal, S. P., & Jaggi, C. K. (1995). Ordering policies of deteriorating items under permissible delay in payments. *Journal of the Operational Research Society, 46*(5), 658–662.

Bhunia, A. K., & Shaikh, A. A. (2015). An application of PSO in a two-warehouse inventory model for deteriorating item under permissible delay in payment with different inventory policies. *Applied Mathematics and Computation, 256*, 831–850.

Bhunia, A. K., Shaikh, A. A., Dhaka, V., Pareek, S., & Cárdenas-Barrón, L. E. (2018). An application of genetic algorithm and PSO in an inventory model for single deteriorating item with variable demand dependent on marketing strategy and displayed stock level. *Scientifica Iranica, 25*, 1641–1655.

Chang, C. T., Teng, J. T., & Goyal, S. K. (2008). Inventory lot-size models under trade credits: A review. *Asia-Pacific Journal of Operational Research, 25*(01), 89–112.

Chung, K. J., & Cárdenas-Barrón, L. E. (2013). The simplified solution procedure for deteriorating items under stock-dependent demand and two-level trade credit in the supply chain management. *Applied Mathematical Modelling, 37*(7), 4653–4660.

Clerc, M. (1999). The swarm and the queen: Towards a deterministic and adaptive particle swarm optimization. In *Proceedings of the 1999 Congress on Evolutionary Computation, 1999. CEC 99* (Vol. 3, pp. 1951–1957). IEEE.

Clerc, M., & Kennedy, J. (2002). The particle swarm-explosion, stability, and convergence in a multidimensional complex space. *IEEE Transactions on Evolutionary Computation, 6*(1), 58–73.

Eberhart, R. C., & Kennedy, J. (1995a). Particle swarm optimization. In *Proceeding of IEEE International Conference on Neural Network*, Perth, Australia, pp. 1942–1948.

Eberhart, R. C., & Kennedy, J. (1995b). A new optimizer using particle swarm theory. In *Proceedings of the Sixth International Symposium on Micro Machine and Human Science, 1995. MHS'95* (pp. 39–43). IEEE.

Garai, T., & Garg, H. (2019). Multi-objective linear fractional inventory model with possibility and necessity constraints under generalised intuitionistic fuzzy set environment. *CAAI Transactions on Intelligence Technology, 4*(3), 175–181.

Ghare, P. M. (1963). A model for an exponentially decaying inventory. *Journal of Industrial Engineering, 14*, 238–243.

Giri, B. C., & Maiti, T. (2013). Supply chain model with price-and trade credit-sensitive demand under two-level permissible delay in payments. *International Journal of Systems Science, 44*(5), 937–948.

Goyal, S. K. (1977). An integrated inventory model for a single supplier-single customer problem. *The International Journal of Production Research, 15*(1), 107–111.

Goyal, S. K. (1985). Economic order quantity under conditions of permissible delay in payments. *Journal of the Operational Research Society, 36*(4), 335–338.

Hariga, M. (1995). An EOQ model for deteriorating items with shortages and time-varying demand. *Journal of the Operational Research Society, 46*(3), 398–404.

He, Y., & Huang, H. (2013). Two-level credit financing for noninstantaneous deterioration items in a supply chain with downstream credit-linked demand. *Discrete Dynamics in Nature and Society, 2013.*

Huang, Y. F. (2003). Optimal retailer's ordering policies in the EOQ model under trade credit financing. *Journal of the Operational Research Society, 54*(9), 1011–1015.

Jaggi, C. K., & Mittal, M. (2003). An EOQ model for deteriorating items with time-dependent demand under inflationary conditions. *Advanced Modeling and Optimization, 5*(2).

Jaggi, C. K., & Mittal, M. (2011). Economic order quantity model for deteriorating items with imperfect quality. *Investigación Operacional, 32*(2), 107–113.

Kaanodiya, K. K., & Pachauri, R. R. (2011). Retailer's optimal ordering policies with two stage credit policies and imperfect quality. *International Business and Management, 3*(1), 77–81.

Min, J., Zhou, Y. W., & Zhao, J. (2010). An inventory model for deteriorating items under stock-dependent demand and two-level trade credit. *Applied Mathematical Modelling, 34*(11), 3273–3285.

Mishra, P., & Shaikh, A. (2017a). Optimal ordering policy for an integrated inventory model with stock dependent demand and order linked trade credits for twin ware house system. *Uncertain Supply Chain Management, 5*(3), 169–186.

Mishra, P., & Shaikh, A. (2017b). Optimal pricing and ordering policies for an integrated inventory model with stock and price sensitive demand. *Dynamics of Continuous, Discrete and Impulsive Systems Series B: Applications & Algorithms, 24*(6), 401–413.

Mishra, P., & Shaikh, A. (2017c). Optimal policies for deteriorating items with preservation and maintenance management when demand is trade credit sensitive. *AMSE Journal of Series-Modelling D, 38*(1), 36–54.

Mishra, P., Shaikh, A., & Talati, I. (2019). Optimal cycle time and payment option for retailer. In *Innovations in infrastructure* (pp. 537–547). Springer.

Mishra, P., Talati, I., & Shaikh, A. (2020). Supply chain network optimization through player selection using multi-objective genetic algorithm. In *Optimization and inventory management* (pp. 281–315). Springer.

Mishra, U., Cárdenas-Barrón, L. E., Tiwari, S., Shaikh, A. A., & Treviño-Garza, G. (2017). An inventory model under price and stock dependent demand for controllable deterioration rate with shortages and preservation technology investment. *Annals of Operations Research, 254*(1–2), 165–190.

Sarkar, B. (2012). An EOQ model with delay in payments and stock dependent demand in the presence of imperfect production. *Applied Mathematics and Computation, 218*(17), 8295–8308.

Sarkar, B., Mandal, B., & Sarkar, S. (2017). Preservation of deteriorating seasonal products with stock-dependent consumption rate and shortages. *Journal of Industrial & Management Optimization, 13*(1), 187–206.

Sarmah, S. P., Acharya, D., & Goyal, S. K. (2007). Coordination and profit sharing between a manufacturer and a buyer with target profit under credit option. *European Journal of Operational Research, 182*(3), 1469–1478.

Shah, N. H. (2015). Manufacturer-retailer inventory model for deteriorating items with price-sensitive credit-linked demand under two-level trade credit financing and profit sharing contract. *Cogent Engineering, 2*(1), 1012989.

Shah, N. H., Jani, M. Y., & Chaudhari, U. (2017). Study of imperfect manufacturing system with preservation technology investment under inflationary environment for quadratic demand: A reverse logistic approach. *Journal of Advanced Manufacturing Systems, 16*(01), 17–34.

Shah, N. H., Patel, D. G., & Shah, D. B. (2014). Optimal policies for deteriorating items with maximum lifetime and two-level trade credits. *International Journal of Mathematics and Mathematical Sciences, 2014*.

Shah, N. H., & Shah, A. D. (2014). Optimal cycle time and preservation technology investment for deteriorating items with price-sensitive stock-dependent demand under inflation. *Journal of Physics: Conference Series, 495*(1), 012017. IOP Publishing.

Shaikh, A. S., & Mishra, P. P. (2018). Optimal policies for items with quadratic demand and time-dependent deterioration under two echelon trade credits. In *Handbook of research on promoting business process improvement through inventory control techniques* (pp. 32–43). IGI Global.

Shaikh, A., & Mishra, P. (2019). Optimal policies for price sensitive quadratic demand with preservation technology investment under inflationary environment. *Journal of Advanced Manufacturing Systems, 18*(02), 325–337.

Shaikh, A., Mishra, P., & Talati, I. (2020). Allocation of order amongst available suppliers using multi-objective genetic algorithm. In *Optimization and inventory management* (pp. 317–329). Springer.

Soni, H., Shah, N. H., & Jaggi, C. K. (2010). Inventory models and trade credit: A review. *Control and Cybernetics, 39*, 867–882.

Teng, J. T., & Chang, C. T. (2009). Optimal manufacturer's replenishment policies in the EPQ model under two levels of trade credit policy. *European Journal of Operational Research, 195*(2), 358–363.

Waliv, R. H., Mishra, U., Garg, H., & Umap, H. P. (2020). A nonlinear programming approach to solve the stochastic multi-objective inventory model using the uncertain information. *Arabian Journal for Science and Engineering, 45*, 6963–6973.

Wu, J., Skouri, K., Teng, J. T., & Ouyang, L. Y. (2014). A note on "optimal replenishment policies for non-instantaneous deteriorating items with price and stock sensitive demand under permissible delay in payment." *International Journal of Production Economics, 155*, 324–329.

Optimization of the Berth Allocation Problem to the Vessels Using Priority Queuing Systems

Venkata S. S. Yadavalli, Olufemi Adetunji, and Rafid Alrikabi

Abstract In this paper, we study the problem of assignment of suitable berths to the vessels under different scenarios of vessel berthing policies, priorities and vessel serving or container handling-off. The problem was solved as a queuing system with non-preemptive priority. The objective was to maximize the utilization of the berth under different service levels. Different scenarios for berthing process of vessels and unloading of containers at the container terminal were considered to evaluate the performance of the system and to obtain the optimal service level parameters. The model considered a system in which different types of containers were managed together in an integrated manner. The steady-state behaviours of the expected waiting time, queue length, server utilization rate and the optimal number of servers necessary to attain given service levels for the different container types were studied experimentally under different conditions of arrival and service rates.

Keywords Berth allocation problem · Berthing priorities · Non-preemptive priority · Queuing model

1 Introduction

The berth allocation problem (BAP) is a dominant issue in a seaport container terminal. It incurs much attention in the maritime industry by many seaports authorities and terminal operators to improve the terminal efficiency and operations planning or to minimize the waiting time of vessels and maximize the berth utilization. There are a lot of incoming vessels or containerships arriving at seaport container terminals at all times, and these vessels need a number of berths along a quay. Each berth can serve one vessel within a few days depending on variables such as vessel type and size, container handling volume, the available number of quay cranes in berthing area, service priority and berth allocation policy.

V. S. S. Yadavalli · O. Adetunji (✉) · R. Alrikabi
Department of Industrial and Systems Engineering, University of Pretoria, Pretoria, South Africa
e-mail: olufemi.adetunji@up.ac.za

N. H. Shah and M. Mittal (eds.), *Soft Computing in Inventory Management*, Inventory Optimization, https://doi.org/10.1007/978-981-16-2156-7_3

Usually, the arriving vessels must wait in a queue until the berths are available to service them. That means, before berthing, the seaport authority assigns a berthing position and a berthing time to each vessel. Most seaports aim to minimize the waiting time of queuing vessels from the time they arrive at the seaport until container-handling operations (loading/loading) begin. After berthing, the vessels stay within the boundaries of the assigned berths, and then, the containers (fully loaded and empty) are unloaded (loaded) from/to the vessels. When the handling process or service is completed, the vessels emerge from their assigned berths and depart from the seaport. The deviation between the actual arrival time and the scheduled arrival time (or the expected arrival time) of the vessels often results in changes to the planning and organizing of quay side and yard side operations; viz, there are many scenarios that deal with how to approach vessel arrival times. When they arrive earlier than the expected a time, they are berthed immediately, or they are kept waiting at a container terminal for a period of time before berthing. This type of arrival time is called the static arrival; i.e., there are no arrival times given for the vessels on the berthing times. A different approach is used when the vessels cannot berth before the expected arrival time; i.e., the arrival times for berthing are fixed. This type of arrival time of vessels is called the dynamic arrival.

There are few studies focused on berth allocation problem, and some studies deal with both berth allocation and quay crane assignment. The following literature review provides more details on this topic: Kim and Moon (2003) suggested a simulated annealing algorithm and formulated a mixed integer linear programming model to minimize the total costs (including the cost due to the non-optimal berthing location of vessels in a container terminal and penalty cost due to delays in the departures of vessels). According to the experimental results that were obtained by using a simulated annealing algorithm and LINDO package for the formulated model, the researchers found that the simulated annealing algorithm obtains solutions that are similar to the optimal solutions found by the mixed integer linear programming model, and the results of the algorithm were near-optimal solutions, and the computational time was within the limits of practical usage. Dai et al. (2004) studied the berth allocation problem and focused on berth allocation planning optimization in a container terminal. Many scenarios and policies were applied to design a berthing system to allocate berthing space to vessels in real time close to their preferred locations at the terminal. The researchers used a simulation model to evaluate the performance of their proposed approach, and they found that the results show that the performance varies according to the various policy parameters adopted by the terminal operator. Furthermore, according to the moderate load scenario, the proposed approach is able to allocate space to over 90% of vessels upon arrival, with more than 80% of them being assigned to the preferred berthing location. Imai et al. (2005) addressed the berth allocation problem in multi-user container terminals (the busy container ports with heavy container traffic), by establishing a heuristic algorithm to minimize the total service times for all ships (the time from arrival to departure and waiting time). The proposed heuristic algorithm is used to solve the problem in two stages; the first stage identifies a solution given the number of partitioned berths, and the second stage relocates the ships that may overlap or be located sparsely in a scheduling space. They found that the algorithm can improve the terminal operation and that it yields a feasible solution to the berth allocation problem (BAP).

Boile et al. (2006) formulated a mixed integer programming model based on a heuristic algorithm to optimize berth allocation with service priorities in a multi-user terminal. The formulated model is used to minimize the weighted total service time (berthing time and handling time) and to find the optimal berth schedule for the assignment of ships to the berthing areas along a quay. The numerical experiments show that the heuristic algorithm is useful to obtain a new berth allocation scheme to deal with the changes in ship arrival times.

Moorthy and Teo (2006) studied the berth allocation problem and analysed the impact of the berth template design problem on container terminal operations. They proposed a robust model and used two methods to evaluate the robustness of the berth template (service-level waiting time and operational cost connectivity). They compared between the results that were obtained by using two models (robust and deterministic) and found that the average delays in the deterministic mode is 1.65 h with a variance of 2.75, whereas the average delay in the robust model is 0.75 h with a variance of 1.13. Furthermore, 27 vessels in the robust model's template have an expected delay of 0 h, as opposed to 13 vessels in the deterministic mode. The results indicate that the robust model is the better choice to solve the problem, and that it is able to find new templates with slightly better waiting time performance, and to keep the number of overlaps between vessels with minimum number during actual operations in a container terminal. Krcum et al. (2007) developed a multi-objective genetic algorithm (using Matlab) to deal with berth and quay cranes assignment problems and to minimize the total costs due to the berthing and quay crane operation (handling operation). The proposed algorithm is a useful technique for finding near-optimal solutions for the problems, and it is used to determine the berthing time and position of each vessel and the number of cranes to be allocated to the vessel. Theofanis et al. (2007) suggested a genetic algorithm heuristic to optimize the berth allocation problem (BAP) and formulated a mixed integer linear programming model to minimize the total weighted service time of all vessels. The scholars studied the discrete BAP and dynamic BAP that deal with calling vessels with various service priorities. The experimental results show that the optimization-based genetic algorithm (OBGA) heuristic is more efficient than the genetic algorithm heuristic without the optimization component in terms of the variance and minimum values of objective function. Imai et al. (2008) proposed a genetic algorithm-based heuristic to address the simultaneous berth and quay allocation problem. The formulated model is used to minimize the total service time (waiting and handling times) and to find the efficient scheduling process of simultaneous berth and crane allocation at a container terminal. The computational experiments show that the proposed algorithm is applicable to solving the problem and determining the berth schedule and quay crane schedule at the same time.

Golias et al. (2009) studied the berth allocation problem and formulated a mixed integer programming model to optimize the vessel arrival time. The proposed model is used to minimize the total waiting and delayed departure time for all vessels. They compared between the numerical results of a genetic algorithm (GA-based heuristic) and CPLEX to investigate the performance of the GA heuristic. The scholars found that their algorithm can be more beneficial for both the carrier and the terminal operator under the proposed berth scheduling policy. Javanshir et al. (2010) modified a mixed integer nonlinear programming model to address the continuous berth allocation problem (CBAP) to achieve the best service time in a container terminal. The modified model is used to minimize the service times of the ships (the time spent from arrival to departure including the waiting time). Many numerical experiments are carried out to find the optimal berthing time and berthing location of each ship, as well as the expected ship delay. According to the outputs and results, they found that the modified model provided better analysis of the berth allocation problem in a more acceptable computational time.

Zeng et al. (2011) studied the disruption management problem of berth allocation in a container terminal and developed a mixed integer programming model and a simulation optimization algorithm to optimize the simultaneous berth allocation (berthing position and berthing order of each vessel) and quay crane scheduling problems. The objective of the paper is to decrease the influence of unforeseen disruptions to operation system and decrease the additional cost resulting from disruptions. They applied a simulation optimization approach to assess the influence of disruptions and optimize the new berth schedule coping with disruptions. The numerical experiments indicate that the algorithm based on local rescheduling and Tabu search can improve the computation efficiency. Shan (2012) applied a genetic algorithm (coded in LINGO 11.0) to optimize the dynamic berth allocation with a discrete layout. The optimization model is used to minimize the total service time (waiting time and handling time) of all ships with the consideration of ships service priority. The proposed algorithm is useful for improving the container terminal management, and it can find a better solution to the problem. Ma et al (2012) focused on berth allocation planning and proposed an integrated model of combining berth allocation problems and quay cranes assignments to improve container terminal performances. The proposed model is used to minimize the total service time (vessel waiting time and handling time) and vessel transfer rate. It is based on a two-level genetic algorithm (TLGA) to maximize the performance of the terminal in terms of service quality. The numerical experiments show that the proposed (TLGA) can achieve better solutions for BAP in serving more important customers and that it is capable of solving the two problems simultaneously.

Hendriks et al. (2013) formulated a mixed integer quadratic programme (MIQP) to deal with both the berth allocation problem (BAP) and yard planning problem (YPP) or yard allocation problem (YAP) simultaneously (case study in PSA Antwerp Terminal). An alternating BAP-YAP heuristic is used to solve the formulated model, and the model is used to minimize the overall straddle carrier travel distance between quay and yard and between yard and hinterland. According to the results that were obtained by using CPLEX 11 to solve the problems, the researchers found that the alternating procedure yields significant reductions in the total straddle carrier driving distance compared with the initial condition. Sheikholeslami et al. (2013) proposed a simulation model (using ARENA simulation package) to address the problem of integrating berth allocation and quay crane assignment. The proposed simulation is applied on Rajaee Port in Iran, and it is used to evaluate the berth allocation planning and the problems in this domain. Three different policies of berth allocation (randomized allocation, length-based allocation and draft-based allocation) are examined by simulation model to test the performance of berth allocation plans. Results obtained from the simulation model indicated that the strategies of length-based allocation and draft-based allocation are dominated by random allocation scenario based on wait time and average anchorage queue length. Most of the researches and studies focused on the optimization of berth allocation problem, and they proposed many models to minimize the total service time for the vessels that arrive at container terminals. The proposed models are based on waiting time, handling time and delay time.

In this paper, the queuing theory (queuing system with non-preemptive priority) is used to study the behaviour and characteristics of berth allocation problem, as well as to understand the assignment of suitable berths to the vessels under different scenarios of berthing policy or priorities and vessel serving. The outline of this study is organized as follows: Sect. (2) discusses and describes briefly the problem of berthing of vessels at container terminals. In Sect. (3), a model is proposed to deal with the problem and to find the system characteristics of the berthing process of vessels from the time they arrive until the time they leave the boundaries of the seaport. In Sect. (4), numerical experiments are presented and the experimental results are discussed. Finally, in Sect. (5), the study is summarized and concluded.

2 Problem Description

When vessels or containerships arrive at a seaport container terminal, they are required to be in a queue before berthing. There are usually a set of incoming vessels that must wait in queue until the berths are available. The quay of a container terminal consists of many berths, each of which can serve one vessel within a few days (see Fig. 1). Sometimes, the berth can handle two small vessels or more, and sometimes, large vessels require two berths along a quay in order to load/unload their containers. Prior to berthing, the expected time of arrival for each visiting vessel depends on several factors such as the departure time of the vessel from the previous seaport, the distance between the origin seaport and the destination seaport, the average operating speed of vessel, weather conditions and other unforeseen events. There are some vessels which arrive at the seaport container terminal earlier or later than the expected time. When the seaport authority assigns a set of berths to a set of vessels, the terminal operator will then allow the vessels to moor at the berths according to the berths scheduling policy and priority. The selection of suitable berths to the vessels depends on many factors such as the length, the drafts and the size of vessels (capacities), the type of service, type and number of quay cranes, the lengths and the depth of berths. Most of container terminals aim to moor the vessels in berthing positions that are as near as possible to the preferable container stacking area in order to facilitate container transhipment from/to the vessels and to minimize the handling time.

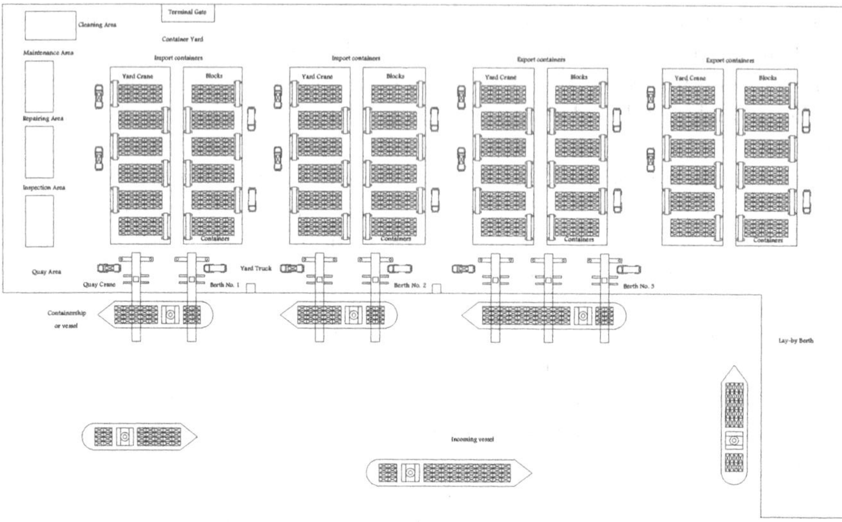

Fig. 1 Schematics of vessels berthing inside a container terminal

After berthing, usually, the incoming vessels are stationed at the assigned berths for a few days for the de-lashing of containers and container handling (loading/unloading) processes. Sometimes, before berthing at the assigned berths, the vessels wait for a short term at lay-by berths., There are many operations and activities that are associated with the arrival of vessels at the seaport (from the time they arrive until the time they leave the boundaries of the seaport). Any delay in the sequence of operations and activities of the vessel berthing process leads to seaport congestion and disruptions in container terminals. Furthermore, the delays incur an additional expenditure, especially if the waiting time of vessels and equipment (Quay Cranes, Yard Trucks, Yard Cranes) are taken into account. The container terminal cannot avoid the seaport congestion or the accumulation problem of large numbers of vessels inside the seaport when the arrival rate of vessels is high. That means the terminal operator must institute many kinds of berthing priorities to serve all vessels such as Berthing On Arrival (BOA), Largest Vessel-First (LVF), Smallest Vessel-First (SVF) and Shortest Service Time First (SSTF). The objective of this research is to apply queuing theory to optimize the vessel berthing process and to improve performance.

3 Mathematical Model

This problem is modelled as a queuing system to understand the behaviour and characteristics of berth allocation problem or the assignment of suitable berths to the vessels under different scenarios of berthing policy or priorities and of vessel serving. When the incoming vessels (or containerships) arrive at the container terminal, they are assigned to berthing positions at determined schedules. The seaports authorities and container terminal operators have to decide how many berths and quay cranes are assigned to these vessels. Usually, the visiting vessels must wait in a queue until the berths are available to service them, and sometimes, the vessels must be subjected to the berth allocation policy or service priority specially, particularly when there are a lot of incoming vessels or containerships arriving at the seaport's container terminals. That means the vessels must spend times in a queue, until the seaport authority assigns a berthing position and a berthing time to each vessel according to the berthing priorities. In general, the incoming vessels must be moored and served within the boundaries of the quay. When the inbound containers arrive at quay side, they are de-lashed and then served by quay cranes, luffing cranes or portainers; i.e., the containers are de-lashed and unloaded from vessel or containership by cranes, and then, they are moved from quay side to the container yard or stacking area by trucks, automated guided vehicles (AGVs) or straddle carriers.

The arrival of the inbound containers at seaport has a rate $\boldsymbol{\lambda}$ and the inter-arrival time (the average interval between consecutive container arrivals) or average time between arrivals (containers) can be expressed as $1/\lambda$. When the arrival vessels (that carry the inbound containers) are subjected to the berth allocation priority, then the arrival rate under priority class k becomes $\boldsymbol{\lambda_k}$ and the average time between arrivals (containers) under priority class k can be expressed as $1/\lambda_{\mathbf{k}}$. After berthing, the containers (fully loaded and empty) are discharged from the vessels, and the service rate of handling-off process (under priority class k) is performed by quay cranes and can be expressed as $\mu_{\mathbf{k}}$, and the mean service time (under priority class k) can be expressed as $1/\mu_{\mathbf{k}}$.

The average utilization (or the utilization factor) of the system is the ratio between the arrival rate and service rate or the ratio between mean service time $1/\mu$ and mean inter-arrival time $1/\lambda$, and can be expressed as $\rho = \frac{\lambda}{\mu}$ or $\rho = \frac{\lambda}{\mathbf{r}*\mu}$, where **r** the number of servers in the system. The utilization factor under priority class k can be expressed as $\rho_k = \frac{\lambda_k}{\mu_k}$.

$$\rho = \sum_{k=1}^{k=\mathbf{p}} \rho_k, \text{ where } k = 1, 2 \ldots p$$

$$\lambda = \sum_{k=1}^{k=p} \lambda_k, \text{ where } k = 1, 2 \ldots p$$

$$\mu = \sum_{k=1}^{k=p} \mu_k, \text{ where } k = 1, 2 \ldots p$$

Actually, in queuing system, there are one or more servers that provide service to the arriving customers. In our case study, the customers are containers and the servers are quay cranes. We assume the queuing system in our case as single server non-preemptive with 2-priorities. In this queuing system, we assume the arrivals follow a Poisson probability distribution at an average rate of **λ** containers per unit time (hour). Also, we assume the service times are distributed exponentially with an average rate of **λ** containers per unit time (hour). We use the state transition diagram shown in Fig. 2 to formulate the state balance equations for the single server non-preemptive priority system at a container terminal and derive the steady-state probabilities by the Markov process method.

Let (N) be maximum number of vessels (or containers) in the system and n the current number of vessels (or containers) in the system. In our case study $N = 2$.

P(n) = the probability that there are (n) vessels (or containers) in the system.

$$(\lambda 1 + \lambda 2)P_{0,0,0} = \mu 2 P_{0,1,2} + \mu 1 P_{1,0,1} \quad (1)$$

$$(\lambda 1 + \lambda 2 + \mu 2)P_{0,1,2} = \lambda 2 P_{0,0,0} + \mu 2 P_{0,2,2} \quad (2)$$

$$(\lambda 1 + \lambda 2 + \mu 1)P_{1,0,1} = \lambda 1 P_{0,0,0} + \mu 1 P_{2,0,1} + \mu 2 P_{1,1,2} \quad (3)$$

$$\mu 1 P_{1,1,1} = \lambda 2 P_{1,0,1} \quad (4)$$

$$\mu 2 P_{0,2,2} = \lambda 2 P_{0,1,2} \quad (5)$$

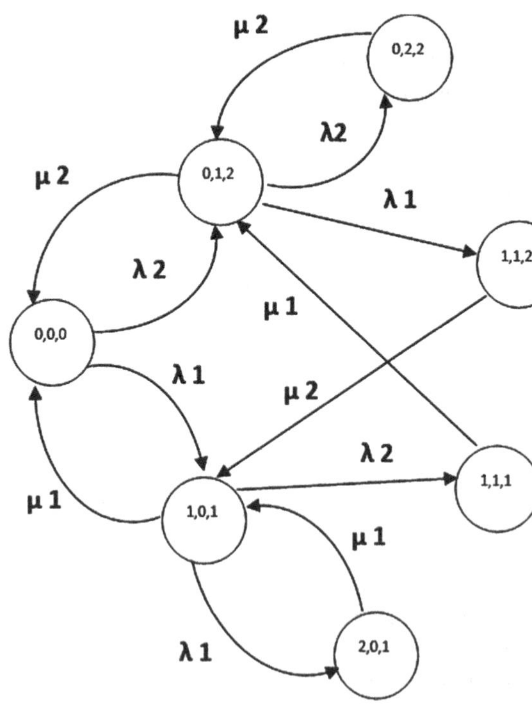

Fig. 2 State transition diagram for a 2-priority, non-preemptive M/M/1/2 queue

$$\mu 2 P_{1,1,2} = \lambda 1 P_{0,1,2} \tag{6}$$

$$\mu 1 P_{2,0,1} = \lambda 1 P_{1,0,1} \tag{7}$$

$$\mathrm{P}_{0,0,0} + \mathrm{P}_{1,0,1} + \mathrm{P}_{2,0,1} + \mathrm{P}_{1,1,1} + \mathrm{P}_{0,1,2} + \mathrm{P}_{0,2,2} + \mathrm{P}_{1,1,2} = 1 \tag{8}$$

To simplify the solution for the above steady-state equations, we suppose $\mathbf{P}_{0,2,2} = \mathbf{Z}$

$$\mathrm{P}_{0,\ 2,\ 2} = \mathrm{Z} \tag{9}$$

Substituting Eq. (9) into Eq. (5), we get

$$\begin{aligned}
\mu 2 P_{0,2,2} &= \lambda 2 P_{0,1,2} \\
\mu 2 Z &= \lambda 2 P_{0,1,2} \\
P_{0,1,2} &= \frac{\mu 2 Z}{\lambda 2}
\end{aligned} \tag{10}$$

Substituting Eqs. (9) and (10) into Eq. (2), we get

$$\begin{aligned}
(\lambda 1 + \lambda 2 + \mu 2) P_{0,1,2} &= \lambda 2 P_{0,0,0} + \mu 2 P_{0,2,2} \\
(\lambda 1 + \lambda 2 + \mu 2) \frac{\mu 2 Z}{\lambda 2} &= \lambda 2 P_{0,0,0} + \mu 2 Z \\
\lambda 2 P_{0,0,0} &= (\lambda 1 + \lambda 2 + \mu 2) \frac{\mu 2 Z}{\lambda 2} - \mu 2 Z \\
\lambda 2 P_{0,0,0} &= \frac{\left(\lambda 1 \mu 2 + \lambda 2 \mu 2 + \mu 2^2\right) Z}{\lambda 2} - \mu 2 Z \\
P_{0,0,0} &= \frac{\left(\lambda 1 \mu 2 + \lambda 2 \mu 2 + \mu 2^2\right) Z}{\lambda 2^2} - \frac{\mu 2 Z}{\lambda 2} \\
P_{0,0,0} &= \frac{\left(\lambda 1 \mu 2 + \mu 2^2\right) Z}{\lambda 2^2}
\end{aligned} \tag{11}$$

Putting Eqs. (10) and (11) into Eq. (1), we get

$$\begin{aligned}
(\lambda 1 + \lambda 2) P_{0,0,0} &= \mu 2 P_{0,1,2} + \mu 1 P_{1,0,1} \\
(\lambda 1 + \lambda 2) \frac{\left(\lambda 1 \mu 2 + \mu 2^2\right) Z}{\lambda 2^2} &= \mu 2 \frac{\mu 2 Z}{\lambda 2} + \mu 1 P_{1,0,1} \\
\mu 1 P_{1,0,1} &= (\lambda 1 + \lambda 2) \frac{\left(\lambda 1 \mu 2 + \mu 2^2\right) Z}{\lambda 2^2} - \mu 2 \frac{\mu 2 Z}{\lambda 2} \\
\mu 1 P_{1,0,1} &= \frac{(\lambda 1 + \lambda 2)\left(\lambda 1 \mu 2 + \mu 2^2\right) Z}{\lambda 2^2} - \frac{\mu 2^2 Z}{\lambda 2}
\end{aligned}$$

$$P_{1,0,1} = \frac{(\lambda 1 + \lambda 2)(\lambda 1\mu 2 + \mu 2^2)Z}{\mu 1\lambda 2^2} - \frac{\mu 2^2 Z}{\mu 1\lambda 2} \tag{12}$$

From Eq. (7) and Eq. (12), we obtain

$$\mu 1 P_{2,0,1} = \lambda 1 P_{1,0,1}$$

$$\mu 1 P_{2,0,1} = \lambda 1\left(\frac{(\lambda 1 + \lambda 2)(\lambda 1\mu 2 + \mu 2^2)Z}{\mu 1\lambda 2^2} - \frac{\mu 2^2 Z}{\mu 1\lambda 2}\right)$$

$$P_{2,0,1} = \left(\frac{\lambda 1}{\mu 1}\right)\left(\frac{(\lambda 1 + \lambda 2)(\lambda 1\mu 2 + \mu 2^2)Z}{\mu 1\lambda 2^2} - \frac{\mu 2^2 Z}{\mu 1\lambda 2}\right) \tag{13}$$

Substituting Eq. (10) into Eq. (6), we get

$$\mu 2 P_{1,1,2} = \lambda 1 P_{0,1,2}$$

$$\mu 2 P_{1,1,2} = \lambda 1 \frac{\mu 2 Z}{\lambda 2}$$

$$\mu 2 P_{1,1,2} = \frac{\lambda 1\mu 2 Z}{\lambda 2}$$

$$P_{1,1,2} = \frac{\lambda 1\mu 2 Z}{\mu 2\lambda 2} \tag{14}$$

Finally, putting Eq. (12) into Eq. (4) a, then we get

$$\mu 1 P_{1,1,1} = \lambda 2 P_{1,0,1}$$

$$\mu 1 P_{1,1,1} = \lambda 2\left(\frac{(\lambda 1 + \lambda 2)(\lambda 1\mu 2 + \mu 2^2)Z}{\mu 1\lambda 2^2} - \frac{\mu 2^2 Z}{\mu 1\lambda 2}\right)$$

$$P_{1,1,1} = \frac{\lambda 2}{\mu 1}\left(\frac{(\lambda 1 + \lambda 2)(\lambda 1\mu 2 + \mu 2^2)Z}{\mu 1\lambda 2^2} - \frac{\mu 2^2 Z}{\mu 1\lambda 2}\right) \tag{15}$$

From Eq. (8), we can find the value of z by using the equations of the probability

$$P_{0,0,0} + P_{1,0,1} + P_{2,0,1} + P_{1,1,1} + P_{0,1,2} + P_{0,2,2} + P_{1,1,2} = 1$$

$$\left(\frac{(\lambda 1\mu 2 + \mu 2^2)Z}{\lambda 2^2}\right) + \left(\frac{(\lambda 1 + \lambda 2)(\lambda 1\mu 2 + \mu 2^2)Z}{\mu 1\lambda 2^2} - \frac{\mu 2^2 Z}{\mu 1\lambda 2}\right)$$
$$+ \left(\left(\frac{\lambda 1}{\mu 1}\right)\left(\frac{(\lambda 1 + \lambda 2)(\lambda 1\mu 2 + \mu 2^2)Z}{\mu 1\lambda 2^2} - \frac{\mu 2^2 Z}{\mu 1\lambda 2}\right)\right)$$
$$+ \left(\left(\frac{\lambda 2}{\mu 1}\right)\left(\frac{(\lambda 1 + \lambda 2)(\lambda 1\mu 2 + \mu 2^2)Z}{\mu 1\lambda 2^2} - \frac{\mu 2^2 Z}{\mu 1\lambda 2}\right)\right)$$

$$+\left(\frac{\mu 2Z}{\lambda 2}\right)+(Z)+\left(\frac{\lambda 1\mu 2Z}{\mu 2\lambda 2}\right) \tag{16}$$

$$\begin{aligned} Z&\left(\left(\frac{(\lambda 1\mu 2+\mu 2^2)}{\lambda 2^2}\right)\right.\\ &+\left(\frac{(\lambda 1+\lambda 2)(\lambda 1\mu 2+\mu 2^2)}{\mu 1\lambda 2^2}-\frac{\mu 2^2}{\mu 1\lambda 2}\right)\\ &+\left(\left(\frac{\lambda 1}{\mu 1}\right)\left(\frac{(\lambda 1+\lambda 2)(\lambda 1\mu 2+\mu 2^2)}{\mu 1\lambda 2^2}-\frac{\mu 2^2}{\mu 1\lambda 2}\right)\right)\\ &+\left(\left(\frac{\lambda 2}{\mu 1}\right)\left(\frac{(\lambda 1+\lambda 2)(\lambda 1\mu 2+\mu 2^2)}{\mu 1\lambda 2^2}-\frac{\mu 2^2}{\mu 1\lambda 2}\right)\right)\\ &\left.+\left(\frac{\mu 2}{\lambda 2}\right)+(1)+\left(\frac{\lambda 1\mu 2}{\mu 2\lambda 2}\right)\right)=1 \end{aligned} \tag{16a}$$

$$\begin{aligned} Z=1/&\left(\left(\frac{(\lambda 1\mu 2+\mu 2^2)}{\lambda 2^2}\right)+\left(\frac{(\lambda 1+\lambda 2)(\lambda 1\mu 2+\mu 2^2)}{\mu 1\lambda 2^2}-\frac{\mu 2^2}{\mu 1\lambda 2}\right)\right.\\ &+\left(\left(\frac{\lambda 1}{\mu 1}\right)\left(\frac{(\lambda 1+\lambda 2)(\lambda 1\mu 2+\mu 2^2)}{\mu 1\lambda 2^2}-\frac{\mu 2^2}{\mu 1\lambda 2}\right)\right)\\ &+\left(\left(\frac{\lambda 2}{\mu 1}\right)\left(\frac{(\lambda 1+\lambda 2)(\lambda 1\mu 2+\mu 2^2)}{\mu 1\lambda 2^2}-\frac{\mu 2^2}{\mu 1\lambda 2}\right)\right)+\left(\frac{\mu 2}{\lambda 2}\right)+(1)\\ &\left.+\left(\frac{\lambda 1\mu 2}{\mu 2\lambda 2}\right)\right) \end{aligned} \tag{16b}$$

$$\begin{aligned} Z=&\left(\left(\frac{(\lambda 1\mu 2+\mu 2^2)}{\lambda 2^2}\right)+\left(\frac{(\lambda 1+\lambda 2)(\lambda 1\mu 2+\mu 2^2)}{\mu 1\lambda 2^2}-\frac{\mu 2^2}{\mu 1\lambda 2}\right)\right.\\ &+\left(\left(\frac{\lambda 1}{\mu 1}\right)\left(\frac{(\lambda 1+\lambda 2)(\lambda 1\mu 2+\mu 2^2)}{\mu 1\lambda 2^2}-\frac{\mu 2^2}{\mu 1\lambda 2}\right)\right)\\ &+\left(\left(\frac{\lambda 2}{\mu 1}\right)\left(\frac{(\lambda 1+\lambda 2)(\lambda 1\mu 2+\mu 2^2)}{\mu 1\lambda 2^2}-\frac{\mu 2^2}{\mu 1\lambda 2}\right)\right)+\left(\frac{\mu 2}{\lambda 2}\right)+(1)\\ &\left.+\left(\frac{\lambda 1\mu 2}{\mu 2\lambda 2}\right)\right)^{-1} \end{aligned} \tag{16c}$$

Then, the steady-state probabilities are:

$$P_{0,2,2}=\left(\left(\frac{(\lambda 1\mu 2+\mu 2^2)}{\lambda 2^2}\right)+\left(\frac{(\lambda 1+\lambda 2)(\lambda 1\mu 2+\mu 2^2)}{\mu 1\lambda 2^2}-\frac{\mu 2^2}{\mu 1\lambda 2}\right)\right.$$

$$+\left(\left(\frac{\lambda 1}{\mu 1}\right)\left(\frac{(\lambda 1+\lambda 2)(\lambda 1\mu 2+\mu 2^2)}{\mu 1\lambda 2^2}-\frac{\mu 2^2}{\mu 1\lambda 2}\right)\right)$$
$$+\left(\frac{\lambda 2}{\mu 1}\left(\frac{(\lambda 1+\lambda 2)(\lambda 1\mu 2+\mu 2^2)}{\mu 1\lambda 2^2}-\frac{\mu 2^2}{\mu 1\lambda 2}\right)\right)+\left(\frac{\mu 2}{\lambda 2}\right)+(1)$$
$$+\left(\frac{\lambda 1\mu 2}{\mu 2\lambda 2}\right)\Bigg)^{-1} \tag{17}$$

$$P_{0,1,2}=\frac{\mu 2}{\lambda 2}*\left(\left(\frac{(\lambda 1\mu 2+\mu 2^2)}{\lambda 2^2}\right)+\left(\frac{(\lambda 1+\lambda 2)(\lambda 1\mu 2+\mu 2^2)}{\mu 1\lambda 2^2}-\frac{\mu 2^2}{\mu 1\lambda 2}\right)\right.$$
$$+\left(\left(\frac{\lambda 1}{\mu 1}\right)\left(\frac{(\lambda 1+\lambda 2)(\lambda 1\mu 2+\mu 2^2)}{\mu 1\lambda 2^2}-\frac{\mu 2^2}{\mu 1\lambda 2}\right)\right)$$
$$+\left(\frac{\lambda 2}{\mu 1}\left(\frac{(\lambda 1+\lambda 2)(\lambda 1\mu 2+\mu 2^2)}{\mu 1\lambda 2^2}-\frac{\mu 2^2}{\mu 1\lambda 2}\right)\right)+\left(\frac{\mu 2}{\lambda 2}\right)+(1)$$
$$+\left(\frac{\lambda 1\mu 2}{\mu 2\lambda 2}\right)\Bigg)^{-1} \tag{18}$$

$$P_{0,0,0}=\frac{(\lambda 1\lambda 2+\lambda 2^2)}{\lambda 2^2}$$
$$*\left(\left(\frac{(\lambda 1\lambda 2+\lambda 2^2)}{\lambda 2^2}\right)+\left(\frac{(\lambda 1+\lambda 2)(\lambda 1\lambda 2+\lambda 2^2)}{\lambda 1\lambda 2^2}-\frac{\lambda 2^2}{\lambda 1\lambda 2}\right)\right.$$
$$+\left(\left(\frac{\lambda 1}{\lambda 1}\right)\left(\frac{(\lambda 1+\lambda 2)(\lambda 1\lambda 2+\lambda 2^2)}{\lambda 1\lambda 2^2}-\frac{\lambda 2^2}{\lambda 1\lambda 2}\right)\right)$$
$$+\left(\frac{\lambda 2}{\lambda 1}\left(\frac{(\lambda 1+\lambda 2)(\lambda 1\lambda 2+\lambda 2^2)}{\lambda 1\lambda 2^2}-\frac{\lambda 2^2}{\lambda 1\lambda 2}\right)\right)+\left(\frac{\lambda 2}{\lambda 2}\right)+(1)$$
$$+\left(\frac{\lambda 1\lambda 2}{\lambda 2\lambda 2}\right)\Bigg)^{-1} \tag{19}$$

$$P_{1,0,1}=\left(\frac{(\lambda 1+\lambda 2)(\lambda 1\mu 2+\mu 2^2)}{\mu 1\lambda 2^2}-\frac{\mu 2^2}{\mu 1\lambda 2}\right)$$
$$*\left(\left(\frac{(\lambda 1\mu 2+\mu 2^2)}{\lambda 2^2}\right)+\left(\frac{(\lambda 1+\lambda 2)(\lambda 1\mu 2+\mu 2^2)}{\mu 1\lambda 2^2}-\frac{\mu 2^2}{\mu 1\lambda 2}\right)\right.$$
$$+\left(\left(\frac{\lambda 1}{\mu 1}\right)\left(\frac{(\lambda 1+\lambda 2)(\lambda 1\mu 2+\mu 2^2)}{\mu 1\lambda 2^2}-\frac{\mu 2^2}{\mu 1\lambda 2}\right)\right)$$
$$+\left(\frac{\lambda 2}{\mu 1}\left(\frac{(\lambda 1+\lambda 2)(\lambda 1\mu 2+\mu 2^2)}{\mu 1\lambda 2^2}-\frac{\mu 2^2}{\mu 1\lambda 2}\right)\right)+\left(\frac{\mu 2}{\lambda 2}\right)+(1)$$

$$+\left(\frac{\lambda 1\mu 2}{\mu 2\lambda 2}\right)\Bigg)^{-1} \tag{20}$$

$$\begin{aligned}
P_{2,0,1} = {} & \left(\frac{\lambda 1}{\mu 1}\right)\left(\frac{(\lambda 1+\lambda 2)(\lambda 1\mu 2+\mu 2^2)}{\mu 1\lambda 2^2}-\frac{\mu 2^2}{\mu 1\lambda 2}\right)\\
& *\left(\left(\frac{(\lambda 1\mu 2+\mu 2^2)}{\lambda 2^2}\right)+\left(\frac{(\lambda 1+\lambda 2)(\lambda 1\mu 2+\mu 2^2)}{\mu 1\lambda 2^2}-\frac{\mu 2^2}{\mu 1\lambda 2}\right)\right.\\
& +\left(\left(\frac{\lambda 1}{\mu 1}\right)\left(\frac{(\lambda 1+\lambda 2)(\lambda 1\mu 2+\mu 2^2)}{\mu 1\lambda 2^2}-\frac{\mu 2^2}{\mu 1\lambda 2}\right)\right)\\
& +\left(\frac{\lambda 2}{\mu 1}\left(\frac{(\lambda 1+\lambda 2)(\lambda 1\mu 2+\mu 2^2)}{\mu 1\lambda 2^2}-\frac{\mu 2^2}{\mu 1\lambda 2}\right)\right)+\left(\frac{\mu 2}{\lambda 2}\right)+(1)\\
& \left.+\left(\frac{\lambda 1\mu 2}{\mu 2\lambda 2}\right)\right)^{-1}
\end{aligned} \tag{21}$$

$$\begin{aligned}
P_{1,1,2} = {} & \frac{\lambda 1\mu 2}{\mu 2\lambda 2} *\left(\left(\frac{(\lambda 1\mu 2+\mu 2^2)}{\lambda 2^2}\right)+\left(\frac{(\lambda 1+\lambda 2)(\lambda 1\mu 2+\mu 2^2)}{\mu 1\lambda 2^2}-\frac{\mu 2^2}{\mu 1\lambda 2}\right)\right.\\
& +\left(\left(\frac{\lambda 1}{\mu 1}\right)\left(\frac{(\lambda 1+\lambda 2)(\lambda 1\mu 2+\mu 2^2)}{\mu 1\lambda 2^2}-\frac{\mu 2^2}{\mu 1\lambda 2}\right)\right)\\
& +\left(\frac{\lambda 2}{\mu 1}\left(\frac{(\lambda 1+\lambda 2)(\lambda 1\mu 2+\mu 2^2)}{\mu 1\lambda 2^2}-\frac{\mu 2^2}{\mu 1\lambda 2}\right)\right)+\left(\frac{\mu 2}{\lambda 2}\right)+(1)\\
& \left.+\left(\frac{\lambda 1\mu 2}{\mu 2\lambda 2}\right)\right)^{-1}
\end{aligned} \tag{22}$$

$$\begin{aligned}
P_{1,1,1} = {} & \left(\frac{\lambda 2}{\mu 1}\left(\frac{(\lambda 1+\lambda 2)(\lambda 1\mu 2+\mu 2^2)}{\mu 1\lambda 2^2}-\frac{\mu 2^2}{\mu 1\lambda 2}\right)\right)\\
& *\left(\left(\frac{(\lambda 1\mu 2+\mu 2^2)}{\lambda 2^2}\right)+\left(\frac{(\lambda 1+\lambda 2)(\lambda 1\mu 2+\mu 2^2)}{\mu 1\lambda 2^2}-\frac{\mu 2^2}{\mu 1\lambda 2}\right)\right.\\
& +\left(\left(\frac{\lambda 1}{\mu 1}\right)\left(\frac{(\lambda 1+\lambda 2)(\lambda 1\mu 2+\mu 2^2)}{\mu 1\lambda 2^2}-\frac{\mu 2^2}{\mu 1\lambda 2}\right)\right)\\
& +\left(\frac{\lambda 2}{\mu 1}\left(\frac{(\lambda 1+\lambda 2)(\lambda 1\mu 2+\mu 2^2)}{\mu 1\lambda 2^2}-\frac{\mu 2^2}{\mu 1\lambda 2}\right)\right)+\left(\frac{\mu 2}{\lambda 2}\right)+(1)\\
& \left.+\left(\frac{\lambda 1\mu 2}{\mu 2\lambda 2}\right)\right)^{-1}
\end{aligned} \tag{23}$$

We suppose the following notations:

$\mathbf{E(W_k)}$: The average time of container spent waiting in the queue or line under priority class k.

$\mathbf{E(L_k^q)}$: The average number of containers waiting in the queue or line under priority class k.

$\mathbf{E(S_k)}$: The average time of container spent waiting in the system, including service under priority class k.

$\mathbf{E(L_k)}$: The average number of containers in the service system under priority class k.

Let $\rho_{\mathbf{k}} = \lambda_{\mathbf{k}}\mathbf{E(B_k)}$ The utilization factor under priority class k.

Then, according to the PASTA property (Poisson Arrivals See Time Averages), can we find $\mathbf{E(L_k^q)}$. First, we find the characteristic of queuing system for the container of class 1. The container of class 1 must wait for the containers of its own class that arrived before and also for the container (if any) in handling-off process (in service).

$$E(W_1) = E(L_1^q) * E(B_1) + \sum_{k=1}^{k=p} \rho_k E(R_k) \tag{24}$$

$$\rho = \sum_{k=1}^{k=p} \rho_k, \text{ where } k = 1, 2 \ldots p \tag{25}$$

$$E(R) = \sum_{k=1}^{k=p} \frac{\rho_k}{\rho} E(R_k), \text{ where } k = 1, 2 \ldots p \tag{26}$$

Substituting Eqs. (25) and (26) into Eq. (24), we get

$$E(W_1) = E\left(L_1^q\right) * E(B_1) + \rho E(R) \tag{27}$$

The term $\rho\,\mathbf{E(R)}$ represents the expected remaining amount of work currently present at the server (quay crane), i.e. handling-off process.

From Little's formula down below and utilization factor under priority class k$\mathbf{E(B_1)}$, we can find $\mathbf{E(W_1)}$

$$E\left(L_1^q\right) = \lambda_1 E(W_1) \tag{28}$$

$$E(W_1) = \lambda_1 E(W_1) * \frac{\rho_1}{\lambda_1} + \rho E(R) \tag{27a}$$

$$E(W_1) = E(W_1) * \rho_1 + \rho E(R) \tag{27b}$$

$$E(W_1) - \rho_1 E(W_1) = \rho E(R) \tag{27c}$$

$$E(W_1)(1-\rho_1)=\rho E(R) \tag{27d}$$

$$E(W_1)=\frac{\rho E(R)}{1-\rho_1} \tag{29}$$

From Eq. (28), we can find the average number of containers class 1 waiting in the queue or in line, $\mathbf{E(L_1^q)}$.

$$E\left(L_1^q\right)=\lambda_1*\frac{\rho E(R)}{1-\rho_1} \tag{30}$$

The average time container class 1 spent waiting in the system, including service $\mathbf{E(S_1)}$, can be expressed as:

$$\mathrm{E(S_1)}=\ \mathrm{E(W_1)}\ +\mathrm{E(B_1)} \tag{31}$$

$$E(S_1)=\frac{\rho E(R)}{1-\rho_1}+\frac{\rho_1}{\lambda_1} \tag{31a}$$

The average number of containers class 1 in the service system $\mathbf{E(L_1)}$ can be expressed as:

$$E(L_1)=E\left(L_1^q\right)+\rho_1 \tag{32}$$

$$E(L_1)=\lambda_1*\frac{\rho E(R)}{1-\rho_1}+\rho_1 \tag{32a}$$

We can also find the characteristic of queuing system for the container of class 2. While the container from this class waits in the queue, it must also wait for the containers for higher priority that arrive late.

$$E(W_k)=\sum_{r=1}^{r=k}E\left(L_r^q\right)*E(B_r)+\rho E(R)+E(W_k)\sum_{r=1}^{r=k-1}\rho_r \tag{33}$$

$$E(W_k)-E(W_k)\sum_{r=1}^{r=k-1}\rho_r=\sum_{r=1}^{r=k}E\left(L_r^q\right)*E(B_r)+\rho E(R) \tag{33a}$$

$$E(W_k)\left(1-\sum_{r=1}^{r=k-1}\rho_r\right)=\sum_{r=1}^{r=k}E\left(L_r^q\right)*E(B_r)+\rho E(R) \tag{33b}$$

From Little's formula, we can find $(\mathbf{W_k})$.

$$E\left(L_k^q\right)=\lambda_k E(W_k)$$

$$E(W_k)\left(1-\sum_{r=1}^{r=k}\rho_r\right)=\sum_{r=1}^{r=k-1}E\left(L_r^q\right)*E(B_r)+\rho E(R) \tag{33c}$$

By replacing k with $k-1$ from Eq. (33b).

$$E(W_k)\left(1-\sum_{r=1}^{r=k}\rho_r\right)=\sum_{r=1}^{r=k-1}E\left(L_r^q\right)*E(B_r)+\rho E(R)=E(W_{k-1})\left(1-\sum_{r=1}^{r=k-2}\rho_r\right) \tag{33d}$$

From the expression $(\mathbf{W}_k)$, we easily drive recursively

$$E(W_k)=\rho E(R)/\left(1-\sum_{r=1}^{r=k}\rho_r\right)\left(1-\sum_{r=1}^{r=k-1}\rho_r\right), wherek=1,2,\ldots p \tag{34}$$

From Little's formula, we can find the average number of containers class 2 (**k = 2**) waiting in the queue or line $\mathbf{E(L_k^q)}$.

$$E\left(L_k^q\right)=\lambda_k*\left(\rho E(R)/\left(1-\sum_{r=1}^{r=k}\rho_r\right)\left(1-\sum_{r=1}^{r=k-1}\rho_r\right)\right) \tag{35}$$

The average time of container class 2 spent waiting in the system, including service $\mathbf{E(S_k)}$ can be expressed as **k = 2**

$$\mathrm{E(S_k)=E(W_k)+E(B_k)} \tag{36}$$

$$E(S_2)=\rho E(R)/\left(1-\sum_{r=1}^{r=k}\rho_r\right)\left(1-\sum_{r=1}^{r=k-1}\rho_r\right)+\frac{\rho_k}{\lambda_k} \tag{36a}$$

The average number of containers class 2(**k = 2**) in the service system $\mathbf{E(L_k)}$ can be expressed as

$$E(L_k)=E\left(L_k^q\right)+\rho_k \tag{37}$$

$$E(L_k)=\lambda_k*\left(\rho E(R)/\left(1-\sum_{r=1}^{r=k}\rho_r\right)\left(1-\sum_{r=1}^{r=k-1}\rho_r\right)\right)+\rho_k \tag{37a}$$

3.1 Assumptions

The following assumptions are made for the model:

1. We consider that each berth along the quay can serve one vessel within a specific time, and there is no overlap in the assigned berths for the vessels. That means the berth cannot handle two small vessels (or more), and the large vessel cannot occupy two berths (or more) along a quay.
2. The length of the berth must be longer than the length of the vessel and the clearance (or the space) between two vessels along a quay must be approximately equal to the width of the biggest vessel; it also must include 15 m for both sides of vessel (the front and the rear of the vessel) to avoid the overlap of vessels in terms of the orientation of the vessels locations within the boundaries of berths.
3. The depth of the berth must be greater than the draft (draught) of the vessel, and the clearance between the keel of the vessel and the channel bottom must be within the guaranteed depth. The depth of berth depends on many factors like: draft of vessel, water level in the channel, sinkage due to vessel speed, unevenness of keel due to loading conditions, wave levels, tidal levels and dredge level.
4. We consider that in the ideal condition, there are enough equipment (cranes, trucks, vehicles, etc.) to perform all tasks, functions and operations at a container terminal. That means there is no delay or waiting in the performance of those tasks or functions in terms of lack in the number of equipment inside a container terminal.
5. When the handling process or service is completed, the vessels leave (depart) the berths and the seaport immediately.
6. The speed of handling-off/on containers from/to the vessel, depends on number of quay cranes, the transshipment rate of quay cranes, the simultaneous operations between quay cranes and yard trucks or automated guided vehicles (AGVs), etc., we assume the service rate of handling-off process for vessels with high priority is the same as that of vessels with low priority, i.e. $\mu = \mu_{\mathbf{kh}} = \mu_{\mathbf{kl}}$.
7. When the vessel with high priority arrives at the container terminal, it can move ahead of all the low priority vessels waiting in the queue, but low priority vessels in service are not interrupted by high priority vessels; i.e., a vessel in service is allowed to complete its service normally even if a vessel of higher priority enters the queue while its service is going on.
8. When the vessels arrive at the seaport earlier than the expected time of arrival, the terminal operator will decide the vessels which will continue the berthing process if there are available berths, and this does not have an effect on the overall berthing strategy.
9. We assume all the vessels moor in berthing positions or locations near the preferable container stacking area.

10. We assume the layout of berths in a container terminal is discrete. That means the quay is divided into a finite set of berths, and each vessel or containership in this layout can occupy a suitable berth within a specific time. Service time for the service centres (de-lashing process, quay cranes and yard trucks) is constant, i.e. static. The arrival of vessels is dynamic, and the vessels cannot berth before the expected arrival time. That means fixed arrival times are given for the vessels berthing times, for all vessels to be scheduled for berthing that have not yet arrived and the arrival times are known in advance.

4 Experimental Results and Discussion

Thirty-two different scenarios for berthing process of vessels and unloading containers at container terminal are considered in order to find the optimal service level and to achieve maximum efficiency of service stations. These scenarios vary from each other in terms of quantities of incoming containers, number of quay cranes (handling-off) that are used to perform the operations, berthing policy and priorities as well as vessel serving.

Tables 1a, b and 2 show the analysis and the probabilities of the single server non-preemptive priority queuing system at a container terminal. Table 3 shows the average waiting times of containers in the queue and in the system (container terminal), as well as the average number of containers waiting in the queue and in the system. Generally, the experimental results show that increment in the number of arrival of containers according to each priority (high or low) leads to increase in the average waiting times of containers in the queue and in the system, respectively, as well as increase the average number of containers waiting in the queue and in the system (when the service centres have the same values of service rate). In the scenarios no. (1) to no. (8), we find the increment in the number of arrival containers class 2 (when the number of arrival containers class 1 remains the same in all scenarios) leads to increase in $\mathbf{E}(\mathbf{W}_2)$, $\mathbf{E}(\mathbf{L}_2^q)$, $\mathbf{E}(\mathbf{L}_2)$ and $\mathbf{E}(\mathbf{S}_2)$, respectively, as shown in Fig. 3. In the scenarios no. (9) to no. (16), we also find that increment in the number of arrival of containers class 1 (when the number of arrival containers class 2 is the same in all scenarios) leads to increase in $\mathbf{E}(\mathbf{W}_1)$, $\mathbf{E}(\mathbf{L}_1^q)$, $\mathbf{E}(\mathbf{L}_1)$ and $\mathbf{E}(\mathbf{S}_1)$ more than the values that are in the in scenarios no. (1) to no. (8), as shown in Fig. 4. Also, the values of $\mathbf{E}(\mathbf{W}_2)$, $\mathbf{E}(\mathbf{L}_2^q)$, $\mathbf{E}(\mathbf{L}_2)$ and $\mathbf{E}(\mathbf{S}_2)$ in scenarios no. (9) to no. (16) are less than the values in scenarios no. (1) to no. (8). The difference is due to the increment in the values of ρ_1 and ρ_2.

In scenarios no. (19) to no. (24), we find when we increase the service rate of the service centres (quay cranes) for container class 1, μ_1, with increment in the number of arrival containers of class 1, λ_1, (while keeping the values of λ_2 and μ_2 unchanged); this leads to reduction in the values of all $\mathbf{E}(\mathbf{W}_1)$, $\mathbf{E}(\mathbf{L}_1^q)$, $\mathbf{E}(\mathbf{L}_1)$ and $\mathbf{E}(\mathbf{S}_1)$ as shown in Fig. 5. In the same manner, for scenarios no. (25) to no. (32), an increment in the service rate of service centres (quay cranes) for container class 2, μ_2, with an increment in the number of arrival of containers class 2, λ_2, (while keeping

Table 1a Analysis of the single server non-preemptive priority queuing system at a container terminal

Scenario	λ_1	λ_2	μ_1	μ_2	$\rho_1 = \lambda_1/\mu_1$	$\rho_2 = \lambda_2/\mu_2$	$1/\lambda_1$	$1/\lambda_2$	$1/\mu_1$
1	0.4	0.42	1.2	1.2	0.3333	0.3500	2.5000	2.3810	0.8333
2	0.4	0.43	1.2	1.2	0.3333	0.3583	2.5000	2.3256	0.8333
3	0.4	0.44	1.2	1.2	0.3333	0.3667	2.5000	2.2727	0.8333
4	0.4	0.45	1.2	1.2	0.3333	0.3750	2.5000	2.2222	0.8333
5	0.4	0.46	1.2	1.2	0.3333	0.3833	2.5000	2.1739	0.8333
6	0.4	0.47	1.2	1.2	0.3333	0.3917	2.5000	2.1277	0.8333
7	0.4	0.48	1.2	1.2	0.3333	0.4000	2.5000	2.0833	0.8333
8	0.4	0.49	1.2	1.2	0.3333	0.4083	2.5000	2.0408	0.8333
9	0.42	0.4	1.2	1.2	0.3500	0.3333	2.3810	2.5000	0.8333
10	0.43	0.4	1.2	1.2	0.3583	0.3333	2.3256	2.5000	0.8333
11	0.44	0.4	1.2	1.2	0.3667	0.3333	2.2727	2.5000	0.8333
12	0.45	0.4	1.2	1.2	0.3750	0.3333	2.2222	2.5000	0.8333
13	0.46	0.4	1.2	1.2	0.3833	0.3333	2.1739	2.5000	0.8333
14	0.47	0.4	1.2	1.2	0.3917	0.3333	2.1277	2.5000	0.8333
15	0.48	0.4	1.2	1.2	0.4000	0.3333	2.0833	2.5000	0.8333
16	0.49	0.4	1.2	1.2	0.4083	0.3333	2.0408	2.5000	0.8333
17	0.72	0.7	1.6	1.5	0.4500	0.4667	1.3889	1.4286	0.6250
18	0.73	0.7	1.65	1.5	0.4424	0.4667	1.3699	1.4286	0.6061
19	0.74	0.7	1.7	1.5	0.4353	0.4667	1.3514	1.4286	0.5882
20	0.75	0.7	1.75	1.5	0.4286	0.4667	1.3333	1.4286	0.5714
21	0.76	0.7	1.8	1.5	0.4222	0.4667	1.3158	1.4286	0.5556
22	0.77	0.7	1.85	1.5	0.4162	0.4667	1.2987	1.4286	0.5405
23	0.78	0.7	1.9	1.5	0.4105	0.4667	1.2821	1.4286	0.5263
24	0.79	0.7	1.95	1.5	0.4051	0.4667	1.2658	1.4286	0.5128
25	0.7	0.72	1.5	1.6	0.4667	0.4500	1.4286	1.3889	0.6667
26	0.7	0.73	1.5	1.65	0.4667	0.4424	1.4286	1.3699	0.6667
27	0.7	0.74	1.5	1.7	0.4667	0.4353	1.4286	1.3514	0.6667
28	0.7	0.75	1.5	1.75	0.4667	0.4286	1.4286	1.3333	0.6667
29	0.7	0.76	1.5	1.8	0.4667	0.4222	1.4286	1.3158	0.6667
30	0.7	0.77	1.5	1.85	0.4667	0.4162	1.4286	1.2987	0.6667
31	0.7	0.78	1.5	1.9	0.4667	0.4105	1.4286	1.2821	0.6667
32	0.7	0.79	1.5	1.95	0.4667	0.4051	1.4286	1.2658	0.6667

Table 1b Analysis of the single server non-preemptive priority queuing system at a container terminal

Scenario	$1/\mu_2$	ρ_1/ρ_2	ρ_2/ρ_1	$\lambda = \lambda_1 + \lambda_2$	$\mu = \mu_1 + \mu_2$	$\rho = \lambda/\mu$	ρ_1/ρ	ρ_2/ρ	Value of Z
1	0.8333	0.9524	1.0500	0.82	2.4	0.3417	0.9756	1.0244	0.0427
2	0.8333	0.9302	1.0750	0.83	2.4	0.3458	0.9639	1.0361	0.0444
3	0.8333	0.9091	1.1000	0.84	2.4	0.3500	0.9524	1.0476	0.0460
4	0.8333	0.8889	1.1250	0.85	2.4	0.3542	0.9412	1.0588	0.0477
5	0.8333	0.8696	1.1500	0.86	2.4	0.3583	0.9302	1.0698	0.0494
6	0.8333	0.8511	1.1750	0.87	2.4	0.3625	0.9195	1.0805	0.0511
7	0.8333	0.8333	1.2000	0.88	2.4	0.3667	0.9091	1.0909	0.0528
8	0.8333	0.8163	1.2250	0.89	2.4	0.3708	0.8989	1.1011	0.0546
9	0.8333	1.0500	0.9524	0.82	2.4	0.3417	1.0244	0.9756	0.0383
10	0.8333	1.0750	0.9302	0.83	2.4	0.3458	1.0361	0.9639	0.0377
11	0.8333	1.1000	0.9091	0.84	2.4	0.3500	1.0476	0.9524	0.0371
12	0.8333	1.1250	0.8889	0.85	2.4	0.3542	1.0588	0.9412	0.0366
13	0.8333	1.1500	0.8696	0.86	2.4	0.3583	1.0698	0.9302	0.0360
14	0.8333	1.1750	0.8511	0.87	2.4	0.3625	1.0805	0.9195	0.0355
15	0.8333	1.2000	0.8333	0.88	2.4	0.3667	1.0909	0.9091	0.0349
16	0.8333	1.2250	0.8163	0.89	2.4	0.3708	1.1011	0.8989	0.0344
17	0.6667	0.9643	1.0370	1.42	3.1	0.4581	0.9824	1.0188	0.0539
18	0.6667	0.9481	1.0548	1.43	3.15	0.4540	0.9746	1.0280	0.0543
19	0.6667	0.9328	1.0721	1.44	3.2	0.4500	0.9673	1.0370	0.0547
20	0.6667	0.9184	1.0889	1.45	3.25	0.4462	0.9606	1.0460	0.0550
21	0.6667	0.9048	1.1053	1.46	3.3	0.4424	0.9543	1.0548	0.0553
22	0.6667	0.8919	1.1212	1.47	3.35	0.4388	0.9485	1.0635	0.0556
23	0.6667	0.8797	1.1368	1.48	3.4	0.4353	0.9431	1.0721	0.0559
24	0.6667	0.8681	1.1519	1.49	3.45	0.4319	0.9380	1.0805	0.0561
25	0.6250	1.0370	0.9643	1.42	3.1	0.4581	1.0188	0.9824	0.0506
26	0.6061	1.0548	0.9481	1.43	3.15	0.4540	1.0280	0.9746	0.0495
27	0.5882	1.0721	0.9328	1.44	3.2	0.4500	1.0370	0.9673	0.0485
28	0.5714	1.0889	0.9184	1.45	3.25	0.4462	1.0460	0.9606	0.0476
29	0.5556	1.1053	0.9048	1.46	3.3	0.4424	1.0548	0.9543	0.0467
30	0.5405	1.1212	0.8919	1.47	3.35	0.4388	1.0635	0.9485	0.0458
31	0.5263	1.1368	0.8797	1.48	3.4	0.4353	1.0721	0.9431	0.0450
32	0.5128	1.1519	0.8681	1.49	3.45	0.4319	1.0805	0.9380	0.0442

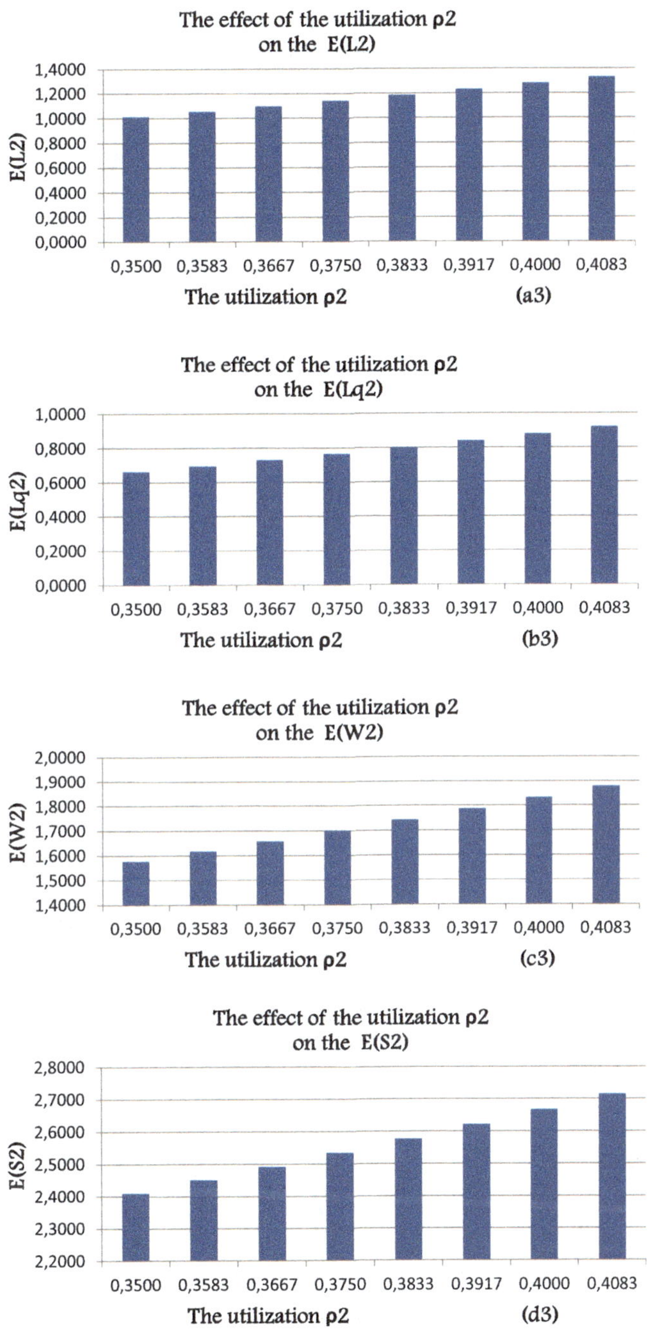

Fig. 3 Relations between all outputs for scenarios from no. (1) to (8)

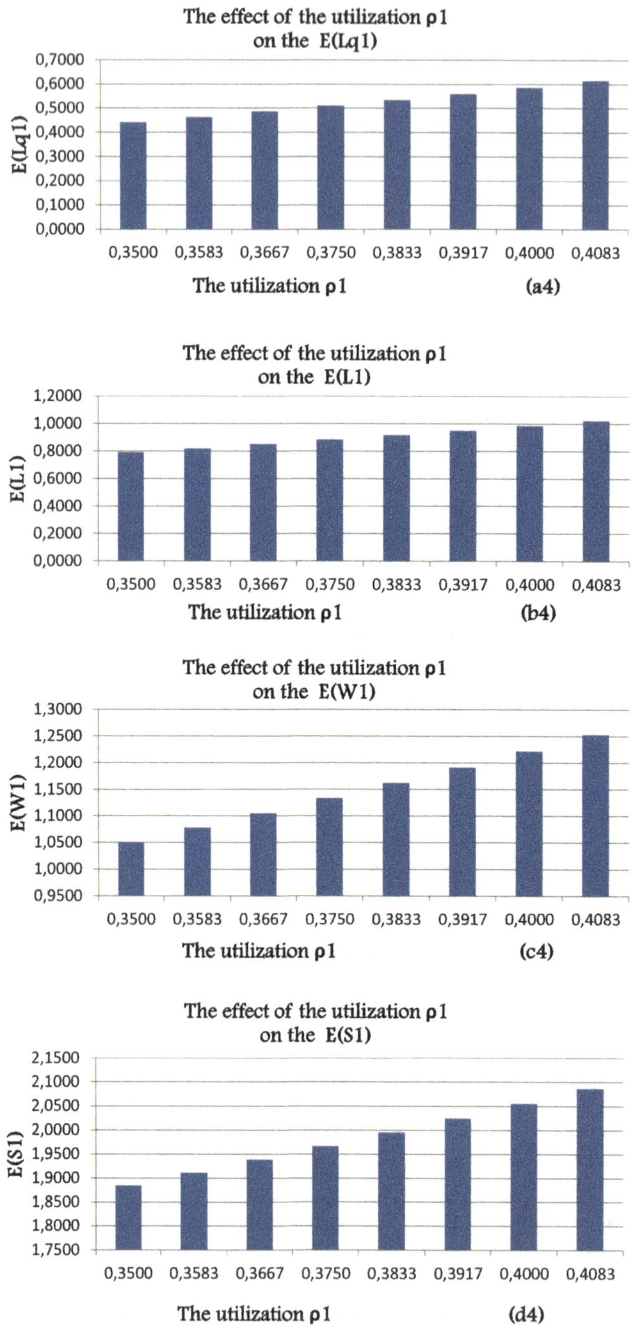

Fig. 4 Relations between all outputs for scenarios from no. (9) to (16)

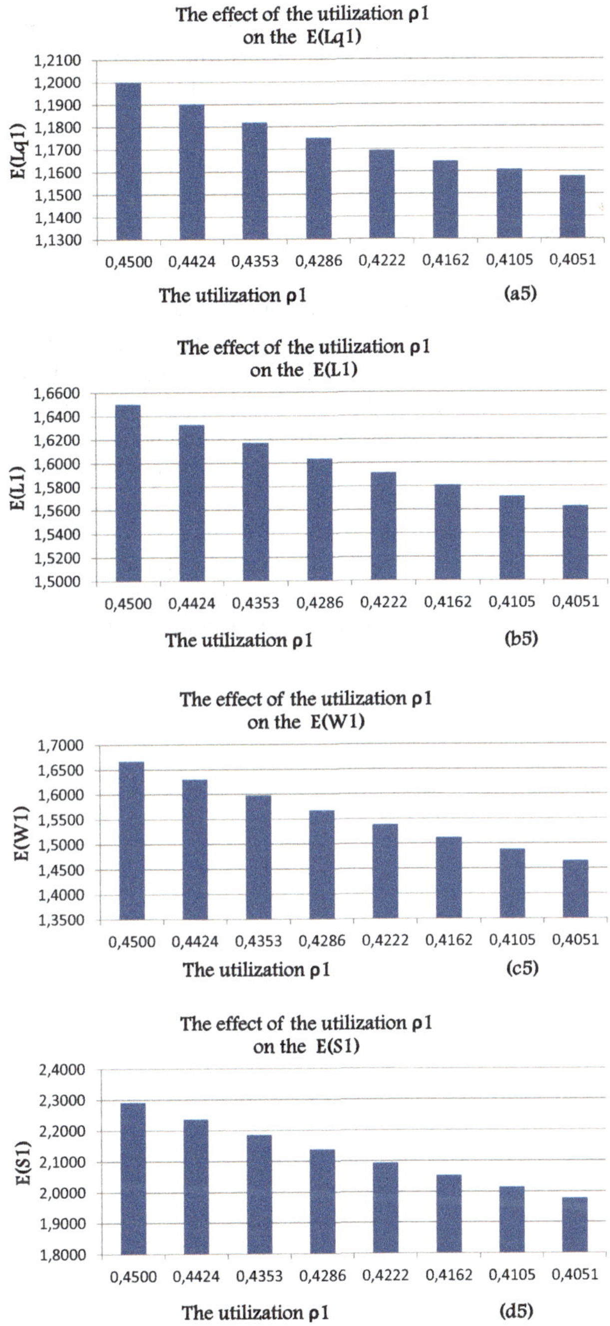

Fig. 5 Relations between all outputs for scenarios from no. (17) to (24)

the values of λ_1 and μ_1 unchanged) leads to reduction in the values of $\mathbf{E(W_2)}$, $\mathbf{E(L_2^q)}$, $\mathbf{E(L_2)}$ and $\mathbf{E(S_2)}$ as shown in Fig. 6. That means when the values of ρ_1 and ρ_2 for the scenarios no. (19) to no. (32) increase, we see all the values of $\mathbf{E(W_k)}$, $\mathbf{E(L_k^q)}$, $\mathbf{E(L_k)}$ and $\mathbf{E(S_k)}$ decrease accordingly.

5 Conclusions

This paper investigates the problem of assignment the suitable berth to the incoming vessel under different scenarios of berthing policy and priorities in order to discharge the vessels. Usually, within a container terminal, the seaport authority assigns a set of berths to a set of incoming vessels, the terminal operator will then allow the vessels to moor at the berths according to the berths scheduling policy and priority.

Our objective of this research is to apply queuing theory to optimize the service level of vessels berthing process and to improve the performance. We consider thirty-two different scenarios for berthing process of vessels and unloading of containers at container terminal to find the optimal service level and to achieve maximum efficiency of service stations. We found the change in the values of ρ_1 and ρ_2 will lead to change the values of $\mathbf{E(W_k)}$, $\mathbf{E(L_k^q)}$, $\mathbf{E(L_k)}$ and $\mathbf{E(S_k)}$ for all scenarios. Also, the increment in the values of λ_k and μ_k will lead sometimes to decrease the values of $\mathbf{E(W_k)}$, $\mathbf{E(L_k^q)}$, $\mathbf{E(L_k)}$ and $\mathbf{E(S_k)}$ for some scenarios.

In future work, we will study the queuing system with multiple server non-preemptive priority or with blocking.

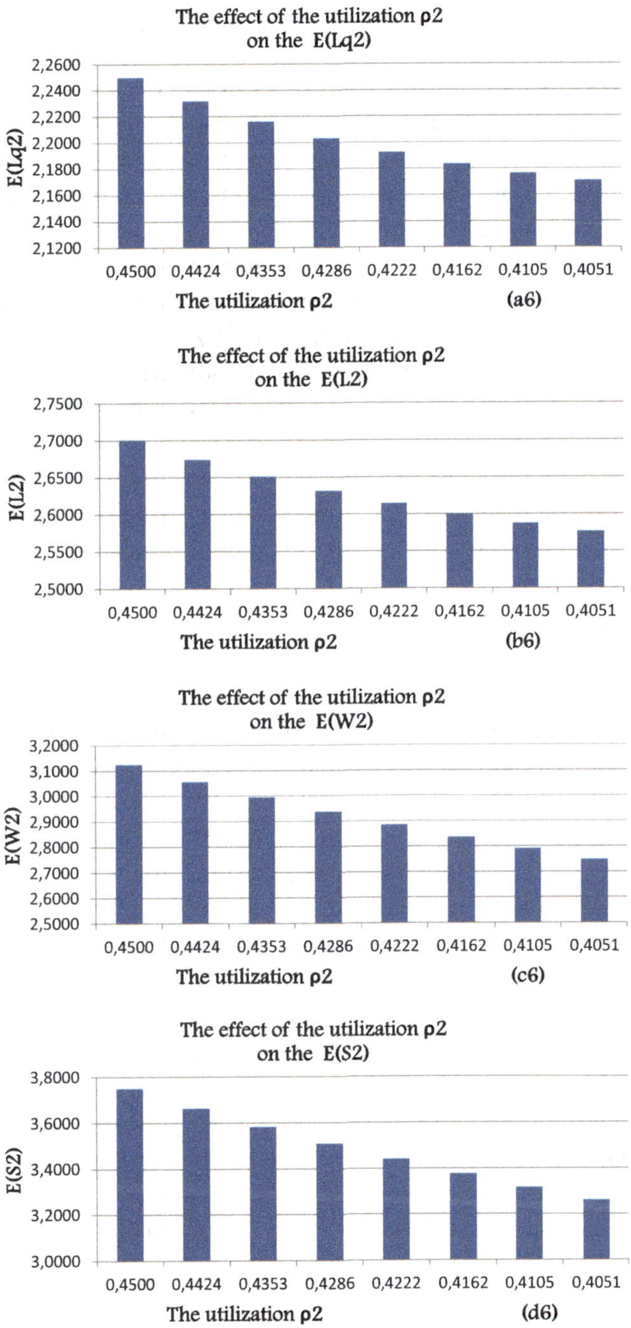

Fig. 6 Relations between all outputs for scenarios from no. (25) to (32)

Table. 2 Probabilities of the single server non-preemptive priority queuing system at a container terminal

Scenario	P 000	P 101	P 201	P 111	P 012	P 022	P 112	$\Sigma P(N)$
1	0.46506	0.19571	0.06524	0.06850	0.12208	0.04273	0.04069	**1**
2	0.46081	0.19489	0.06496	0.06983	0.12384	0.04438	0.04128	**1**
3	0.45662	0.19406	0.06469	0.07116	0.12557	0.04604	0.04186	**1**
4	0.45247	0.19324	0.06441	0.07247	0.12726	0.04772	0.04242	**1**
5	0.44837	0.19243	0.06414	0.07376	0.12891	0.04941	0.04297	**1**
6	0.44432	0.19161	0.06387	0.07505	0.13052	0.05112	0.04351	**1**
7	0.44031	0.19080	0.06360	0.07632	0.13209	0.05284	0.04403	**1**
8	0.43635	0.18999	0.06333	0.07758	0.13363	0.05457	0.04454	**1**
9	0.46506	0.20296	0.07104	0.06765	0.11483	0.03828	0.04019	**1**
10	0.46081	0.20565	0.07369	0.06855	0.11308	0.03769	0.04052	**1**
11	0.45662	0.20826	0.07636	0.06942	0.11137	0.03712	0.04084	**1**
12	0.45247	0.21081	0.07905	0.07027	0.10969	0.03656	0.04113	**1**
13	0.44837	0.21329	0.08176	0.07110	0.10804	0.03601	0.04142	**1**
14	0.44432	0.21571	0.08449	0.07190	0.10642	0.03547	0.04168	**1**
15	0.44031	0.21806	0.08722	0.07269	0.10484	0.03495	0.04193	**1**
16	0.43635	0.22035	0.08998	0.07345	0.10328	0.03443	0.04217	**1**
17	0.36616	0.21673	0.09753	0.09482	0.11546	0.05388	0.05542	**1**
18	0.37061	0.21544	0.09531	0.09140	0.11634	0.05429	0.05662	**1**
19	0.37485	0.21416	0.09322	0.08818	0.11714	0.05466	0.05779	**1**
20	0.37888	0.21290	0.09124	0.08516	0.11787	0.05501	0.05894	**1**
21	0.38274	0.21165	0.08936	0.08231	0.11855	0.05532	0.06006	**1**
22	0.38642	0.21043	0.08759	0.07962	0.11916	0.05561	0.06117	**1**
23	0.38995	0.20923	0.08589	0.07709	0.11972	0.05587	0.06225	**1**
24	0.39332	0.20805	0.08429	0.07469	0.12023	0.05611	0.06332	**1**
25	0.35923	0.22012	0.10272	0.10566	0.11246	0.05061	0.04920	**1**
26	0.36042	0.22044	0.10287	0.10728	0.11196	0.04953	0.04750	**1**
27	0.36151	0.22072	0.10300	0.10889	0.11146	0.04852	0.04590	**1**
28	0.36252	0.22096	0.10312	0.11048	0.11097	0.04756	0.04439	**1**
29	0.36345	0.22117	0.10321	0.11206	0.11049	0.04665	0.04297	**1**
30	0.36431	0.22135	0.10330	0.11363	0.11001	0.04579	0.04162	**1**
31	0.36511	0.22150	0.10337	0.11518	0.10953	0.04497	0.04035	**1**
32	0.36584	0.22162	0.10342	0.11672	0.10906	0.04418	0.03915	**1**

Table 3 Performance measures of the single server non-preemptive priority queuing system at a container terminal

Scenario	E (W_1)	E (Lq$_1$)	E (S_1)	E (L_1)	E (W_2)	E (Lq$_2$)	E (S_2)	E (L_2)
1	1.0250	0.4100	1.8583	0.7433	1.5769	0.6623	2.4103	1.0123
2	1.0375	0.4150	1.8708	0.7483	1.6169	0.6953	2.4502	1.0536
3	1.0500	0.4200	1.8833	0.7533	1.6579	0.7295	2.4912	1.0961
4	1.0625	0.4250	1.8958	0.7583	1.7000	0.7650	2.5333	1.1400
5	1.0750	0.4300	1.9083	0.7633	1.7432	0.8019	2.5766	1.1852
6	1.0875	0.4350	1.9208	0.7683	1.7877	0.8402	2.6210	1.2319
7	1.1000	0.4400	1.9333	0.7733	1.8333	0.8800	2.6667	1.2800
8	1.1125	0.4450	1.9458	0.7783	1.8803	0.9213	2.7136	1.3297
9	1.0513	0.4415	1.8846	0.7915	1.5769	0.6308	2.4103	0.9641
10	1.0779	0.4635	1.9113	0.8218	1.6169	0.6468	2.4502	0.9801
11	1.1053	0.4863	1.9386	0.8530	1.6579	0.6632	2.4912	0.9965
12	1.1333	0.5100	1.9667	0.8850	1.7000	0.6800	2.5333	1.0133
13	1.1622	0.5346	1.9955	0.9179	1.7432	0.6973	2.5766	1.0306
14	1.1918	0.5601	2.0251	0.9518	1.7877	0.7151	2.6210	1.0484
15	1.2222	0.5867	2.0556	0.9867	1.8333	0.7333	2.6667	1.0667
16	1.2535	0.6142	2.0869	1.0226	1.8803	0.7521	2.7136	1.0854
17	1.6667	1.2000	2.2917	1.6500	3.1250	2.1875	3.7917	2.6542
18	1.6304	1.1902	2.2365	1.6326	3.0571	2.1399	3.7237	2.6066
19	1.5972	1.1819	2.1855	1.6172	2.9948	2.0964	3.6615	2.5630
20	1.5667	1.1750	2.1381	1.6036	2.9375	2.0563	3.6042	2.5229
21	1.5385	1.1692	2.0940	1.5915	2.8846	2.0192	3.5513	2.4859
22	1.5123	1.1645	2.0529	1.5807	2.8356	1.9850	3.5023	2.4516
23	1.4881	1.1607	2.0144	1.5712	2.7902	1.9531	3.4568	2.4198
24	1.4655	1.1578	1.9783	1.5629	2.7478	1.9235	3.4145	2.3902
25	1.7188	1.2031	2.3854	1.6698	3.1250	2.2500	3.7500	2.7000
26	1.7045	1.1932	2.3712	1.6598	3.0571	2.2317	3.6631	2.6741
27	1.6912	1.1838	2.3578	1.6505	2.9948	2.2161	3.5830	2.6514
28	1.6786	1.1750	2.3452	1.6417	2.9375	2.2031	3.5089	2.6317
29	1.6667	1.1667	2.3333	1.6333	2.8846	2.1923	3.4402	2.6145
30	1.6554	1.1588	2.3221	1.6255	2.8356	2.1834	3.3762	2.5997
31	1.6447	1.1513	2.3114	1.6180	2.7902	2.1763	3.3165	2.5869
32	1.6346	1.1442	2.3013	1.6109	2.7478	2.1708	3.2607	2.5759

References

Abdorreza, S., Ilati, G., & Hassannayebi, E. (2013). A simulation model for the problem in integrated berth allocation and quay crane assignment. *Journal of Basic and Applied Scientific Research, 3*(8), 343–354.

Akio, I., Sun, X., Nishimura, E., & Papadimitriou, S. (2005). Berth allocation in a container port: Using a continuous location space approach. *Transportation Research Part B, 39*, 199–221.

Akio, I., Chen, H. S., Nishimura, E., & Papadimitriou, S. (2008). The simultaneous berth and quay crane allocation problem. *Transportation Research Part E, 44*, 900–920.

Boile, M., Sotirios, T., & Mihalis, G. (2006). Berth allocation with service priorities: A linear reformulation. In *Proceedings of the 5th WSEAS Int. Conf. on System Science and Simulation in Engineering*, Tenerife, Canary Islands, Spain, December 16–18 (pp 72–77).

Dai, J., Wuqin, L., Rajeeva, M., & Chung-Piaw, T. (2004) Berth allocation planning optimization in container terminal. National University of Singapore Academic Research Grant R-314–000–030–112.

Golias Mihalis, M., Georgios, K. S., Maria, B., Sotirios, T., & Marianthi, G. I. The berth allocation problem: Optimizing vessel arrival time. *Maritime Economics & Logistics, 11*(4), 358–377.

Hendriks, M. P. M., Lefeber, E., & Udding, J. T. (2012). Simultaneous berth allocation and yard planning at tactical level. *Or Spectrum, 2013*(35), 441–456. https://doi.org/10.1007/s00291-012-0305-4 Publishedonline:9September2012,©Springer-Verlag.

Hwan, K., Kyung, C. M. (2003) Berth scheduling by simulated annealing. *Transportation Research Part B, 37*, 541–560

Javanshir, H., & Seyed-Alizadeh Ganji, S. R. (2010). Optimal allocation of ships to quay length in container ports. *Journal of Industrial and Systems Engineering, 3*(4), 275–290.

Krčum, M., Gudelj, A., & Vlahinić, S. (2007). Genetic Algorithm for Solving Berth and Quay Cranes Assignment problems. In *2nd International Conference on Ports and Waterways* (pp. 165-177), supported by the Ministry of Science, Education and Sports of the Republic of Croatia.

Ma, H. L., Chan, F. T. S., Chung, S. H., & Wong, C. S. (2012, July). Berth allocation planning for improving container terminal performances. In *Proceedings of the International Conference on Industrial Engineering and Operations Management Istanbul, Turkey*, July 3–6, 2012 (pp. 502–508).

Rajeeva, M., & Teo, C.-P. (2006). Berth management in container terminal: The template design problem. *Or Spectrum, 28*(4), 495–518.

Shan, T. (2012) Genetic algorithm for dynamic berth allocation problem with discrete layout. In *The 2nd International Conference on Computer Application and System Modeling* (2012) (261–264). Atlantis Press.

Theofanis, S., Maria, B., & Mihalis, G. (2007) An optimization based genetic algorithm Heuristic for the berth allocation problem. In *2007 IEEE Congress on Evolutionary Computation (CEC 2007)* (pp 4439–4445).

Zeng, Q., Xiangpei, H., Wen, J. Wang, & Yan, F. (2011) Disruption management model and its algorithms for berth allocation problem in container terminals. *International Journal of Innovative Computing, Information and Control, 7*(5(B)), 2763–2773.

Fuzzy Inventory Model for Deteriorating Items in a Supply Chain System with Time Dependent Demand Rate

Srabani Shee and Tripti Chakrabarti

Abstract An inventory model for a single deteriorating item under fuzzy environment has been presented in this paper. Here demand rate is considered to be constant for some time period, post which the same is a linear function of time. This situation is common during the time of a new product launch in the market. As the product becomes popular, its demand increases with time although it remains constant during the initial days. Cycle time is considered to be constant in most of the models. However, practically it has been observed that it is difficult to pro-actively predict the cycle time. Because of this problem, cycle time has been considered as uncertain and has been further described as Symmetric Triangular Fuzzy number. The Signed Distance method has been used for defuzzification of the total cost function. For illustration of the process for finding the total optimal cost and the cycle time, numerical examples have been considered. The effects of changing parameter values on the optimal solution of the system have been demonstrated through Sensitivity Analysis.

Keywords Supply chain management · Constant and time dependent demand rate · Deterioration · Symmetric triangular fuzzy number · Signed distance method

1 Introduction

The most important and difficult role that inventory plays in supply chain is that of facilitating the balancing of demand and supply. To effectively manage the forward and reverse flows in the supply chain, firms have to deal with upstream supplier exchanges and downstream customer demands. Uncertainty is another key issue to deal with in order to define effective Supply Chain inventory policies. Demand, supply (e.g., lead time), various relevant cost, backorder costs, deterioration rate, etc.

S. Shee (✉) · T. Chakrabarti
Department of Applied Mathematics, University of Calcutta, 92 A.P.C. Road, Kolkata 700009, India

T. Chakrabarti
Basic Science, Techno India University, Kolkata, India

N. H. Shah and M. Mittal (eds.), *Soft Computing in Inventory Management*, Inventory Optimization, https://doi.org/10.1007/978-981-16-2156-7_4

are usually uncertain. To solve these types of practical problems, we use the Fuzzy Set Theory. Bellman and Zadeh (1970) first studied fuzzy set theory to solve decision making problem. Then, Dubois and Prade (1978) introduced some operations on fuzzy number. Thereafter, Park (1987) developed fuzzy set theoretical interpretation of EOQ. Several researchers like Wu and Yao (2003), Wang et al. (2007), Hu et al. (2010), Jaggi et al. (2013), Yao and Chiang (2003), Wang et al. (2007), Kao and Hsu (2002), Dutta et al. (2005), Roy and Samanta (2009) have developed different types of inventory model under Fuzzy environment. In this area, a lot of research papers have been published by several researchers, viz. Bera et al. (2013), He et al. (2013), Dutta and Kumar (2015), Mishra et al. (2015), etc. Priyan and Manivannan (2017) developed an optimal inventory modeling of supply chain system involving quality inspection errors in fuzzy situation.

Lin et al. (2000) and Mishra et al. (2015) developed an economic order quantity model that focused on time varying demand and deteriorating items. After that, Ghosh and Chaudhuri (2004) proposed an inventory model with Weibull distribution rate of deterioration, time quadratic demand and shortages. A lot of research papers have been published by several researchers, viz. Wang and Chen (2001), Pal et al. (2006), Bera et al. (2013), He et al. (2013), Dutta and Kumar (2015), etc.

This paper has presented a Fuzzy supply chain inventory model in which the demand rate is constant for some time and then it increases or decreases according to the popularity of the product. This type of situation occurs when a new product is launched in the market. When the product becomes popular the demand of the product increases with time. It is also assumed that the cycle time is taken as Symmetric Triangular Fuzzy number. In addition, expressions for order quantity, cycle time and the total average cost (for both the models) are obtained. The convexity of the total cost function is established to ensure the existence of a unique optimal solution. The problem is solved by using LINGO 17.0 software.

2 Assumptions and Notations

The proposed model is developed under the following notations and assumptions:

Notations

1. $I(t)$ is the inventory level at time $t(\geq 0)$.
2. Demand $R(t) = \begin{cases} a, & \text{for } 0 \leq t \leq \mu \\ a + b(t - \mu), & \text{for } \mu \leq t \leq T \end{cases}$.
3. θ is the rate of deterioration.
4. q is the number of items received at the beginning of the period.
5. C is the deterioration cost per unit.
6. C_1 is the inventory holding cost per unit per-unit-time.
7. C_2 is the setup cost per cycle.
8. μ is the time point at which deterioration starts and also demand increases with time.

9. T is the cycle length.
10. $\tilde{T}$ is the fuzzy cycle length.
11. $K(t)$ is the total inventory cost of the system per unit time.
12. $\widetilde{K(t)}$ is the fuzzy total inventory cost of the system.

Assumptions

1. The deterioration cost, holding cost and ordering cost remain constant over time.
2. There is no deterioration for the period $[0, \mu]$. The deterioration rate is constant, say θ, for the period $[\mu, T]$, which is practically very small.
3. A single item is considered over a prescribed period of T units of time.
4. The cycle time is uncertain and we assume it as symmetric triangular fuzzy number.
5. The replenishment is instantaneous.
6. Lead time is zero.
7. There is no replacement or repair of deteriorated items.
8. Shortage is not allowed.

3 Mathematical Model

The inventory cycle starts at time $t = 0$ with the inventory level q. During the time interval $[0, \mu]$, the inventory level decreases due to the constant demand a units per unit time. After time $t = \mu$, the inventory level gradually decreases mainly to meet demands and partly for deterioration and falls to zero at time $t = T$. The cycle then repeats itself after time T.

This model is represented by the following diagram:

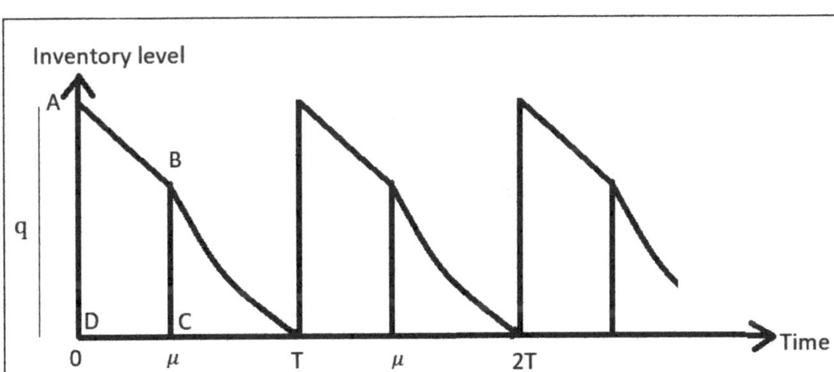

Now, the total demand for the time period $[0, \mu]$, is $= a\mu$.

Therefore, the inventory level is decreased by the factor $a\mu$ and $(q - a\mu)$ inventory is left for the time period $[\mu, T]$.

The holding cost for the period $[0, \mu]$ is

$$= C_1(\text{Area of trapezium } ABCD)$$
$$= C_1 \cdot \frac{1}{2}[q + (q - a\mu)]\mu$$
$$= C_1\mu\left[(q - a\mu) + \frac{a\mu}{2}\right]$$

Then, the differential equation governing the instantaneous state of $I(t)$ during the time interval $\mu \leq t \leq t_1$ is,

$$\frac{\mathrm{d}I(t)}{\mathrm{d}t} = -\theta I(t) - [a + b(t - \mu)], \quad 0 \leq t \leq t_1 \tag{1}$$

where $t_1 = (T - \mu)$, the origin has been shifted just for the sake of mathematical simplicity.

With the boundary conditions, $t = 0,\ I(t) = (q - a\mu)$ and $t = t_1,\ I(t) = 0$.

Solving the differential equation we get,

$$\mathrm{e}^{\theta t}I(t) - (q - a\mu) = -\int_0^t [a + b(t - \mu)]\mathrm{e}^{\theta t}\mathrm{d}t$$

At $t = t_1,\ I(t) = 0$

$$\therefore (q - a\mu) = \int_0^{t_1} [a + b(t - \mu)]\mathrm{e}^{\theta t}\mathrm{d}t \tag{2}$$

We know that $\mathrm{e}^{\theta t} = \sum_{n=0}^{\infty} \frac{(\theta t)^n}{n!}$. Using this exponential expansion in Eq. (2) and then integrating term bay term we have,

$$(q - a\mu) = (a - b\mu)\sum_{n=0}^{\infty} \frac{\theta^n}{n!}\frac{t_1^{n+1}}{n+1} + b\sum_{n=0}^{\infty} \frac{\theta^n}{n!}\frac{t_1^{n+2}}{n+2} \tag{3}$$

Now, the holding cost for the time period $(0, t_1)$ is

$$= C_1\frac{1}{2}(q - a\mu)t_1$$

Total amount of inventory that has deteriorated during this cycle is

$$= (q - a\mu) - \int_0^{t_1} [a + b(t - \mu)]\mathrm{e}^{\theta t}\mathrm{d}t$$

$$= (q - a\mu) - (a - b\mu)t_1 - \frac{1}{2}bt_1^2 \tag{4}$$

Therefore, the total inventory cost per unit time is,

$$\begin{aligned}
K(T) &= \text{inventory carrying cost} + \text{deterioration cost} + \text{set up cost} \\
&= \frac{1}{T}\Bigg[C_1\mu(q - a\mu) + C_1\frac{a\mu^2}{2} + \frac{1}{2}C_1(q - a\mu)t_1 \\
&\quad + C\left\{(q - a\mu) - (a - b\mu)t_1 - \frac{1}{2}bt_1^2\right\} + C_2\Bigg] \\
&= \frac{1}{T}\left[(q - a\mu)\left\{C_1\mu + \frac{1}{2}C_1t_1 + C\right\} + C_1\frac{a\mu^2}{2} - C(a - b\mu)t_1 - \frac{C}{2}bt_1^2 + C_2\right] \\
&= \frac{1}{T}\Bigg[(C_1\mu + C)\left\{(a - b\mu)\sum_{n=0}^{\infty}\frac{\theta^n}{n!}\frac{(T-\mu)^{n+1}}{n+1} + b\sum_{n=0}^{\infty}\frac{\theta^n}{n!}\frac{(T-\mu)^{n+2}}{n+2}\right\} \\
&\quad + \frac{C_1}{2}\left\{(a - b\mu)\sum_{n=0}^{\infty}\frac{\theta^n}{n!}\frac{(T-\mu)^{n+2}}{n+1} + b\sum_{n=0}^{\infty}\frac{\theta^n}{n!}\frac{(T-\mu)^{n+3}}{n+2}\right\} \\
&\quad + C_1\frac{a\mu^2}{2} - C(a - b\mu)(T - \mu) - \frac{C}{2}b(T - \mu)^2 + C_2\Bigg]
\end{aligned}$$

Since θ is very small, the terms involving θ^n with $n(> 1)$ can be neglected. Hence, retaining the terms in the summation for $n = 0$ and $n = 1$ only, we have,

$$\begin{aligned}
K(T) &= \frac{1}{T}\Bigg[P\left\{A(T-\mu) + \frac{A\theta}{2}(T-\mu)^2 + \frac{b}{2}(T-\mu)^2 + \frac{b\theta}{3}(T-\mu)^3\right\} \\
&\quad + \frac{C_1}{2}\left\{A(T-\mu)^2 + \frac{A\theta}{2}(T-\mu)^3 + \frac{b}{2}(T-\mu)^3 + \frac{b\theta}{3}(T-\mu)^4\right\} \\
&\quad + C_1\frac{a\mu^2}{2} - CAT + CA\mu - \frac{C}{2}b(T-\mu)^2 + C_2\Bigg] \\
&= \frac{C_1b\theta}{6}T^3 + \left(-\frac{2}{3}\mu C_1b\theta + \frac{Pb\theta}{3} + \frac{C_1A\theta}{4} + \frac{C_1b}{4}\right)T^2 \\
&\quad + \left(C_1b\theta\mu^2 - Pb\theta\mu - \frac{3C_1A\theta\mu}{4} - \frac{3C_1b\mu}{4} + \frac{PA\theta}{2} + \frac{Pb}{2} + \frac{C_1A}{2} - \frac{Cb}{2}\right)T \\
&\quad + \Big(-\frac{2}{3}C_1b\theta\mu^3 + Pb\theta\mu^2 + \frac{3}{4}C_1A\theta\mu^2 + \frac{3}{4}C_1b\mu^2 - PA\theta\mu - Pb\mu \\
&\quad - C_1A\mu + Cb\mu + PA - CA\Big) + \Bigg(\frac{C_1b\theta\mu^4}{6} - \frac{Pb\theta\mu^3}{3} - \frac{C_1A\theta\mu^3}{4} - \frac{C_1b\mu^3}{4} \\
&\quad + \frac{PA\theta\mu^2}{2} + \frac{Pb\mu^2}{2} + \frac{C_1A\mu^2}{2} - \frac{Cb\mu^2}{2} - PA\mu + CA\mu + C_1\frac{a\mu^2}{2} + C_2\Bigg)\frac{1}{T} \\
&= U_1T^3 + V_1T^2 + W_1T + X_1 + Y_1\frac{1}{T}
\end{aligned} \tag{5}$$

where, $P = (C_1\mu + C)$ and $A = (a - b\mu)$

$U_1 = \frac{C_1b\theta}{6}$

$V_1 = \left(-\frac{2}{3}\mu C_1b\theta + \frac{Pb\theta}{3} + \frac{C_1A\theta}{4} + \frac{C_1b}{4}\right)$

$$W_1 = \left(C_1 b\theta\mu^2 - Pb\theta\mu - \tfrac{3C_1 A\theta\mu}{4} - \tfrac{3C_1 b\mu}{4} + \tfrac{PA\theta}{2} + \tfrac{Pb}{2} + \tfrac{C_1 A}{2} - \tfrac{Cb}{2} \right)$$

$$X_1 = \left(-\frac{2}{3}C_1 b\theta\mu^3 + Pb\theta\mu^2 + \frac{3}{4}C_1 A\theta\mu^2 + \frac{3}{4}C_1 b\mu^2 - PA\theta\mu - Pb\mu \right.$$
$$\left. -C_1 A\mu + Cb\mu + PA - CA \right)$$

$$Y_1 = \left(\frac{C_1 b\theta\mu^4}{6} - \frac{Pb\theta\mu^3}{3} - \frac{C_1 A\theta\mu^3}{4} - \frac{C_1 b\mu^3}{4} + \frac{PA\theta\mu^2}{2} + \frac{Pb\mu^2}{2} + \frac{C_1 A\mu^2}{2} \right.$$
$$\left. -\frac{Cb\mu^2}{2} - PA\mu + CA\mu + C_1\frac{a\mu^2}{2} + C_2 \right)$$

Now, let us describe the cycle time T as triangular fuzzy number $\tilde{T} = (T - \Delta, T, T + \Delta)$.

So, from Eq. (5) the total Fuzzy cost function is

$$\widetilde{K(T)} = U_1\tilde{T}^3 + V_1\tilde{T}^2 + W_1\tilde{T} + X_1 + Y_1\frac{1}{\tilde{T}} \tag{6}$$

From the definition of the signed distance method, we have,

$$\mathrm{d}\left(\tilde{A}, 0\right) = \frac{1}{2}\int_0^1 [A_{\mathrm{L}}(\alpha) + A_{\mathrm{U}}(\alpha)]\mathrm{d}\alpha$$

where, $\tilde{A} = (a, b, c),\ A_{\mathrm{L}}(\alpha) = a + (b - a)\alpha,\ A_{\mathrm{U}}(\alpha) = c - (c - b)\alpha.$

Now, $T_{\mathrm{L}}(\alpha) = (T - \Delta) + \Delta\alpha,\ T_{\mathrm{U}}(\alpha) = (T + \Delta) - \Delta\alpha.$

Therefore,

$$\begin{aligned}
\mathrm{d}\left(\tilde{T}, 0\right) &= \frac{1}{2}\int_0^1 [T_{\mathrm{L}}(\alpha) + T_{\mathrm{U}}(\alpha)]\mathrm{d}\alpha \\
&= \frac{1}{2}\int_0^1 [(T - \Delta) + \Delta\alpha + (T + \Delta) - \Delta\alpha]\mathrm{d}\alpha \\
&= \frac{1}{2}\int_0^1 2T\mathrm{d}\alpha = T
\end{aligned} \tag{7}$$

And

$$\mathrm{d}\left(\frac{1}{\tilde{T}}, 0\right) = \frac{1}{2}\int_0^1 \left[\left(\frac{1}{\tilde{T}}\right)_{\mathrm{L}}(\alpha) + \left(\frac{1}{\tilde{T}}\right)_{\mathrm{U}}(\alpha)\right]\mathrm{d}\alpha$$

$$= \frac{1}{2}\int_0^1 \left[\frac{1}{T + \Delta - \Delta\alpha} + \frac{1}{T - \Delta + \Delta\alpha}\right] d\alpha$$

$$= \frac{1}{2\Delta} \ln\left(\frac{T + \Delta}{T - \Delta}\right) \tag{8}$$

From (6), (7) and (8) we have

$$\widetilde{K(T)} = U_1 T^3 + V_1 T^2 + W_1 T + X_1 + \frac{1}{2\Delta} Y_1 \ln\left(\frac{T + \Delta}{T - \Delta}\right) \tag{9}$$

To minimize $K(T)$ the necessary condition is

$$\frac{dK(T)}{dT} = 0$$

By simplifying $\frac{dK(T)}{dT} = 0$ we get a bi-quadratic equation in T, which is,

$$3U_1 T^4 + 2V_1 T^3 + W_1 T^2 - Y_1 = 0 \tag{10}$$

We can solve Eq. (5) by Newton–Raphson's method for a positive T (T^* say).
If $\frac{d^2 K(T)}{dT^2} > 0$ for $T = T^*$, then T^* will be an optimal solution.
Hence, $K(T)$ is strictly convex.
Substituting the value of $T = T^*$ in (5), the optimum average cost $K(T^*)$ can also be determined.

4 Numerical Example

To illustrate the results obtained for the suggested model, a numerical example with the following parameter values is considered.

$$a = 20\,\text{units},\ b = 0.2,\ \mu = 0.4\,\text{days},\ \theta = 0.02,$$

$$C = \text{Rs. } 18\,\text{per unit},$$

$$C_1 = \text{Rs. } 0.50\,\text{per unit per day},\ C_2 = \text{Rs. } 80.$$

We obtain for crisp model optimum total cost is $K(T^*) = 50.4065$ per day.
And cycle time is $T^* = 2.975$ days.
For fuzzy model total cost $\widetilde{K(T^*)} = 53.5294$ and cycle time $\widetilde{T^*} = 3.016$.
The convexity of the total cost function is shown in Fig. 1.

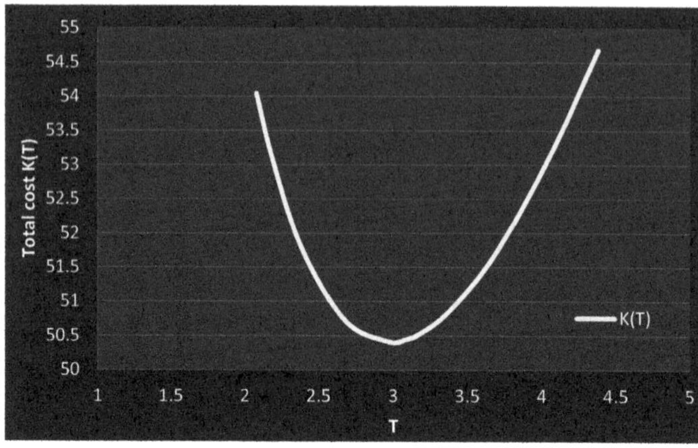

Fig. 1 Convexity of cost function w. r. t. T

5 Sensitivity Analysis

Sensitivities of the parameters are shown in Tables 1, 2, 3, 4 and 5 and graphically illustrated in Figs. 2, 3, 4, 5, 6, 7, 8, 9, 10 and 11.

Table 1 Sensitivity on μ

Change value		Crisp model		Fuzzy model	
		$K(T^*)$	T^*	$\widetilde{K(T^*)}$	$\widetilde{T}^*$
μ	0.1	52.5818	2.954	53.5589	2.995
	0.2	51.8308	2.960	53.5247	3.001
	0.3	51.1057	2.967	53.5148	3.008
	0.4	50.4065	2.975	53.5294	3.016
	0.5	49.7332	2.985	53.5684	3.025
	0.6	49.0858	2.996	53.6318	3.036
	0.7	48.4643	3.009	53.7195	3.049

Table 2 Sensitivity on C_2

Change value		Crisp model		Fuzzy model	
		$K(T^*)$	T^*	$\widetilde{K(T^*)}$	$\widetilde{T}^*$
C_2	60	43.2216	2.591	46.3794	2.637
	70	46.9379	2.790	50.0764	2.834
	80	50.4065	2.975	53.5294	3.016
	90	53.6722	3.148	56.7822	3.187
	100	56.7680	3.312	59.8670	3.348

Table 3 Sensitivity on C_1

Change value		Crisp model		Fuzzy model	
		$K(T^*)$	T^*	$\widetilde{K(T^*)}$	$\widetilde{T^*}$
C_1	0.10	36.0927	4.069	39.0516	4.098
	0.30	43.8291	3.393	46.8647	3.428
	0.50	50.4065	2.975	53.5294	3.016
	0.70	56.2313	2.684	59.4507	2.729
	0.90	61.5158	2.465	64.8401	2.514

Table 4 Sensitivity on C

Change value		Crisp model		Fuzzy model	
		$K(T^*)$	T^*	$\widetilde{K(T^*)}$	$\widetilde{T^*}$
C	14	48.5454	3.112	50.0011	3.151
	16	49.4898	3.041	52.2789	3.081
	18	50.4065	2.975	53.5294	3.016
	20	51.2974	2.614	54.7544	2.955
	22	52.1641	2.855	55.9556	2.898

Table 5 Sensitivity on θ

Change value		Crisp model		Fuzzy model	
		$K(T^*)$	T^*	$\widetilde{K(T^*)}$	$\widetilde{T^*}$
θ	0.01	45.8050	3.349	47.4191	3.385
	0.015	48.1976	3.154	50.5652	3.183
	0.02	50.4065	2.975	53.5294	3.016
	0.025	52.4629	2.832	56.3430	2.875
	0.03	54.3902	2.709	59.0291	2.753

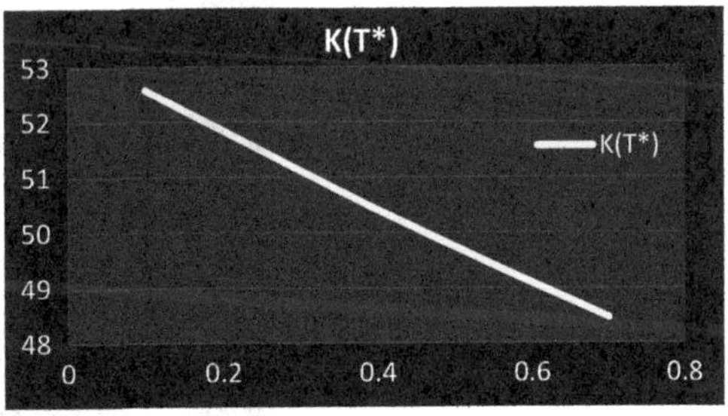

Fig. 2 Impact of μ on $K(T^*)$: crisp model (from Table: 1)

Fig. 3 Impact of μ on $\widetilde{K(T^*)}$: fuzzy model (from Table: 1)

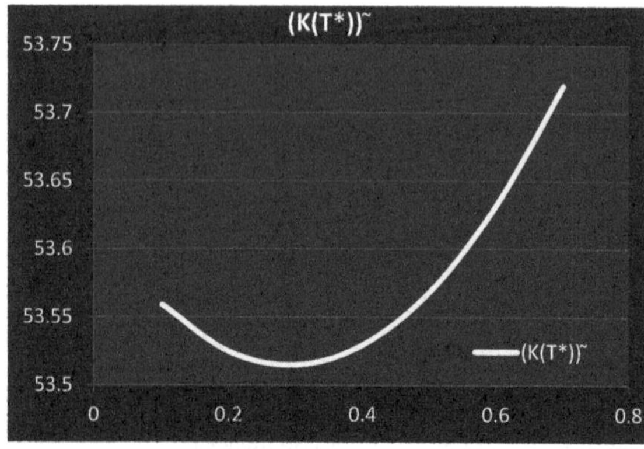

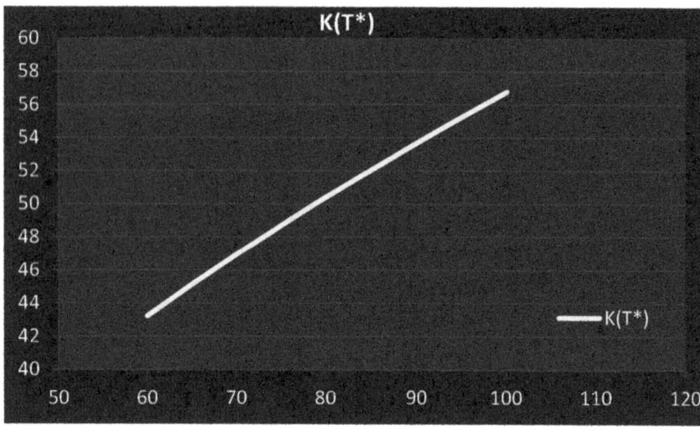

Fig. 4 Impact of C_2 on $K(T^*)$: crisp model (from Table: 2)

Fig. 5 Impact of C_2 on $\widetilde{K(T^*)}$: fuzzy model (from Table: 2)

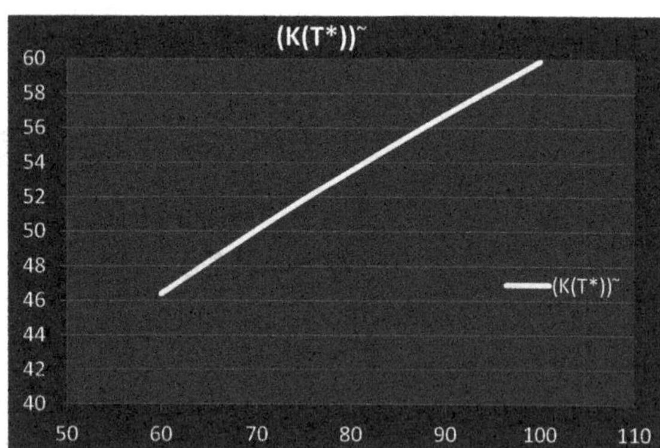

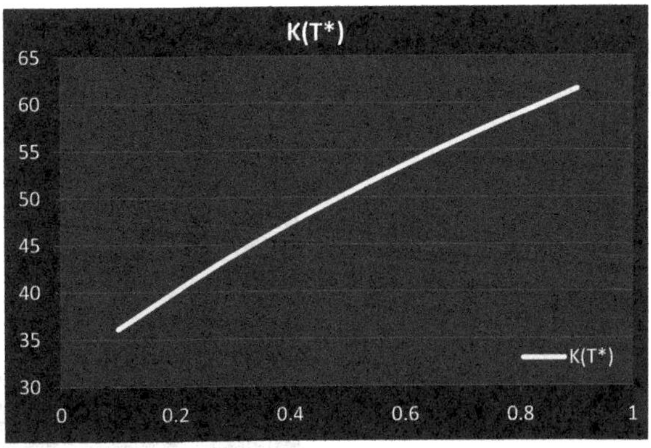

Fig. 6 Impact of C_1 on $K(T^*)$: crisp model (from Table: 3)

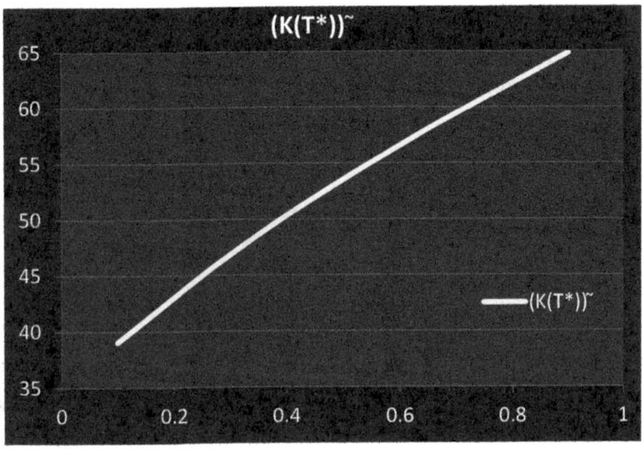

Fig. 7 Impact of C_1 on $\widetilde{K(T^*)}$: fuzzy model (from Table: 3)

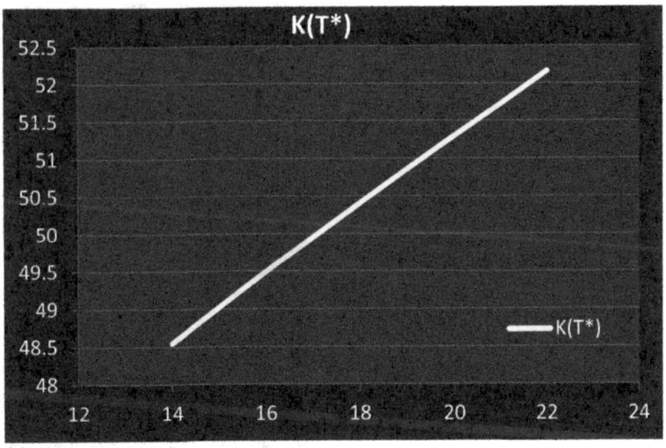

Fig. 8 Impact of C on $K(T^*)$: crisp model (from Table: 4)

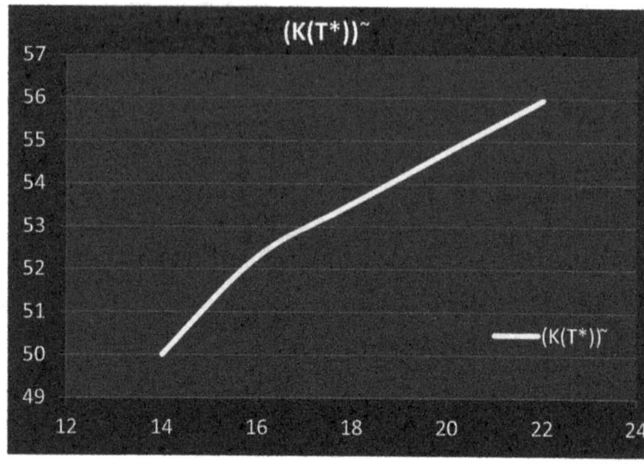

Fig. 9 Impact of C on $\widetilde{K(T^*)}$: fuzzy model (from Table: 4)

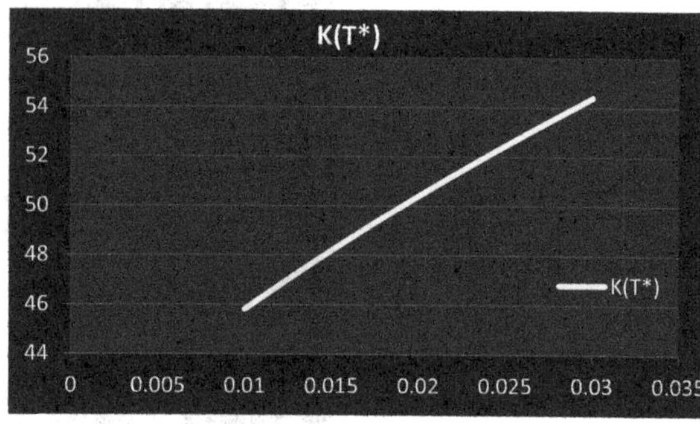

Fig. 10 Impact of θ on $K(T^*)$: crisp model (from Table: 5)

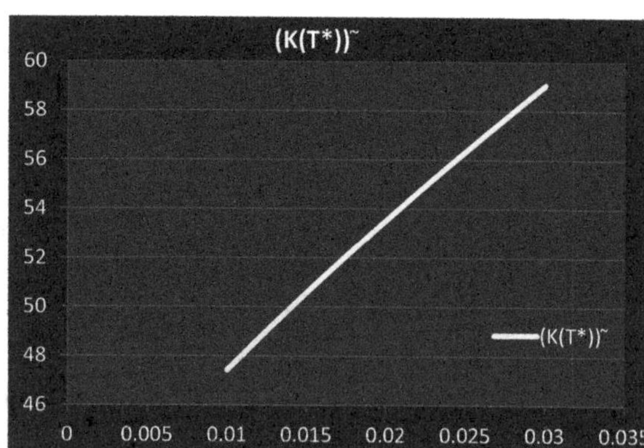

Fig. 11 Impact of θ on $\widetilde{K(T^*)}$: fuzzy model (from Table: 5)

Observations

It is observed from the tables that:

(i) In crisp model, if the parameter μ is increased (or decreased), the value of optimum cycle time increases (or decreases) while the optimal total cost decreases (or increases). Further, in fuzzy model, if the parameter μ

is increased (or decreased) the value of optimum cycle time increases (or decreases) while the optimal cost increases.

(ii) The increases (or decrease) in setup cost C_2 increases (or decreases) the total inventory cost for both the models.

(iii) The total cost (for both the models) increases (or decreases) as the holding cost C_1 per unit time increases (or decreases).

(iv) With the increase (or decrease) of the rate of deterioration θ, the total inventory cost (for the two models) also increase (or decrease).

(v) As the deterioration cost C per unit increase (or decrease), the total costs for the two models also increase (or decrease).

6 Conclusion

In the present chapter, we have dealt with a fuzzy inventory model where we have introduced the cycle time T as a Triangular Symmetric Fuzzy number. It is assumed the demand rate is constant for some time and then as a linear function of time. In our real life, we generally find that the cycle time is uncertain. So keeping this situation in mind we have tried to compare crisp model with the fuzzy model and have observed that the cycle time and the total cost obtained by fuzzy model is greater than those obtained by crisp model. The sensitivity analysis shows that the total cost of both the model increases as the cost associated with the model increases. In future, researchers can do more work about several types of demand, variable cost, etc.

References

Bellman, R. E., & Zadeh, L. A. (1970). Decision-making in a fuzzy environment. *Management Science, 17*(4), 141–164.

Bera, U. K., Bhunia, A. K., & Maiti, M. (2013). Optimal partial backordering two-storage inventory model for deteriorating items with variable demand. *International Journal of Operational Research, 16*(1), 96.

Dubois, D., & Prade, H. (1978). Operations on fuzzy numbers. *International Journal of Systems Science, 9*(6), 613–626.

Dutta, D., & Kumar, P. (2015). A partial backlogging inventory model for deteriorating items with time-varying demand and holding cost. *International Journal of Mathematics in Operational Research, 7*(3), 281.

Dutta, P., Chakraborty, D., & Roy, A. R. (2005). A single-period inventory model with fuzzy random variable demand. *Mathematical and Computer Modelling, 41*(8–9), 915–922.

Ghosh, S. K., & Chaudhuri, K. S. (2004). An order-level inventory model for a deteriorating item with Weibull distribution deterioration, time-quadratic demand and shortages. *AMO-Advanced Modeling and Optimization, 6*(1), 21–35.

He, W., Wei, H. E., & Fuyuan, X. U. (2013). Inventory model for deteriorating items with time-dependent partial backlogging rate and inventory level-dependent demand rate. *Journal of Computer Applications, 33*(8), 2390–2393.

Hu, J., Guo, C., Xu, R., & Ji, Y. (2010). Fuzzy economic order quantity model with imperfect quality and service level. In *2010 Chinese Control and Decision Conference* [Internet]. Available from https://doi.org/10.1109/ccdc.2010.5498441

Jaggi, C. K., Pareek, S., Sharma, A., & Nidhi. (2013). Fuzzy inventory model for deteriorating items with time-varying demand and shortages. *American Journal of Operational Research, 2*(6), 81–92.

Kao, C., & Hsu, W. K. (2002). A single-period inventory model with fuzzy demand. *Computers & Mathematics with Applications, 43*(6–7), 841–848.

Lin, C., Tan, B., & Lee, W. C. (2000). An EOQ model for deteriorating items with time-varying demand and shortages. *International Journal of System Science, 31*(3), 391–400.

Mishra, N., Mishra, S. P., Mishra, S., Panda, J., & Misra, U. K. (2015). Inventory model of deteriorating items for linear holding cost with time dependent demand. *Mathematical Journal of Interdisciplinary Sciences, 4*(1), 29–36.

Pal, A. K., Bhunia, A. K., & Mukherjee, R. N. (2006). Optimal lot size model for deteriorating items with demand rate dependent on displayed stock level (DSL) and partial backordering. *European Journal of Operational Research, 175*(2), 977–991.

Park, K. S. (1987). Fuzzy-set theoretic interpretation of economic order quantity. *IEEE Transactions on Systems, Man, and Cybernetics, 17*(6), 1082–1084.

Priyan, S., & Manivannan, P. (2017). Optimal inventory modelling of supply chain system involving quality inspection errors and fuzzy effective rate. *OPSEARCH, 54*, 21–43.

Roy, A., & Samanta, G. P. (2009). Fuzzy continuous review inventory model without backorder for deteriorating items. *Electronic Journal of Applied Statistical Analysis, 2*, 58–66.

Wang, T. Y., & Chen, L. H. (2001). A production lot size inventory model for deteriorating items with time-varying demand. *International Journal of Systems Science, 32*(6), 745–751.

Wang, X., Tang, W., & Zhao, R. (2007). Fuzzy economic order quantity inventory models without backordering. *Tsinghua Science and Technology, 12*(1), 91–96.

Wu, K., & Yao, J.-S. (2003). Fuzzy inventory with backorder for fuzzy order quantity and fuzzy shortage quantity. *European Journal of Operational Research, 150*(20), 320–352.

Yao, J. S., & Chiang, J. (2003). Inventory without backorder with fuzzy total cost and fuzzy storing cost defuzzified by centroid and signed distance. *European Journal of Operational Research, 148*(2), 401–409.

Credit Financing in a Two-Warehouse Inventory Model with Fuzzy Deterioration and Weibull Demand

Aastha, Sarla Pareek, and Vinti Dhaka

Abstract In the inventory system, usually demand and deterioration rate consider as in deterministic form. But, in the practical situation, these rates are uncertain in nature. In this case, demand increases as the number of customer increases. Furthermore, there is some limitation with the storage space. So, for keeping the inventory, retailer has to need extra space or rent warehouse (RW) with unlimited capacity. RW has better preserving facilities for keeping products for long time without any deterioration. So, RW has higher holding cost as compared with OW holding cost. In this paper, demand considered as a Weibull and deterioration in fuzzy sense; here, the supplier give some time period to pay the amount to the customer which is known as one level permissible delay in payments. The main objective is to find the optimum solution by using triangular fuzzy number. Numerical example provides the optimal solution of crisp and fuzzy model and sensitivity analysis also carried on different parameters.

1 Introduction

The inventory models maintain inventory level. In the last few years, researchers attracted toward inventory systems. It is well known that the first model of inventory was developed by Harris (1913). Harris introduced EOQ model in which demand is assumed to be known and constant. After that, lots of research works have been done in this field. Many works have been done by extending the Harris (1913) model. There are considered lots of assumption in this model to come close to real-life situation.

In the basic EOQ model, rate of demand was assumed to be constant. But in reality, demand can not be deterministic, it should vary with time. Sometimes, it depends upon situation. So, there is always some uncertainty in demand. Silver and Moon (1969) were the first researchers to modify the EOQ formula for the case of varying demand.

Aastha (✉) · S. Pareek · V. Dhaka
Department of Mathematics and Statistics, Banasthali Vidyapith, Banasthali, India
e-mail: dhakavinti@gmail.com

N. H. Shah and M. Mittal (eds.), *Soft Computing in Inventory Management*, Inventory Optimization, https://doi.org/10.1007/978-981-16-2156-7_5

Usually, it is assumed that lifetime of an item is infinite when it is in storage. Goyal (1985)'s inventory model assumed that the lifetime of the product is infinite within the storage time. In reality, the effect of deterioration cannot be ignored in inventory models. Deterioration is outlined as decay, alternate, harm, spoilage, or obsolescence in the effect of decreasing usefulness from its usual rationale. It is assumed that items are start deteriorating as soon as they arrive in the warehouse. Generally, it is assumed as known and constant. But, it cannot be predefined. There must be an uncertainty in rate of deterioration of the products. Hence, it is preferably taken as in fuzzy.

Nowadays, the seller wants to attract the buyer to purchase products in large quantities; for this, seller always uses new techniques. Credit financing is the most common technique used by seller to attract buyer. In this, the seller offers some time period to buyer to pay the amount of the purchase. But if the customer do not pay the amount in this time, then the customer have to pay the interest on that amount. The credit financing policy seems to be a beneficial option for buyer with limited payment at one time. Possibly, Haley and Higgins (1973) were the first researchers in proposing credit policy in inventory models.

Furthermore, everyone wants to increase their customers. The availability of products in the system is common factor to attract customers. But due to limited storage capacity in own warehouse, the seller has require large space for store the inventory. To deal such type of situations, seller uses OW and RW. Also, deterioration of items in both the warehouse is not same as RW has better preserving facility to keep products from deterioration for some time.

In this paper, deterioration is taken as fuzzy value which is solved by triangular fuzzy number and defuzzify by graded mean integration method. Demand follows the pattern of Weibull distribution. This model is solved in two-warehouse environment and investigated under credit period policy.

2 Literature Study

A replenishment policy for items had been developed by Wee (1997) where demand depends upon price. Chen et al. (2003) established an inventory model having demand depends upon time and deterioration in the form of Weibull. After that, Ghosh et al. (2006) developed an inventory model by taking demand as in Weibull form. Also, he considered shortages in his model. By taking demand depends upon stock, a model was developed by Shah et al. (2011) with advance payment policy. Later on, Shah et al. Shah et al. (2012b) developed an integrated inventory model with advance payment policy and quadratic demand. Bhunia et al. (2018) developed a model for deteriorating items where demand was taken as variable. A two-warehouse inventory model was developed by Chandra (2020) in which stock-dependent demand was taken under credit financing policy.

Furthermore, the deterioration in items had been extremely considered by Nahmias (1982), Raafat (1991), Bakker et al. (2012), Pareek and Dhaka (2015) in inventory models. After these models, deterioration of items depend upon time with partial backlogging in exponential had been considered by Dye et al. (2007). An inventory model had been developed by Sarkar and Sarkar (2013a) on considering deterioration of items varies with time and demand depends upon stock. Also, deterioration as a fuzzy number was considered by few researchers. A model was established by De et al. (2003) by assuming demand and deterioration both in fuzzy sense. Roy et al. (2007) presented a model with fuzzy deterioration over a random planning horizon in two storage facility. Fuzzy EOQ model was developed by Halim et al. (2008). In this model, fuzzy deterioration was considered with stochastic demand. Mishra and Mishra (2011) proposed a model where deterioration of items was taken as in fuzzy sense and credit policy was also considered in this model. After that, an inventory model was developed in which deterioration rate can be controlled using some techniques. In this model, stock and price-dependent demand was considered. This model was developed by Mishra et al. (2017). Also, not all the items deteriorated instantaneously when they stored in warehouse. This is non-instantaneous deterioration situation. So, based on this phenomena, some models was developed. A model was developed by Shaikh et al. (2017) based on this phenomena with demand depends upon stock and price. Again, a model was generated on non-instantaneous deteriorating items under two-warehouse environment by Shaikh et al. (2019). Impact of deterioration showed in an integrated inventory model by Lin et al. (2019) where credit policy was also considered.

Nowadays, the effect of trade credit also attracts researcher. An EOQ model first developed by Goyal (1985) under credit financing policy and then this model had been extended with a constant deterioration rate by Shah (1993), Aggarwal and Jaggi (1995), and Hwang and Shinn (1997). After that, a probabilistic inventory model had been described by Shah and Shah (1998) where advance payment policy was considered. A model for deterioration in items with credit financing developed by yang (2004) under two-warehouse environment. Mahata and Goswami (2006) had been described a fuzzy EPQ model under advance payment policy. Also, they considered that items start deterioration when they arrive in inventory. Liang and Zhou (2011) presented a inventory model with permissible delay in payments and deterioration of items under two-warehouse environment. Shah et al. (2012a) described a fuzzy EOQ model with trade credit. Liao et al. (2012), Guchhait et al. (2013) generated inventory models in two-warehouse environment under advance payment policy by assuming that the rate of deterioration of items is same for both the warehouse. Bhunia et al. (2014) proposed a model for deteriorating items under credit financing. This model was generated in two-warehouse environment and backlogging. There was a model developed by Maihami et al. (2017). In this model, researcher showed the trade credit effect on inventory model. Also, demand and deterioration were considered as probabilistic in nature. A model was developed under credit financing policy when demand depends upon stock by Dhaka et al. (2019).

However, storing of items are an essential crisis in inventory models, the basic inventory models are commonly proposed with limited space in single warehouse, but due to high demand of items, the retailer may buy more items that can be stored in own warehouse (OW). But due to limited space in own warehouse, another warehouse such as RW with unlimited capacity is also required to store the goods. To know more in this field, see the models of Sarma (1987), Goswami and Chaudhuri (1992), Pakkala and Archary (1992), Benkherouf (1997), Bhunia and Matti (1998), Yang (2004), Yang (2006), Lee (2006), Banerjee and Agrawal (2008), Jaggi et al. (2013), Sett et al. (2016), Sarkar and Sharmila (2017). Jaggi et al. (2014) described a model in two-warehouse environment by considering deterioration in items. Also, they assumed backlogging and credit financing in this model. Shabani et al. (2016) developed an inventory model under advance payment policy in two storage environment. Here, both demand and deterioration rate considered in fuzzy sense. A model was developed with demand as ramp type and deterioration in Weibull distribution under two storage environment by Chakraborty et al. (2018). A sustainable inventory model was developed for two storage system by Mashud et al. (2020). In this model, demand was based on price whereas deterioration was taken as non instantaneous. Also, another model was developed for two warehouses with non-instantaneous concept by Khan et al. (2020) but this model was developed under credit policy by considering shortages (Table 1).

In this model, demand follows Weibull distribution where deterioration is used in fuzzy sense. The fuzzy solution used in the model is more simplified which provides more generalized results.

3 Preliminieries

Before start the fuzzy model, here is the description of fuzzy number.

A graded mean integration method based on the integral value of graded mean h-level of the generaliZed fuzzy number was developed by Chen and Hsieh (1999) for defuzzifying fuzzy numbers.

A fuzzy number $\tilde{A} = (a, b, c)$ where $a < b < c$ and defined on R is called a triangular fuzzy number if its membership function is:

$$\mu = \begin{cases} \dfrac{x-a}{b-a}, & a \le x \le b \\ \dfrac{c-x}{c-b}, & b \le x \le c \\ 0, & \text{otherwise} \end{cases}$$

When $a = b = c$, we have fuzzy point $(c, c, c) = \tilde{c}$.

Table 1 Literature review of inventory models under two-warehouse environment from 2011 to 2020

Author	Deterioration	Demand	Trade credit
Mishra and Mishra (2011)	Fuzzy	Linear	Yes
Liang and Zhou (2011)	Constant	Constant	Yes
Tripathy and Pradhan (2011)	Variable	Constant	Yes
Liao et al. (2012)	Constant	Constant	Yes
Sarkar (2012)	Time varying	Constant	Yes
Sett et al. (2012)	Time varying	Quadratic	No
Guchhait et al. (2013)	Constant	Variable	Yes
Sarker and Sarkar (2013a)	Time varying	Stock dependent	No
Sarkar and Sarkar (2013b)	Stochastic	Constant	No
Ghoreishi et al. (2014)	Non-instantaneous	Price and time dependent	Yes
Jaggi et al. (2014)	Constant	Price dependent	Yes
Pareek and Dhaka (2015)	Constant	Constant	No
Sarkar et al. (2015)	Time varying	Constant	Yes
Shabani et al. (2016)	Fuzzy	Fuzzy	Yes
Bhunia et al. (2016)	Constant	Constant	Yes
Sarkar et al. (2017)	Time varying	Constant	No
Tiwari et al. (2017)	Non instantaneous	Stock dependent	No
Jaggi et al. (2019)	Constant	Stochastic	Yes
Tiwari et al. (2019)	Non instantaneous	Constant	Yes
Khan et al. (2020)	Non instantaneous	Constant	Yes
This paper	Fuzzy	Weibull	Yes

The family of all triangular fuzzy numbers on R is denoted as

$$F_N = \{(a, b, c) | a < b < c \forall a, b, c \in R\}$$

The α-cut of $\tilde{A} = (a, b, c) \in F_N, 0 \leq \alpha \leq 1$ is

$$A(\alpha) = [A_L(\alpha), A_R(\alpha)]$$

where, $A_L(\alpha) = a + (b - a)\alpha$ and $A_R(\alpha) = c - (c - b)\alpha$ are the left and right end-points of $A(\alpha)$.

If $A = (a, b, c)$ is a triangular fuzzy number then the graded mean integration representation of $\tilde{A}$ is defined as:

$$P(\tilde{A}) = \frac{\int_0^{W_A} h\left(\frac{L^{-1}(h) + R^{-1}(h)}{2}\right) dh}{\int_0^{W_A} hdh}$$

with $0 < h \leq W_A$ and $0 < W_A \leq 1$

$$P(A) = \frac{1}{2}\left[\frac{\int_0^1 h\{a + h(b-a) + c - h(c-a)\} dh}{\int_0^1 hdh}\right] P(\tilde{A}) = \frac{a + 4b + c}{6}$$

4 Assumptions and Notation

The following assumptions and notation have been carried out in the paper.

4.1 Assumptions

The inventory model is based on the following assumptions:

- There is limited capacity W in OW and unlimited capacity in RW. The items of RW are consumed first and than from OW for the profitable reasons.
- The seller can accumulate revenue and earn interest from the very beginning that his/her customer pays for the amount of purchasing cost to the seller until the end of the credit period offered by the supplier.
- There is an infinite replenishment rate and the lead time is zero.
- θ_1 is the deterioration rate in OW and θ_2 is in RW. $\theta_1 \neq \theta_2$. The rate of deterioration in RW is smaller than the rate of deterioration in OW as the RW has better storing facilities than OW.
- The inventory system considered a single item.
- Demand $D(t) = \alpha\beta t^{\beta-1}$ is assumed to be a function of time i.e. where α and β are positive constants and $\alpha \geq 0, 0 \leq \beta \leq 1$
- There is no shortages in the model.

4.2 Notation

The following notation are used in the model:

- T is time period of each cycle (unit of time).
- t_w is time where level of inventory reaches to W (unit of time).
- W is stored units in OW (units).
- A is ordering cost (\$/order).
- M is trade credit period of retailer offered by the supplier (unit of time).
- P is sales price per unit (\$/unit).
- I_e is interest earn (/\$/unit/unit of time).
- c is purchasing price (rupee/unit).
- h_o is holding cost in OW (\$/unit/unit of time).
- I_p is interest charges by the supplier (/\$/unit/unit of time).
- h_r is holding cost in RW (\$/unit/unit of time).
- $I_r(t)$ is the inventory level at time $t \in [0, t_w]$ in RW (units).
- $I_o(t)$ is the inventory level at time $t \in [0, T]$ in OW.(units)
- $D = \alpha\beta t^{\beta-1}$ is total demand $0 < \alpha << 1, \beta > 1$ (unit/unit of time).
- θ_1 is rate of deterioration in OW $0 \leq \theta_1 \leq 1$.
- $\tilde{\theta_1}$ is the fuzzy deterioration rate in OW $0 \leq \tilde{\theta_1} \leq 1$.
- θ_2 is deterioration rate in RW $0 \leq \theta_2 \leq 1$.
- $\tilde{\theta_2}$ is the fuzzy deterioration rate in RW $0 \leq \tilde{\theta_2} \leq 1$.
- TC_1 is the total inventory cost per unit time (\$).
- $\tilde{TC_1}$ is the total fuzzy inventory cost per unit time (\$).

5 Mathematical Model

Let $I_o(t)$ be the level of inventory in OW at $[0, T]$ and $I_r(t)$ be the level of inventory in RW at $[0, t_w]$ with initial OW kept W units and rest stored in RW. The inventory of OW is used only after use of the stock kept in RW. The stock kept in RW exhausts due to demand and deterioration during the interval $[0, t_w]$. In OW, the inventory W gradually decreases due to deterioration only during $[0, t_w]$ and due to demand and deterioration during $[t_w, T]$. At the time T, both RW and OW becomes empty (Fig. 1).

5.1 Crisp Model

The level of inventory in RW and OW at time $t \in [0, t_w]$ has these differential equations:

$$\frac{dI_r}{dt} = -\alpha\beta t^{\beta-1} - \theta_2 I_r(t), \qquad 0 \leq t \leq t_w \tag{1}$$

Fig. 1 Time-inventory status

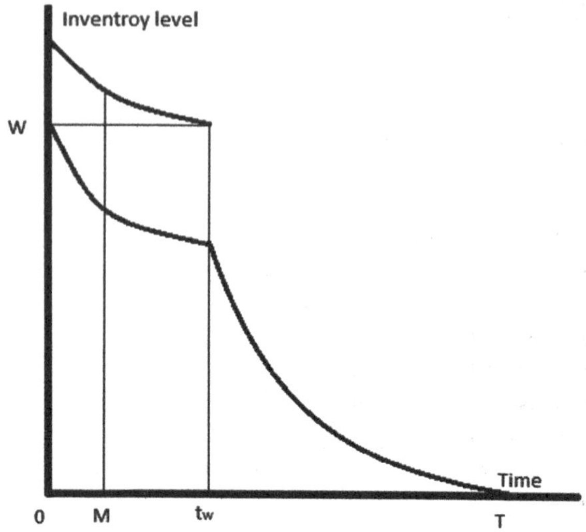

with the boundary conditions $I_r(t_w) = 0$ and

$$\frac{dI_o(t)}{dt} = -\theta_1 I_o(t), \qquad 0 \le t \le t_w \tag{2}$$

with the initial conditions $I_o(0) = W$,

during the interval $[t_w, T]$, the level of inventory in OW, has this differential equation:

$$\frac{dI_o(t)}{dt} = -\alpha\beta t^{\beta-1} - \theta_1 I_o(t), \qquad t_w \le t \le T \tag{3}$$

The solution from Eqs. (1) to (3 is:

$$I_r(t) = \alpha[t_w^{\beta} e^{\frac{\theta_2 t_w \beta}{\beta+1}} - t^{\beta} e^{\frac{\theta_2 t \beta}{\beta+1}}]e^{-\theta_2 t}, \qquad 0 \le t \le t_w \tag{4}$$

$$I_o(t) = We^{-\theta_1 t}, \qquad 0 \le t \le t_w \tag{5}$$

$$I_o(t) = \alpha[T^{\beta} e^{\frac{\theta_1 T \beta}{\beta+1}} - t^{\beta} e^{\frac{\theta_1 t \beta}{\beta+1}}]e^{-\theta_1 t}, \qquad t_w \le t \le T \tag{6}$$

Using the continuity of $I_o(t)$ at time $t = t_w$

$$I_o(t_w) = We^{-\theta_1 t_w}$$

$$I_o(t_w) = \alpha \left[T^{\beta} e^{\frac{\theta_1 T \beta}{\beta+1}} - t_w^{\beta} e^{\frac{\theta_1 t_w \beta}{\beta+1}} \right] e^{-\theta_1 t_w}$$

which implies that

$$T = \left[\frac{\frac{W}{\alpha} + t_w^{\beta} e^{\frac{\theta_1 t_w \beta}{\beta+1}}}{\frac{\alpha\beta}{\beta+1}} \right]^{\beta(\beta+1)} \tag{7}$$

Annual ordering cost is

$$C_r = \frac{A}{T} \tag{8}$$

Annual holding cost of RW is

$$C_{h1} = h_r \int_0^{t_w} I_r(t)dt$$

$$C_{h1} = \frac{h_r \alpha}{T} \left[\frac{t_w^{\beta}}{\theta_2} \left(e^{\frac{\theta_2 t_w \beta}{\beta+1}} - e^{\frac{-\theta_2 t_w}{\beta+1}} \right) + \left(\frac{(\beta+2)t_w^{\beta+1} - \theta_2 t_w^{\beta+2}}{(\beta+1)(\beta+2)} \right) \right] \tag{9}$$

Annual holding cost of OW is

$$C_{h2} = h_o \int_0^{T} I_o(t)dt$$

$$\begin{aligned} C_{h2} = {} & \frac{h_o W}{T\theta_1}(1 - e^{-\theta_1 t_w}) + \frac{h_o \alpha T^{\beta-1} e^{\frac{\theta_1 T \beta}{\beta+1}}}{\theta_1}(e^{-\theta_1 t_w} - e^{-\theta_1 T}) \\ & + h_o \alpha \frac{((T^{\beta} - T t_w^{\beta+1})(\beta+2) - \theta_1 (T^{\beta+1} - t_w^{\beta+2}))}{(\beta+1)(\beta+2)} \end{aligned} \tag{10}$$

Annual cost of deterioration in RW and OW is

$$C_{\theta} = \theta_2 \int_0^{t_w} I_r(t)dt + \theta_1 \int_0^{T} I_o(t)\mathrm{d}t$$

$$\begin{aligned} C_{\theta} = {} & \alpha\theta_2 t_w^{\beta} \left[\frac{e^{\frac{\theta_2 t_w \beta}{\beta+1}}}{\theta_2}(1 - e^{-\theta_2 t_w}) - \frac{t_w(\beta+2) - \theta_2 t_w}{(\beta+1)(\beta+2)} \right] + (1 - e^{-\theta_1 t_w} - e^{-\theta_1 T}) + \\ & \alpha T^{\beta} e^{\frac{\theta_1 T \beta}{\beta+1}} e^{-\theta_1 t_w} - \frac{(T^{\beta+1} - t_w^{\beta+1})(\beta+2) - \theta_1 (T^{\beta+2} - t_w^{\beta+1})}{(\beta+1)(\beta+2)} \end{aligned} \tag{11}$$

Now there are three cases arises:
Case 1: $M \leq t_w \leq T$
Case 2: $t_w < M \leq T$
Case 3: $M > T$

5.1.1 Case 1: $M \leq t_w \leq T$

In this case, buyer has to pay an interest charges. Also at the same time he earns interest on the income till M:

$$C_{e1} = \frac{pI_e}{T}\int_0^M \alpha\beta t^\beta dt$$

$$C_{e1} = \frac{pI_e\alpha\beta M^{\beta+1}}{T(\beta+1)} \tag{12}$$

Further, Interest payable is:

$$C_{p1} = \frac{cI_p}{T}\left[\int_M^{t_w} I_r(t)dt + \int_M^{t_w} I_o(t) + \int_{t_w}^T I_o(t)\right]$$

$$C_{p1} = \frac{cI_p}{T}\left[\frac{\alpha t_w^\beta e^{\frac{\theta_2\beta}{\beta+1}}}{2}(e^{-\theta_2 M} - e^{-\theta_2 t_w}) + \frac{(\beta+2)(M^{\beta+1} - T^{\beta+1}) + \theta_1(T^{\beta+2} - t_w^{\beta+2})}{(\beta+1)(\beta+2)}\right]$$
$$+ \frac{cI_p}{T}\left[\frac{W(e^{-\theta_1 M} - e^{-\theta_1 t_w})}{\theta_1} + \frac{\theta_2(t_w^{\beta+2} - M^{\beta+2})}{(\beta+1)(\beta+2)} + \frac{\alpha T^\beta e^{\frac{\theta_1 T\beta}{\beta+1}}}{\theta_1}(e^{-\theta_1 t_w} - e^{-\theta_1 T})\right] \tag{13}$$

Now, the total cost is:

$$TC_1(T, t_w) = C_r + C_{h1} + C_{h2} + C_\theta + C_{p1} - C_{e1} \tag{14}$$

5.1.2 Case 2: $t_w < M \leq T$

Interest will be paid:

$$C_{p2} = \frac{cI_p}{T}\int_T^M I_o(t)dt$$

$$C_{p2} = cI_p\alpha\left[\frac{T^{\beta-1}e^{\frac{\theta_1 T\beta}{\beta+1}}}{\theta_1}(e^{-\theta_1 M} - e^{-\theta_1 T}) - \frac{(\beta+2)(T^{\beta} - TM^{\beta+1}) - \theta_1(T^{\beta+1} + TM^{\beta+2})}{(\beta+1)(\beta+2)}\right] \tag{15}$$

The interest will be earn as follows:

$$C_{e2} = \frac{pI_e}{T}\int_0^M \alpha\beta t^{\beta} dt$$

$$C_{e2} = \frac{pI_e\alpha\beta M^{\beta+1}}{T(\beta+1)} \tag{16}$$

Now, the total cost is:

$$TC_2(T, t_w) = C_r + C_{h1} + C_{h2} + C_{\theta} + C_{p2} - C_{e2} \tag{17}$$

5.1.3 Case 3: $M > T$

In this case, the buyer gets a larger credit period M which is after T. Then, the buyer earns interest, no need to pay interest charges:

$$C_{e3} = pI_e \int_0^T \int_0^t \alpha\beta t^{\beta-1} dudt$$

$$C_{e3} = pI_e\alpha\beta\left(\frac{T^{\beta}+1}{\beta+1}\right) \tag{18}$$

Now, the total cost is:

$$TC_3(T, t_w) = C_r + C_{h1} + C_{h2} + C_{\theta} - C_{e3} \tag{19}$$

6 Fuzzy Model

In reality, it is not easy to define all the parameter accurately as there is always an uncertainty in the environment. So, in this model $\tilde{\theta_1}$, $\tilde{\theta_2}$ assumes to be in fuzzy sense.

Let $\tilde{\theta_1} = (\theta_{11}, \theta_{12}, \theta_{13})$ and $\tilde{\theta_2} = (\theta_{21}, \theta_{22}, \theta_{23})$ are consider in the form of triangular fuzzy numbers.

6.1 Case 1: $M \leq t_w \leq T$

Total cost per unit time in fuzzy sense

$$\widetilde{TC_1}(T, t_w) = \frac{A}{T} + \frac{h_r\alpha}{T}\left[\frac{t_w^{\beta}}{\widetilde{\theta_2}}\left(e^{\frac{\widetilde{\theta_2}t_w\beta}{\beta+1}} - e^{\frac{-\widetilde{\theta_2}t_w}{\beta+1}}\right) + \left(\frac{(\beta+2)t_w^{\beta+1} - \widetilde{\theta_2}t_w^{\beta+2}}{(\beta+1)(\beta+2)}\right)\right]$$
$$+ A_1 + \alpha\widetilde{\theta_2}t_w^{\beta}\left[\frac{e^{\frac{\widetilde{\theta_2}t_w\beta}{\beta+1}}}{\widetilde{\theta_2}}(1 - e^{-}\widetilde{\theta_2}t_w) - \left(\frac{t_w(\beta+2) - \widetilde{\theta_2}t_w}{(\beta+1)(\beta+2)}\right)\right]$$
$$+ W(1 - e^{-\widetilde{\theta_1}t_w}) + \alpha T^{\beta}e^{\frac{\widetilde{\theta_1}T\beta}{\beta+1}}e^{-\widetilde{\theta_1}t_w} - e^{-\widetilde{\theta_1}T}$$
$$- \frac{(T^{\beta+1} - t_w^{\beta+1})(\beta+2) - \widetilde{\theta_1}(T^{\beta+2} - t_w^{\beta+1})}{(\beta+1)(\beta+2)} + \frac{pI_e\alpha\beta M^{\beta+1}}{T(\beta+1)} + A_2$$

$$\underline{\widetilde{TC_1}(T, t_w)} = \frac{A}{T} + \frac{h_r\alpha}{T}\left[\begin{array}{l}\frac{t_w^{\beta}}{(\widetilde{\theta_{21}}, \widetilde{\theta_{22}}, \widetilde{\theta_{23}})}\left(e^{\frac{(\widetilde{\theta_{21}}, \widetilde{\theta_{22}}, \widetilde{\theta_{23}})t_w\beta}{\beta+1}} - e^{\frac{-(\widetilde{\theta_{21}}, \widetilde{\theta_{22}}, \widetilde{\theta_{23}})t_w}{\beta+1}}\right) \\ + \frac{(\beta+2)t_w^{\beta+1} - (\widetilde{\theta_{21}}, \widetilde{\theta_{22}}, \widetilde{\theta_{23}})t_w^{\beta+2}}{(\beta+1)(\beta+2)}\end{array}\right]$$
$$+ h_oA_3 + \alpha T^{\beta}e^{\frac{(\widetilde{\theta_{11}}, \widetilde{\theta_{12}}, \widetilde{\theta_{13}})T\beta}{\beta+1}}\left[e^{-(\widetilde{\theta_{11}}, \widetilde{\theta_{12}}, \widetilde{\theta_{13}})t_w} - e^{-(\widetilde{\theta_{11}}, \widetilde{\theta_{12}}, \widetilde{\theta_{13}})T}\right]$$
$$+ W(1 - e^{-(\widetilde{\theta_{11}}, \widetilde{\theta_{12}}, \widetilde{\theta_{13}})t_w}) + \alpha(\widetilde{\theta_{21}}, \widetilde{\theta_{12}}, \widetilde{\theta_{13}})t_w^{\beta}$$
$$\times\left[\begin{array}{l}\frac{e^{\frac{(\widetilde{\theta_{21}}, \widetilde{\theta_{12}}, \widetilde{\theta_{13}})t_w\beta}{\beta+1}}}{(\widetilde{\theta_{21}}, \widetilde{\theta_{22}}, \widetilde{\theta_{23}})}(1 - e^{-}(\widetilde{\theta_{21}}, \widetilde{\theta_{22}}, \widetilde{\theta_{23}})t_w) \\ - \frac{t_w(\beta+2) - (\widetilde{\theta_{21}}, \widetilde{\theta_{12}}, \widetilde{\theta_{13}})t_w}{(\beta+1)(\beta+2)}\end{array}\right]$$
$$- \frac{T^{\beta+1}(\beta+2) - (\widetilde{\theta_{11}}, \widetilde{\theta_{12}}, \widetilde{\theta_{13}})T^{\beta+2} - t_w^{\beta+1}(\beta+2) + (\widetilde{\theta_{11}}, \widetilde{\theta_{12}}, \widetilde{\theta_{13}})t_w^{\beta+1}}{(\beta+1)(\beta+2)}$$
$$+ \frac{pI_e\alpha\beta M^{\beta+1}}{T(\beta+1)} + \frac{cI_p}{T}A_4$$

Using graded mean integration method for defuzzification of TC_1

$$\tilde{TC_1}(T, t_w) = \frac{(\tilde{TC_a} + 4\tilde{TC_b} + \tilde{TC_c})}{6}$$

For the values of $A_1, A_2, A_3, \tilde{TC_a}, \tilde{TC_b}, \tilde{TC_c}$ see the appendix.

6.2 Case 2: $t_w < M \leq T$

Total cost per unit time in fuzzy sense

$$\widetilde{TC_2}(T,t_w) = \frac{A}{T} + \frac{h_r\alpha}{T}\left[\frac{t_w^{\beta}}{\widetilde{\theta_2}}\left(e^{\frac{\widetilde{\theta_2}t_w\beta}{\beta+1}} - e^{\frac{-\widetilde{\theta_2}t_w}{\beta+1}}\right) + \left(\frac{(\beta+2)t_w^{\beta+1} - \widetilde{\theta_2}t_w^{\beta+2}}{(\beta+1)(\beta+2)}\right)\right]$$
$$+ \frac{h_o\alpha T^{\beta-1}e^{\frac{\widetilde{\theta_1}T\beta}{\beta+1}}}{\widetilde{\theta_1}}(e^{-\widetilde{\theta_1}t_w} - e^{-\widetilde{\theta_1}T}) + \frac{h_oW}{T\widetilde{\theta_1}}(1-e^{-\widetilde{\theta_1}t_w}) + \frac{pI_e\alpha\beta M^{\beta+1}}{T(\beta+1)}$$
$$+ \alpha\theta_2 t_w^{\beta}\left[\frac{e^{\frac{\theta_2 t_w\beta}{\beta+1}}}{\widetilde{\theta_2}}(1-e^{-}\widetilde{\theta_2}t_w)\right]$$
$$\times h_o\alpha\frac{(T^{\beta}(\beta+2) - \widetilde{\theta_1}T^{\beta+1} - T(t_w^{\beta+1}(\beta+2) - \widetilde{\theta_1}t_w^{\beta+2}))}{(\beta+1)(\beta+2)}$$
$$- \alpha\theta_2 t_w^{\beta}\left[\frac{t_w(\beta+2) - \widetilde{\theta_2}t_w}{(\beta+1)(\beta+2)}\right] + W(1-e^{-\widetilde{\theta_1}t_w}) + \alpha T^{\beta}e^{\frac{\widetilde{\theta_1}T\beta}{\beta+1}}e^{-\widetilde{\theta_1}t_w}$$
$$- e^{-\widetilde{\theta_1}T} - \frac{T^{\beta+1}(\beta+2) - \widetilde{\theta_1}T^{\beta+2} - t_w^{\beta+1}(\beta+2) + \widetilde{\theta_1}t_w^{\beta+1}}{(\beta+1)(\beta+2)}$$
$$+ cI_p\alpha\left[\begin{array}{l}\dfrac{T^{\beta-1}e^{\frac{\widetilde{\theta_1}T\beta}{\beta+1}}}{\widetilde{\theta_1}}(e^{-\widetilde{\theta_1}M} - e^{-\widetilde{\theta_1}T}) \\ -\left(\dfrac{(\beta+2)T^{\beta} - \widetilde{\theta_1}T^{\beta+1} - T(\beta+2)M^{\beta+1} + \widetilde{\theta_1}M^{\beta+2}}{(\beta+1)(\beta+2)}\right)\end{array}\right]$$

Using graded mean integration method for defuzzification of TC_2

$$\tilde{TC_2}(T,t_w) = \frac{(\tilde{TC_a} + 4\tilde{TC_b} + \tilde{TC_c})}{6}$$

In case 2, we do the same process as in case 1.

6.3 Case 3: $M > T$

Total cost unit time in fuzzy sense

$$\widetilde{TC_3}(T, t_w) = \frac{A}{T} + \frac{h_r\alpha}{T}\left[\frac{t_w^\beta}{\widetilde{\theta_2}}\left(e^{\frac{\widetilde{\theta_2} t_w \beta}{\beta+1}} - e^{\frac{-\widetilde{\theta_2} t_w}{\beta+1}}\right) + \left(\frac{(\beta+2)t_w^{\beta+1} - \widetilde{\theta_2} t_w^{\beta+2}}{(\beta+1)(\beta+2)}\right)\right]$$
$$+ \frac{h_o W}{T\widetilde{\theta_1}}(1 - e^{-\widetilde{\theta_1} t_w}) + \frac{h_o \alpha T^{\beta-1} e^{\frac{\widetilde{\theta_1} T \beta}{\beta+1}}}{\widetilde{\theta_1}}(e^{-\widetilde{\theta_1} t_w} - e^{-\widetilde{\theta_1} T})$$
$$+ h_o\alpha\frac{((T^\beta - Tt_w^{\beta+1})(\beta+2) - \widetilde{\theta_1}(T^{\beta+1} - Tt_w^{\beta+2}))}{(\beta+1)(\beta+2)}$$
$$+ \alpha\widetilde{\theta_2} t_w^\beta\left[\frac{e^{\frac{\widetilde{\theta_2} t_w \beta}{\beta+1}}}{\widetilde{\theta_2}}(1 - e^{-}\widetilde{\theta_2} t_w) - \frac{t_w(\beta+2) - \widetilde{\theta_2} t_w}{(\beta+1)(\beta+2)}\right]$$
$$+ \alpha T^\beta e^{\frac{\widetilde{\theta_1} T \beta}{\beta+1}} e^{-\widetilde{\theta_1} t_w} - e^{-\widetilde{\theta_1} T} + W(1 - e^{-\widetilde{\theta_1} t_w})$$
$$- \frac{T^{\beta+1}(\beta+2) - \widetilde{\theta_1} T^{\beta+2} - t_w^{\beta+1}(\beta+2) + \widetilde{\theta_1} t_w^{\beta+1}}{(\beta+1)(\beta+2)}$$
$$- pI_e\alpha\beta\left(\frac{T^\beta + 1}{\beta+1}\right)$$

Using graded mean integration method for defuzzification of TC_3

$$\tilde{TC_3}(T, t_w) = \frac{(\tilde{TC_a} + 4\tilde{TC_b} + \tilde{TC_c})}{6}$$

In case 3, we do the same process as in case 1. To find the optimal cost, the given conditions should be satisfied. $\frac{\partial(TC)}{\partial(T)} = 0$ and $\frac{\partial(TC)}{\partial(t_w)} = 0$

Further, for total cost $\tilde{TC}(T, t_w)$ to be convex, $\left(\frac{\partial^2(TC)}{\partial(t_w^2)}\right)\left(\frac{\partial^2(TC)}{\partial(T^2)}\right) - \left(\frac{\partial^2(TC)}{\partial(t_w)\partial(T)}\right)^2 > 0$ must be satisfied.

7 Numerical Examples

An example is taken for this model to validate the results:
For crisp model $A = 200$ \$/order, $\alpha = 0.5$ units/year, $\beta = 4$ units/year, $e = 2.5$, c = 10 \$/unit, $I_p = 0.15$/\$/unit/year, $h_r = 1$ \$/unit/year, $p = 12$ \$/unit, $h_o = 0.5$ units/year, $W = 50$ units, $\theta_1 = 0.9$, $I_e = 0.12$/\$/unit/year, $\theta_2 = 0.02$, $M = \frac{25}{365}$ year and **for fuzzy model** $A = 200$ \$/order, $\alpha = 0.5$ units/year, $\beta = 4$ units/year, $e = 2.5$, $c = 10$ \$/unit,

h_o = 0.5 \$/unit/year, I_e = 0.12/\$/unit/year, h_r = 1 \$/unit/year, p = 12 \$/unit, I_p = 0.15/\$/unit/year, W = 50 units, $\theta_1 = 0.9$, $\theta_2 = 0.02$, $M = \frac{25}{365}$ year. Here parameteric values are opted from Shabani et al. (2016)

7.1 Crisp Model Versus Fuzzy Model

Crisp				Fuzzy			
t_w	T	Z	Case	t_w	T	Z	Case
1.673	2.117	338.284	1	1.127	1.862	305.785	1
1.076	2.570	613.389	2	1.755	1.765	364.719	2
0.767	1.755	280.719	3	0.621	1.816	228.560	3

As, we see that from the numerical example, the fuzzy solution gives maximum optimal value in comparison to the crisp solution.

8 Sensitivity Analysis

Here is the study of the effects of changes in parameter β, θ_1, θ_2 and M in all the cases. Rest of the parameters are same as in example.

From Table 2, the value of total cost (Z) is increasing with the increment in the value of (T, t_w). But, from Table 3, the value of total cost is decreasing having the decreasing effect on the value of (T, t_w), except the first value of β. So, fuzzy model is more optimal with respect to crisp model (Figs. 2, 3,4, 5, 6 and 7).

Table 2 Sensitivity analysis for case 1 in crisp manner

Parameter	Value	t_w	T	Z
β	4	1.235	2.269	291.256
	6	1.673	2.117	338.284
	8	1.117	1.580	381.877
θ_1	0.5	1.140	2.5781	204.011
	0.7	2.134	3.027	246.222
	0.9	1.235	2.269	291.256
θ_2	0.02	1.235	2.269	291.256
	0.05	1.243	2.275	291.414
	0.08	1.253	2.280	291.582
M	15/365	1.233	2.269	292.068
	25/365	1.235	2.2699	291.256
	35/365	1.237	2.270	290.461

Table 3 Sensitivity analysis for case 1 in fuzzy manner

Parameter	Value	t_w	T	Z
β	4	2.022	3.011	375.521
	6	1.127	1.862	305.785
	8	1.090	1.6184	341.220
θ_1	0.5	0.671	2.695	135.035
	0.7	1.126	2.557	203.791
	0.9	2.022	3.011	375.521
θ_2	0.02	2.022	3.011	375.521
	0.05	2.074	2.981	247.089
	0.08	2.010	2.934	248.766
M	15/365	2.137	3.029	245.970
	25/365	2.022	3.011	375.521
	35/365	2.139	3.029	244.513

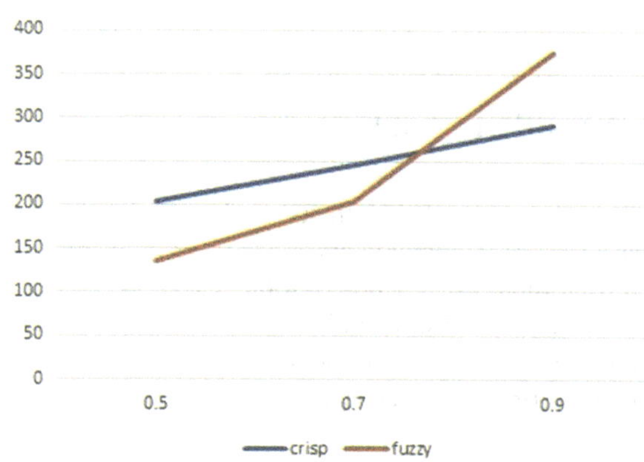

Fig. 2 Graphical representation case 1 profit in crisp and fuzzy with respect to θ_1 parameter

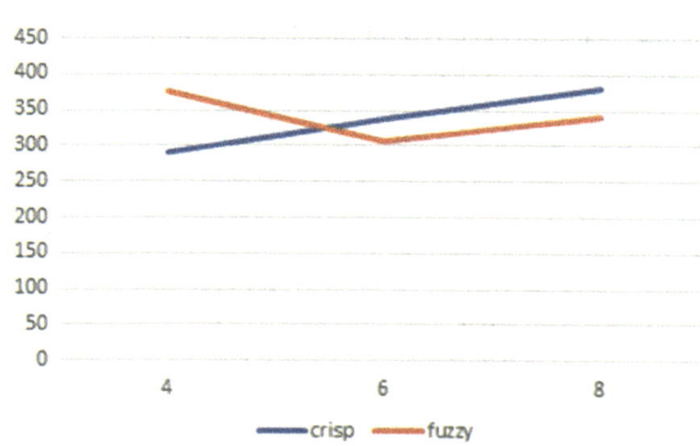

Fig. 3 Graphical representation case 1 profit in crisp and fuzzy with respect to β parameter

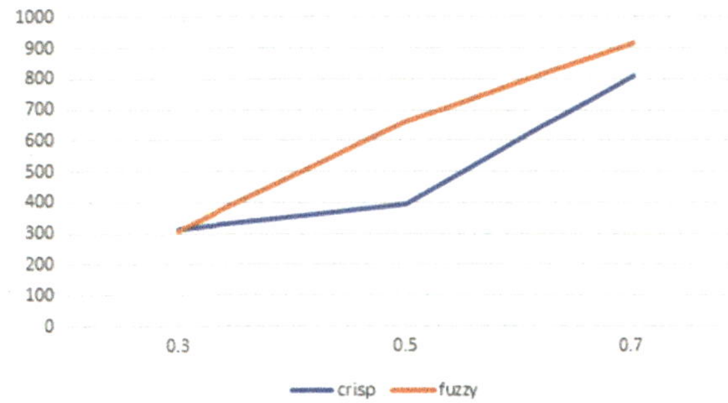

Fig. 4 Graphical representation case 2 profit in crisp and fuzzy with respect to θ_1 parameter

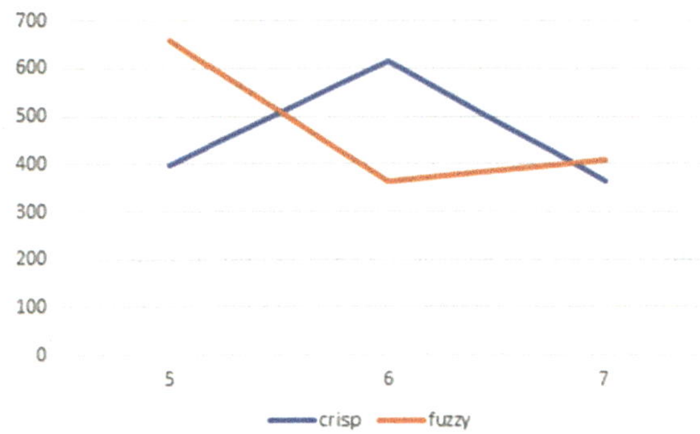

Fig. 5 Graphical representation case 2 profit in crisp and fuzzy with respect to β parameter

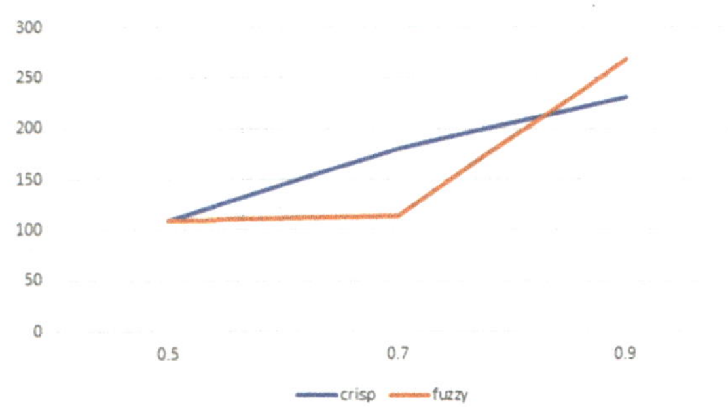

Fig. 6 Graphical representation case 3 profit in crisp and fuzzy with respect to θ_1 parameter

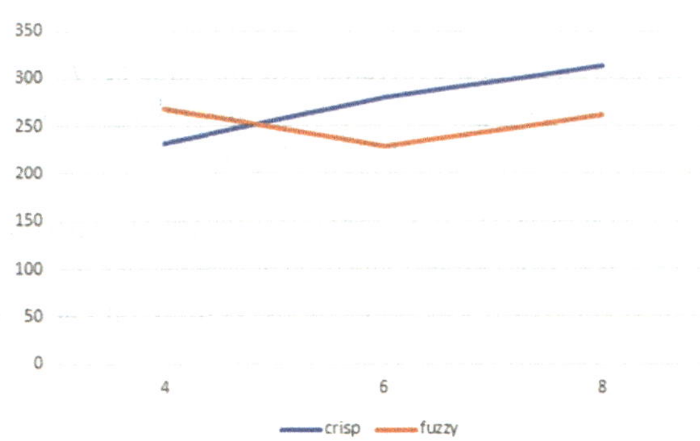

Fig. 7 Graphical representation case 3 profit in crisp and fuzzy with respect to β parameter

Table 4 Sensitivity analysis for case 2 in crisp manner

Parameter	Value	t_w	T	Z
β	5	2.112	2.331	395.765
	6	1.076	2.570	613.389
	7	1.745	1.750	362.435
θ_1	0.3	1.612	1.858	312.541
	0.5	2.112	2.331	395.765
	0.7	2.384	2.957	810.135
θ_2	0.02	2.112	2.331	395.765
	0.03	2.112	2.322	395.175
	0.04	2.112	2.314	394.721
M	15/365	2.111	2.331	396.721
	25/365	2.112	2.331	395.765
	35/365	2.113	2.332	394.818

Table 5 Sensitivity analysis for case 2 in fuzzy manner

Parameter	Value	t_w	T	Z
β	5	1.062	2.592	659.995
	6	1.755	1.765	364.719
	7	2.134	2.379	409.801
θ_1	0.3	1.656	1.895	308.022
	0.5	1.062	2.592	659.995
	0.7	2.395	3.046	918.355
θ_2	0.02	1.062	2.592	659.995
	0.03	2.134	2.370	409.050
	0.04	2.134	2.314	408.458
M	15/365	2.133	2.379	410.813
	25/365	1.062	2.592	659.995
	35/365	2.135	2.379	408.799

In Table 4, with the increment in the value of (T, t_w), the value of total cost (Z) is going to increasing. But, in Table 5, the value of total cost having decreasing effect on the value of (T, t_w), except the first value of β. So, fuzzy model is more optimal with respect to crisp model.

From Table 6, the value of total cost (Z) is increasing with the increasing value of (T, t_w). But, from table 7, the total cost is decreasing with the value of (T, t_w), except the first value of β. So, fuzzy model is more optimal with respect to crisp model.

Table 6 Sensitivity analysis for case 3 in crisp manner

Parameter	Value	t_w	T	Z
β	4	0.784	2.207	231.729
	6	0.767	1.755	280.719
	8	0.775	1.545	313.876
θ_1	0.5	0.145	2.512	110.272
	0.7	0.604	2.344	180.131
	0.9	0.784	2.207	231.729
θ_2	0.02	0.784	2.207	231.729
	0.05	0.785	2.207	231.744
	0.08	0.785	2.208	231.760
M	15/365	0.784	2.207	231.729
	25/365	0.7847	2.207	231.729
	35/365	0.784	2.207	231.729

Table 7 Sensitivity analysis for case 3 in fuzzy manner

Parameter	Value	t_w	T	Z
β	4	0.361	2.324	268.822
	6	0.621	1.816	228.560
	8	0.651	1.584	261.616
θ_1	0.5	0.145	2.512	110.272
	0.7	0.173	2.480	113.681
	0.9	0.361	2.324	268.822
θ_2	0.02	0.361	2.324	268.822
	0.05	0.606	2.328	181.091
	0.08	0.606	2.328	181.095
M	15/365	0.606	2.328	181.087
	25/365	0.361	2.324	268.822
	35/365	0.606	2.328	181.087

9 Conclusion

In this paper, we have proposed the effect of fuzzy deterioration as well as Weibull demand under credit financing in two-warehouse environment. The study associated with some types of inventory such as seasonal food items inventory, newly launch fashion items, etc. The model is motivated by the fact that there is always an uncertainty in demand and the deterioration rate such as for physical goods. So, it is worthwhile to take the deterioration rate in fuzzy number as well as demand in Weibull distribution. The rate of deterioration is represented by triangular fuzzy number. Nowadays, the credit financing policy has become a advertisement tool to attract customers. Customer has to purchase items in a very large quantity without immediately payment. In trade credit policy, seller offers some credit period to pay. But beyond this time, buyer has to pay an interest. Here, graded mean integration method is used for defuzzification to calculate the total cycle time as well as total cost of the model. From the numerical study and sensitivity analysis with respect to different key parameters, it is observed that fuzzy model is more optimal than crisp model.

10 Managerial Insights

Here, fuzzy model is more optimal with respect to crisp model. The above results show the significance of the model. This model can be extended in several forms. It can be more realistic if this model can be extended with types of demand such as advertisement-dependent demand, ramp type demand or two level and three level trade credit policy or if one may assume variable lead time also, one can take nonlinear holding cost. Further, this model can be extended under carbon emission constraints with international supply chain.

Appendix

$$A_1 = h_o \left[\begin{array}{l} \frac{W}{T\widetilde{\theta_1}}(1 - e^{-\widetilde{\theta_1} t_w}) + \frac{\alpha T^{\beta-1} e^{\frac{\widetilde{\theta_1} T\beta}{\beta+1}}}{\widetilde{\theta_1}}(e^{-\widetilde{\theta_1} t_w} - e^{-\widetilde{\theta_1} T}) \\ + \alpha \frac{\left((T^\beta - Tt_w^{\beta+1})(\beta+2) - \widetilde{\theta_1}(T^{\beta+1} + Tt_w^{\beta+2})\right)}{(\beta+1)(\beta+2)} \end{array} \right]$$

$$A_2 = \frac{cI_p}{T} \left[\begin{array}{l} \frac{(\beta+2)(t_w^{\beta+1} - M^{\beta+1}) - \widetilde{\theta_2}(t_w^{\beta+2} - M^{\beta+2})}{(\beta+1)(\beta+2)} \\ + \frac{W(e^{-\widetilde{\theta_1} M} - e^{-\widetilde{\theta_1} t_w})}{\widetilde{\theta_1}} + \frac{\alpha T^\beta e^{\frac{\widetilde{\theta_1} T\beta}{\beta+1}}}{\widetilde{\theta_1}}(e^{-\widetilde{\theta_1} t_w} - e^{-\widetilde{\theta_1} T}) \end{array} \right]$$
$$- \frac{cI_p}{T} \left[\frac{\alpha t_w^\beta e^{\frac{\widetilde{\theta_2}\beta}{\beta+1}}}{\widetilde{\theta_2}}(e^{-\widetilde{\theta_2} M} - e^{-\widetilde{\theta_2} t_w}) \right]$$

$$\begin{aligned} A_3 = & \frac{W}{T(\widetilde{\theta_{11}}, \widetilde{\theta_{12}}, \widetilde{\theta_{13}})}(1 - e^{-(\widetilde{\theta_{11}}, \widetilde{\theta_{12}}, \widetilde{\theta_{13}}) t_w}) \\ & + \frac{\alpha T^{\beta-1} e^{\frac{(\widetilde{\theta_{11}}, \widetilde{\theta_{12}}, \widetilde{\theta_{13}})}{T\beta\beta+1}}}{(\widetilde{\theta_{11}}, \widetilde{\theta_{12}}, \widetilde{\theta_{13}})} \left(e^{-(\widetilde{\theta_{11}}, \widetilde{\theta_{12}}, \widetilde{\theta_{13}}) t_w} - e^{-(\widetilde{\theta_{11}}, \widetilde{\theta_{12}}, \widetilde{\theta_{13}}) T}\right) \\ & + \alpha \frac{((T^\beta - Tt_w^{\beta+1})(\beta+2) - (\widetilde{\theta_{11}}, \widetilde{\theta_{12}}, \widetilde{\theta_{13}})(T^{\beta+1} - Tt_w^{\beta+2}))}{(\beta+1)(\beta+2)} \end{aligned}$$

$$A_4 = \left[\begin{array}{l} \dfrac{\alpha t_w^{\beta} e^{\frac{(\widetilde{\theta_{21}},\widetilde{\theta_{22}},\widetilde{\theta_{23}})\beta}{\beta+1}}}{(\widetilde{\theta_{21}},\widetilde{\theta_{22}},\widetilde{\theta_{23}})}\left(e^{-(\widetilde{\theta_{21}},\widetilde{\theta_{22}},\widetilde{\theta_{23}})M} - e^{-(\widetilde{\theta_{21}},\widetilde{\theta_{22}},\widetilde{\theta_{23}})t_w}\right) \\ - \dfrac{(\beta+2)(t_w^{\beta+1} - M^{\beta+1}) - (\widetilde{\theta_{21}},\widetilde{\theta_{22}},\widetilde{\theta_{23}})(t_w^{\beta+2} - M^{\beta+2})}{(\beta+1)(\beta+2)} \end{array}\right]$$

$$+ \left[\begin{array}{l} \dfrac{W\left(e^{-(\widetilde{\theta_{11}},\widetilde{\theta_{12}},\widetilde{\theta_{13}})M} - e^{-(\widetilde{\theta_{11}},\widetilde{\theta_{12}},\widetilde{\theta_{13}})t_w}\right)}{(\widetilde{\theta_{11}},\widetilde{\theta_{12}},\widetilde{\theta_{13}})} \\ + \dfrac{\alpha T^{\beta} e^{\frac{(\widetilde{\theta_{11}},\widetilde{\theta_{12}},\widetilde{\theta_{13}})T\beta}{\beta+1}}}{(\widetilde{\theta_{11}},\widetilde{\theta_{12}},\widetilde{\theta_{13}})}\left(e^{-(\widetilde{\theta_{11}},\widetilde{\theta_{12}},\widetilde{\theta_{13}})t_w} - e^{-(\widetilde{\theta_{11}},\widetilde{\theta_{12}},\widetilde{\theta_{13}})T}\right) \end{array}\right]$$

$$- \left[\frac{(\beta+2)T^{\beta+1} - (\widetilde{\theta_{11}},\widetilde{\theta_{12}},\widetilde{\theta_{13}})T^{\beta+2} - (\beta+2)t_w^{\beta+1} + (\widetilde{\theta_{11}},\widetilde{\theta_{12}},\widetilde{\theta_{13}})t_w^{\beta+2}}{(\beta+1)(\beta+2)}\right]$$

$$\underline{*\widetilde{TC_a}(T,t_w)} = \frac{A}{T} + \frac{h_r\alpha}{T}\left[\begin{array}{l} \dfrac{t_w^{\beta}}{\widetilde{\theta_{21}}}\left(e^{\frac{\widetilde{\theta_{21}}t_w\beta}{\beta+1}} - e^{\frac{-\widetilde{\theta_{21}}t_w}{\beta+1}}\right) \\ + \left(\dfrac{(\beta+2)t_w^{\beta+1} - \widetilde{\theta_{21}}t_w^{\beta+2}}{(\beta+1)(\beta+2)}\right) \end{array}\right]$$

$$+ \frac{h_oW}{T\widetilde{\theta_{11}}}(1 - e^{-\widetilde{\theta_{11}}t_w}) + \frac{h_o\alpha T^{\beta-1}e^{\frac{\widetilde{\theta_{11}}T\beta}{\beta+1}}}{\widetilde{\theta_{11}}}(e^{-\widetilde{\theta_{11}}t_w} - e^{-\widetilde{\theta_{11}}T})$$

$$+ h_o\alpha\frac{(T^{\beta}(\beta+2) - \widetilde{\theta_{11}}T^{\beta+1} - T(t_w^{\beta+1}(\beta+2) - \widetilde{\theta_{11}}t_w^{\beta+2}))}{(\beta+1)(\beta+2)}$$

$$+ \alpha\widetilde{\theta_{21}}t_w^{\beta}\left[\frac{e^{\frac{\widetilde{\theta_{21}}t_w\beta}{\beta+1}}}{\widetilde{\theta_{21}}}(1 - e^{-}\widetilde{\theta_{21}}t_w) - \frac{t_w(\beta+2) - \widetilde{\theta_{21}}t_w}{(\beta+1)(\beta+2)}\right]$$

$$+ W(1 - e^{-\widetilde{\theta_{11}}t_w}) + \alpha T^{\beta}e^{\frac{\widetilde{\theta_{11}}T\beta}{\beta+1}}e^{-\widetilde{\theta_{11}}t_w} - e^{-\widetilde{\theta_{11}}T}$$

$$- \frac{T^{\beta+1}(\beta+2) - \widetilde{\theta_{11}}T^{\beta+2} - t_w^{\beta+1}(\beta+2) + \widetilde{\theta_{11}}t_w^{\beta+1}}{(\beta+1)(\beta+2)}$$

$$+ \frac{pI_e\alpha\beta M^{\beta+1}}{T(\beta+1)} + \frac{cI_p}{T}\left[\frac{\alpha t_w^{\beta}e^{\frac{\widetilde{\theta_{21}}\beta}{\beta+1}}}{\widetilde{\theta_{21}}}(e^{-\widetilde{\theta_{21}}M} - e^{-\widetilde{\theta_{21}}t_w})\right]$$

$$- \frac{cI_p}{T}\left[\begin{array}{l} \dfrac{(\beta+2)(t_w^{\beta+1} - M^{\beta+1}) - \widetilde{\theta_{21}}(t_w^{\beta+2} - M^{\beta+2})}{(\beta+1)(\beta+2)} \\ + \dfrac{W(e^{-\widetilde{\theta_{11}}M} - e^{-\widetilde{\theta_{11}},t_w})}{\widetilde{\theta_{11}}} + \dfrac{\alpha T^{\beta}e^{\frac{\widetilde{\theta_{11}}T\beta}{\beta+1}}}{\widetilde{\theta_{11}}}(e^{-\widetilde{\theta_{11}}t_w} - e^{-\widetilde{\theta_{11}}T}) \end{array}\right]$$

$$- \frac{cI_p}{T}\left[\frac{(\beta+2)T^{\beta+1} - \widetilde{\theta_{11}}T^{\beta+2} - (\beta+2)t_w^{\beta+1} + \widetilde{\theta_{11}}t_w^{\beta+2}}{(\beta+1)(\beta+2)}\right]$$

$$\underline{\widetilde{*TC_b(T,t_w)}} = \frac{A}{T} + \frac{h_r\alpha}{T}\left[\begin{array}{l}\frac{t_w^{\beta}}{\widetilde{\theta_{22}}}\left(e^{\frac{\widetilde{\theta_{22}}t_w\beta}{\beta+1}} - e^{\frac{-\widetilde{\theta_{22}}t_w}{\beta+1}}\right)\\ +\left(\frac{(\beta+2)t_w^{\beta+1}-\widetilde{\theta_{22}}t_w^{\beta+2}}{(\beta+1)(\beta+2)}\right)\end{array}\right]$$

$$+\frac{h_oW}{T\widetilde{\theta_{12}}}(1-e^{-\widetilde{\theta_{12}}t_w}) + \frac{h_o\alpha T^{\beta-1}e^{\frac{\widetilde{\theta_{12}}T\beta}{\beta+1}}}{\widetilde{\theta_{12}}}(e^{-\widetilde{\theta_{12}}t_w}-e^{-\widetilde{\theta_{12}}T})$$

$$+h_o\alpha\frac{(T^{\beta}(\beta+2)-\widetilde{\theta_{12}}T^{\beta+1}-T(t_w^{\beta+1}(\beta+2)-\widetilde{\theta_{12}}t_w^{\beta+2}))}{(\beta+1)(\beta+2)}$$

$$+\alpha\widetilde{\theta_{22}}t_w^{\beta}\left[\frac{e^{\frac{\widetilde{\theta_{22}}t_w\beta}{\beta+1}}}{\widetilde{\theta_{22}}}(1-e^{-}\widetilde{\theta_{22}}t_w) - \frac{t_w(\beta+2)-\widetilde{\theta_{22}}t_w}{(\beta+1)(\beta+2)}\right]$$

$$+W(1-e^{-\widetilde{\theta_{12}}t_w}) + \alpha T^{\beta}e^{\frac{\widetilde{\theta_{12}}T\beta}{\beta+1}}e^{-\widetilde{\theta_{12}}t_w} - e^{-\widetilde{\theta_{12}}T}$$

$$-\frac{T^{\beta+1}(\beta+2)-\widetilde{\theta_{12}}T^{\beta+2}-t_w^{\beta+1}(\beta+2)+\widetilde{\theta_{12}}t_w^{\beta+1}}{(\beta+1)(\beta+2)}$$

$$+\frac{pI_e\alpha\beta M^{\beta+1}}{T(\beta+1)} + \frac{cI_p}{T}\left[\frac{\alpha t_w^{\beta}e^{\frac{\widetilde{\theta_{22}}\beta}{\beta+1}}}{\widetilde{\theta_{22}}}\left(e^{-\widetilde{\theta_{22}}M}-e^{-\widetilde{\theta_{22}}t_w}\right)\right]$$

$$-\frac{cI_p}{T}\left[\begin{array}{l}\frac{(\beta+2)(t_w^{\beta+1}-M^{\beta+1})-\widetilde{\theta_{22}}(t_w^{\beta+2}-M^{\beta+2})}{(\beta+1)(\beta+2)}\\ +\frac{W(e^{-\widetilde{\theta_{12}}M}-e^{-\widetilde{\theta_{12}}t_w})}{\widetilde{\theta_{12}}} + \frac{\alpha T^{\beta}e^{\frac{\widetilde{\theta_{12}}T\beta}{\beta+1}}}{\widetilde{\theta_{12}}}(e^{-\widetilde{\theta_{12}}t_w}-e^{-\widetilde{\theta_{12}}T})\end{array}\right]$$

$$--\frac{cI_p}{T}\left[\frac{(\beta+2)T^{\beta+1}-\widetilde{\theta_{12}}T^{\beta+2}-(\beta+2)t_w^{\beta+1}+\widetilde{\theta_{12}}t_w^{\beta+2}}{(\beta+1)(\beta+2)}\right]$$

$$\underline{*\widetilde{TC_c}(T,t_w)} = \frac{A}{T} + \frac{h_r\alpha}{T}\left[\frac{t_w^\beta}{\widetilde{\theta_{23}}}\left(e^{\frac{\widetilde{\theta_{23}}t_w\beta}{\beta+1}} - e^{\frac{-\widetilde{\theta_{23}}t_w}{\beta+1}}\right) + \left(\frac{(\beta+2)t_w^{\beta+1} - \widetilde{\theta_{23}}t_w^{\beta+2}}{(\beta+1)(\beta+2)}\right)\right]$$

$$+ \frac{h_o W}{T\widetilde{\theta_{13}}}(1 - e^{-\widetilde{\theta_{13}}t_w}) + \frac{h_o\alpha T^{\beta-1}e^{\frac{\widetilde{\theta_{13}}T\beta}{\beta+1}}}{\widetilde{\theta_{13}}}(e^{-\widetilde{\theta_{13}}t_w} - e^{-\widetilde{\theta_{13}}T})$$

$$+ h_o\alpha\frac{(T^\beta(\beta+2) - \widetilde{\theta_{13}}T^{\beta+1} - T(t_w^{\beta+1}(\beta+2) - \widetilde{\theta_{13}}t_w^{\beta+2}))}{(\beta+1)(\beta+2)}$$

$$+ \alpha\widetilde{\theta_{23}}t_w^\beta\left[\frac{e^{\frac{\widetilde{\theta_{23}}t_w\beta}{\beta+1}}}{\widetilde{\theta_{23}}}(1 - e^{-}\widetilde{\theta_{23}}t_w) - \frac{t_w(\beta+2) - \widetilde{\theta_{23}}t_w}{(\beta+1)(\beta+2)}\right]$$

$$+ W(1 - e^{-\widetilde{\theta_{13}}t_w}) + \alpha T^\beta e^{\frac{\widetilde{\theta_{13}}T\beta}{\beta+1}}e^{-\widetilde{\theta_{13}}t_w} - e^{-\widetilde{\theta_{13}}T}$$

$$- \frac{T^{\beta+1}(\beta+2) - \widetilde{\theta_{13}}T^{\beta+2} - t_w^{\beta+1}(\beta+2) + \widetilde{\theta_{13}}t_w^{\beta+1}}{(\beta+1)(\beta+2)}$$

$$+ \frac{pI_e\alpha\beta M^{\beta+1}}{T(\beta+1)} + \frac{cI_p}{T}\left[\frac{\alpha t_w^\beta e^{\frac{\widetilde{\theta_{23}}\beta}{\beta+1}}}{\widetilde{\theta_{23}}}\left(e^{-\widetilde{\theta_{23}}M} - e^{-\widetilde{\theta_{23}}t_w}\right)\right]$$

$$- \frac{cI_p}{T}\left[\begin{array}{l}\dfrac{(\beta+2)(t_w^{\beta+1} - M^{\beta+1}) - \widetilde{\theta_{23}}(t_w^{\beta+2} - M^{\beta+2})}{(\beta+1)(\beta+2)} \\ + \dfrac{W(e^{-\widetilde{\theta_{13}}M} - e^{-\widetilde{\theta_{13}}t_w})}{\widetilde{\theta_{13}}} + \dfrac{\alpha T^\beta e^{\frac{\widetilde{\theta_{13}}T\beta}{\beta+1}}}{\widetilde{\theta_{13}}}(e^{-\widetilde{\theta_{13}}t_w} - e^{-\widetilde{\theta_{13}}T})\end{array}\right]$$

$$- \frac{cI_p}{T}\left[\frac{(\beta+2)T^{\beta+1} - \widetilde{\theta_{13}}T^{\beta+2} - (\beta+2)t_w^{\beta+1} + \widetilde{\theta_{13}}t_w^{\beta+2}}{(\beta+1)(\beta+2)}\right]$$

References

Aggarwal, S., & Jaggi, C. (1995). Ordering policies of deteriorating items under permissible delay in payments. *Journal of the operational Research Society*, *46*(5), 658–662.

Bakker, M., Riezebos, J., & Teunter, R. H. (2012). Review of inventory systems with deterioration since 2001. *European Journal of Operational Research*, *221*(2), 275–284.

Banerjee, S., & Agrawal, S. (2008). A two-warehouse inventory model for items with three-parameter weibull distribution deterioration, shortages and linear trend in demand. *International Transactions in Operational Research*, *15*(6), 755–775.

Benkherouf, L. (1997). A deterministic order level inventory model for deteriorating items with two storage facilities. *International Journal of Production Economics*, *48*(2), 167–175.

Bhunia, A., & Maiti, M. (1998). A two warehouse inventory model for deteriorating items with a linear trend in demand and shortages. *Journal of the Operational Research Society*, *49*(3), 287–292.

Bhunia, A. K., Jaggi, C. K., Sharma, A., & Sharma, R. (2014). A two-warehouse inventory model for deteriorating items under permissible delay in payment with partial backlogging. *Applied Mathematics and Computation, 232*, 1125–1137.
Bhunia, A. K., Shaikh, A. A., Dhaka, V., Pareek, S., & Cárdenas-Barrón, L. E. (2018). An application of genetic algorithm and pso in an inventory model for single deteriorating item with variable demand dependent on marketing strategy and displayed stock level. *Scientia Iranica, 25*(3), 1641–1655.
Bhunia, A. K., Shaikh, A. A., & Sahoo, L. (2016). A two-warehouse inventory model for deteriorating item under permissible delay in payment via particle swarm optimisation. *International Journal of Logistics Systems and Management, 24*(1), 45–69.
Chakraborty, D., Jana, D. K., & Roy, T. K. (2018). Two-warehouse partial backlogging inventory model with ramp type demand rate, three-parameter weibull distribution deterioration under inflation and permissible delay in payments. *Computers & Industrial Engineering, 123*, 157–179.
Chandra, S. (2020). Two warehouse inventory model for deteriorating items with stock dependent demand under permissible delay in payment. *Journal of Mathematical and Computational Science (JMCS), 10*(4), 1131–1149.
Chen, S.-H., & Hsieh, C. H. (1999). Graded mean integration representation of generalized fuzzy number.
De Kumar, S., Kundu, P., & Goswami, A. (2003). An economic production quantity inventory model involving fuzzy demand rate and fuzzy deterioration rate. *Journal of Applied Mathematics and Computing, 12*(1–2), 251.
Dhaka, V., Pareek, S., & Mittal, M. (2019). Stock-dependent inventory model for imperfect items under permissible. *Optimization and Inventory Management*, 181.
Dye, C.-Y., Hsieh, T.-P., & Ouyang, L.-Y. (2007). Determining optimal selling price and lot size with a varying rate of deterioration and exponential partial backlogging. *European Journal of Operational Research, 181*(2), 668–678.
Ghoreishi, M., Mirzazadeh, A., & Kamalabadi, I. N. (2014). Optimal pricing and lot-sizing policies for an economic production quantity model with non-instantaneous deteriorating items, permissible delay in payments, customer returns, and inflation. *Proceedings of the Institution of Mechanical Engineers, Part B: Journal of Engineering Manufacture, 228*(12), 1653–1663.
Ghosh, S., Goyal, S., & Chaudhuri, K. (2006). An inventory model with weibull demand rate, finite rate of production and shortages. *International Journal of Systems Science, 37*(14), 1003–1009.
Goswami, A., & Chaudhuri, K. (1992). An economic order quantity model for items with two levels of storage for a linear trend in demand. *Journal of the Operational Research Society, 43*(2), 157–167.
Goyal, S. K. (1985). Economic order quantity under conditions of permissible delay in payments. *Journal of the Operational Research Society, 36*(4), 335–338.
Guchhait, P., Maiti, M. K., & Maiti, M. (2013). Two storage inventory model of a deteriorating item with variable demand under partial credit period. *Applied Soft Computing, 13*(1), 428–448.
Haley, C. W. & Higgins, R. C. (1973). Inventory policy and trade credit financing. *Management Science*, 20(4-part-i), 464–471.
Halim, K., Giri, B., & Chaudhuri, K. (2008). Fuzzy economic order quantity model for perishable items with stochastic demand, partial backlogging and fuzzy deterioration rate. *International Journal of Operational Research, 3*(1–2), 77–96.
Harris, F. W. (1913). How many parts to make at once.
Hwang, H., & Shinn, S. W. (1997). Retailer's pricing and lot sizing policy for exponentially deteriorating products under the condition of permissible delay in payments. *Computers & Operations Research, 24*(6), 539–547.
Jaggi, C. K., Gupta, M., & Tiwari, S. (2019). Credit financing in economic ordering policies for deteriorating items with stochastic demand and promotional efforts in two-warehouse environment. *International Journal of Operational Research, 35*(4), 529–550.

Jaggi, C. K., Pareek, S., Khanna, A., & Sharma, R. (2014). Credit financing in a two-warehouse environment for deteriorating items with price-sensitive demand and fully backlogged shortages. *Applied Mathematical Modelling*, *38*(21–22), 5315–5333.

Jaggi, C. K., Pareek, S., Verma, P., & Sharma, R. (2013). Ordering policy for deteriorating items in a two-warehouse environment with partial backlogging. *International Journal of Logistics Systems and Management*, *16*(1), 16–40.

Khan, M. A.-A., Shaikh, A. A., Panda, G. C., Bhunia, A. K., & Konstantaras, I. (2020). Non-instantaneous deterioration effect in ordering decisions for a two-warehouse inventory system under advance payment and backlogging. *Annals of Operations Research*, 1–33.

Kumar Sett, B., Sarkar, S., Sarkar, B., & Young Yun, W. (2016). Optimal replenishment policy with variable deterioration for fixed lifetime products. *Scientia Iranica*, *23*(5), 2318–2329.

Lee, C. C. (2006). Two-warehouse inventory model with deterioration under FIFO dispatching policy. *European Journal of Operational Research*, *174*(2), 861–873.

Liang, Y., & Zhou, F. (2011). A two-warehouse inventory model for deteriorating items under conditionally permissible delay in payment. *Applied Mathematical Modelling*, *35*(5), 2221–2231.

Liao, J.-J., Huang, K.-N., & Chung, K.-J. (2012). Lot-sizing decisions for deteriorating items with two warehouses under an order-size-dependent trade credit. *International Journal of Production Economics*, *137*(1), 102–115.

Lin, F., Jia, T., Wu, F., & Yang, Z. (2019). Impacts of two-stage deterioration on an integrated inventory model under trade credit and variable capacity utilization. *European Journal of Operational Research*, *272*(1), 219–234.

Mahata, G., & Goswami, A. (2006). Production lot-size model with fuzzy production rate and fuzzy demand rate for deteriorating item under permissible delay in payments. *Opsearch*, *43*(4), 358–375.

Maihami, R., Karimi, B., & Ghomi, S. M. T. F. (2017). Effect of two-echelon trade credit on pricing-inventory policy of non-instantaneous deteriorating products with probabilistic demand and deterioration functions. *Annals of Operations Research*, *257*(1–2), 237–273.

Mashud, A. H. M., Wee, H.-M., Sarkar, B., & Li, Y.-H. C. (2020). A sustainable inventory system with the advanced payment policy and trade-credit strategy for a two-warehouse inventory system. *Kybernetes*.

Ming Chen, J., & Shun Lin, C. (2003). Optimal replenishment scheduling for inventory items with weibull distributed deterioration and time-varying demand. *Journal of Information and Optimization Sciences*, *24*(1), 1–21.

Mishra, S. S., & Mishra, P. (2011). A (q, r) model for fuzzified deterioration under cobweb phenomenon and permissible delay in payment. *Computers & Mathematics with Applications*, *61*(4), 921–932.

Mishra, U., Cárdenas-Barrón, L. E., Tiwari, S., Shaikh, A. A., & Treviño-Garza, G. (2017). An inventory model under price and stock dependent demand for controllable deterioration rate with shortages and preservation technology investment. *Annals of Operations Research*, *254*(1–2), 165–190.

Nahmias, S. (1982). Perishable inventory theory: A review. *Operations research*, *30*(4), 680–708.

Pakkala, T., & Achary, K. (1992). A deterministic inventory model for deteriorating items with two warehouses and finite replenishment rate. *European Journal of Operational Research*, *57*(1), 71–76.

Pareek, S., & Dhaka, V. (2015). Fuzzy eoq models for deterioration items under discounted cash flow approach when supplier credits are linked to order quantity. *International Journal of Logistics Systems and Management*, *20*(1), 24–41.

Raafat, F. (1991). Survey of literature on continuously deteriorating inventory models. *Journal of the Operational Research society*, *42*(1), 27–37.

Roy, A., Maiti, M. K., Kar, S., & Maiti, M. (2007). Two storage inventory model with fuzzy deterioration over a random planning horizon. *Mathematical and Computer Modelling*, *46*(11–12), 1419–1433.

Sarkar, B. (2012). An eoq model with delay in payments and time varying deterioration rate. *Mathematical and Computer Modelling*, *55*(3–4), 367–377.
Sarkar, B., & Saren, S. (2017). Ordering and transfer policy and variable deterioration for a warehouse model. *Hacettepe Journal of Mathematics and Statistics*, *46*(5), 985–1014.
Sarkar, B., Saren, S., & Cárdenas-Barrón, L. E. (2015). An inventory model with trade-credit policy and variable deterioration for fixed lifetime products. *Annals of Operations Research*, *229*(1), 677–702.
Sarkar, B., & Sarkar, S. (2013a). An improved inventory model with partial backlogging, time varying deterioration and stock-dependent demand. *Economic Modelling*, *30*, 924–932.
Sarkar, B., Ullah, M., & Kim, N. (2017). Environmental and economic assessment of closed-loop supply chain with remanufacturing and returnable transport items. *Computers & Industrial Engineering*, *111*, 148–163.
Sarkar, M., & Sarkar, B. (2013b). An economic manufacturing quantity model with probabilistic deterioration in a production system. *Economic Modelling*, *31*, 245–252.
Sarma, K. (1987). A deterministic order level inventory model for deteriorating items with two storage facilities. *European Journal of Operational Research*, *29*(1), 70–73.
Sett, B. K., Sarkar, B., & Goswami, A. (2012). A two-warehouse inventory model with increasing demand and time varying deterioration. *Scientia Iranica*, *19*(6), 1969–1977.
Shabani, S., Mirzazadeh, A., & Sharifi, E. (2016). A two-warehouse inventory model with fuzzy deterioration rate and fuzzy demand rate under conditionally permissible delay in payment. *Journal of Industrial and Production Engineering*, *33*(2), 134–142.
Shah, N., Pareek, S., & Sangal, I. (2012a). Eoq in fuzzy environment and trade credit. *International Journal of Industrial Engineering Computations*, *3*(2), 133–144.
Shah, N. H. (1993). A lot-size model for exponentially decaying inventory when delay in payments is permissible. *Cahiers du Centre d'études de recherche opérationnelle*, *35*(1–2), 115–123.
Shah, N. H., Gor, A. S., & Jhaveri, C. A. (2012b). Optimal pricing and ordering policy for an integrated inventory model with quadratic demand when trade credit linked to order quantity. *Journal of Modelling in Management*.
Shah, N. H., Patel, A., & Lou, K. (2011). Optimal ordering and pricing policy for price sensitive stock-dependent demand under progressive payment scheme. *International Journal of Industrial Engineering Computations*, *2*(3), 523–532.
Shah, N. H., & Shah, Y. (1998). A discrete-in-time probabilistic inventory model for deteriorating items under conditions of permissible delay in payments. *International Journal of Systems Science*, *29*(2), 121–125.
Shaikh, A. A., Cárdenas-Barrón, L. E., & Tiwari, S. (2019). A two-warehouse inventory model for non-instantaneous deteriorating items with interval-valued inventory costs and stock-dependent demand under inflationary conditions. *Neural Computing and Applications*, *31*(6), 1931–1948.
Shaikh, A. A., Mashud, A. H. M., Uddin, M. S., & Khan, M. A.-A. (2017). Non-instantaneous deterioration inventory model with price and stock dependent demand for fully backlogged shortages under inflation. *International Journal of Business Forecasting and Marketing Intelligence*, *3*(2), 152–164.
Silver, E. A., & Meal, H. C. (1969). A simple modification of the eoq for the case of a varying demand rate. *Production and inventory management*, *10*(4), 52–65.
Tiwari, S., Ahmed, W., & Sarkar, B. (2019). Sustainable ordering policies for non-instantaneous deteriorating items under carbon emission and multi-trade-credit-policies. *Journal of Cleaner Production*, *240*, 118183.
Tiwari, S., Jaggi, C. K., Bhunia, A. K., Shaikh, A. A., & Goh, M. (2017). Two-warehouse inventory model for non-instantaneous deteriorating items with stock-dependent demand and inflation using particle swarm optimization. *Annals of Operations Research*, *254*(1–2), 401–423.
Tripathy, P., & Pradhan, S. (2011). An integrated partial backlogging inventory model having weibull demand and variable deterioration rate with the effect of trade credit. *International Journal of Scientific & Engineering Research*, *2*(4), 1–4.

Wee, H.-M. (1997). A replenishment policy for items with a price-dependent demand and a varying rate of deterioration. *Production Planning & Control*, *8*(5), 494–499.
Yang, H.-L. (2004). Two-warehouse inventory models for deteriorating items with shortages under inflation. *European Journal of Operational Research*, *157*(2), 344–356.
Yang, H.-L. (2006). Two-warehouse partial backlogging inventory models for deteriorating items under inflation. *International Journal of Production Economics*, *103*(1), 362–370.

Two-Warehouse Inventory of Sugar Industry Model for Deteriorating Items with Inflation Using Differential Evolution

Ajay Singh Yadav, Navin Ahlawat, Anupam Swami, and Mohammed Abid

Abstract In this article, the warehouse of the sugar industry system was created for the growing commodity demand and demand with an increase in dual warehouses using different variables. Warelo its warehouse (OW) has a capacity of W units; the warehouse (RW) has unlimited capacity. At this point, we think the sugar industry is holding higher RW records than at EW using different evolution. Sugar companies are allowed to quit, and the sugar industry will get worse in the near future, fluctuating when they make various changes. There is also an effect of an increase in the various costs associated with the marketing of sugar systems using different variables. Numerical symbols are also used to study the behavior of the model using different variables. Reduction costs are used to obtain a statement of total costs in other areas using a different evolution method.

Keywords Inventory · Partially backlogged · Deteriorating items · Inflation · Two-warehouse · Differential evolution

1 Introduction

Most analysts have increased EOQ performance to a minimum. Some researchers have discussed the plans of the sugar industry and which system to favor. The biggest disadvantage of the system over time is that it shows a change in price demands per minute. This is not surprising in stocks and markets. In recent years, more and more

A. S. Yadav
Department of Mathematics, SRM Institute of Science and Technology, Delhi-NCR Campus, Ghaziabad, Uttar Pradesh, India

N. Ahlawat
Department of Computer Science, SRM Institute of Science and Technology, Delhi-NCR Campus, Ghaziabad, Uttar Pradesh, India

A. Swami
Department of Mathematics, Government Post Graduate College, Sambhal, Uttar Pradesh, India

M. Abid (✉)
SRM Institute of Science and Technology, Delhi-NCR Campus, Ghaziabad, Uttar Pradesh, India

N. H. Shah and M. Mittal (eds.), *Soft Computing in Inventory Management*, Inventory Optimization, https://doi.org/10.1007/978-981-16-2156-7_6

models have been developed and are looking for change faster than ever before. For seasonal products such as clothing and spirits, there is a need for these products in the early stages and at the end of the season. Now the demand for these products changes rather than decreasing rapidly. These questions are believed to be relevant. These conditions can be demonstrated by rising prices. An important factor in the history of the sugar industry is how to fix the negatives that arise during times of scarcity or scarcity. With most of these models developed, researchers speculated that the deficit could be delayed or even disappear altogether. The first, called the last or the last, represents the world and the uncontrolled world. In the second case, also known as the lost market, we assume that the incomparable demand is completely lost. On top of that, if a shortage arises, some buyers want to wait for an order where others are buying from other retailers. In most cases, customers notice a delay in shipping and may have to wait a long time to process their first order. For example, in the case of high-end products and technology products with a shorter lifespan, the customer's need to wait reduces the waiting time. Therefore, the longer wait time for an additional extension will determine whether the fish is received backwards or not. In most cases, it is useful in times of shortness, long wait, little adjusting backwards. That is, in the case of a reasonable business environment, the surplus percentage will change depending on the waiting period for the next take. Many researchers have adapted the sugar industry policy to use it to "delay time." DE uses two different unrelated systems to control the transition, which makes it unique to other algorithms. As in GA, special people were created. Three other people are selected for each. The vector velocity is generated by increasing the difference in weight (differential velocity) between the two components. Redesign or restructuring is one of the major tasks of AG, but it works in partnership with DE. If everyone is treated in this way, health status is assessed. If the value of a new person is better than the value of the old, replace the old with the new. This process is repeated until a large number of generations have changed.

2 Related Works

Demand was believed to be a fluctuating function of time and that the backlog of unmet demand was a decreasing function of waiting time. Yadav and Swami (Yadav & Swami, 2018a, 2019a; Yadav et al., 2020f) "A model with a partial backlog in production inventory and lot size with time-varying operating costs and female decline." "Integrated supply chain model for material spoilage with linear demand based on inventory in an inaccurate and inflationary environment." "A flexible volume two-stage model with fluctuating demand and inflationary holding costs." Yadav et al. (Yadav & Swami, 2018b; Yadav et al., 2016, 2017a, 2019, 2020h, 2020j) "Supply chain inventory model for two warehouses with soft IT optimization." "Multi-objective optimization for the stock model of electronic components and the degradation of double-bearing elements using a genetic algorithm." "An inflation inventory model for spoilage under two storage systems." "Chemical industry supply chain for warehouses with distribution centers using the Artificial Bee Colony algorithm." "Management of the supply chain for electronic components of industrial electronics development for warehouses and their environmental impact using the particle swarm optimization algorithm." "Cost method for reliability considerations for the LOFO inventory model with warehouse for chemical industry." Pandey et al. (Yadav et al., 2020b) "An analysis of the inventory optimization of the marble industry based on genetic algorithms and particle swarm optimization." Malik et al. (Yadav et al., 2020c) "Security mechanism implemented in gateway service providers." Yadav et al. (2020h, 2020i, 2020k, 2020l) "proposed the supply chain management of the National Blood Bank Center for the application of blockchain using a genetic algorithm." "Provided drug industry supply chain management for blockchain applications using artificial neural networks." "Suggested the red wine industry to manage the supply chain of distribution centers using neural networks." "A supply chain management for the rosé wine industry for storage using a genetic algorithm." "Providing supply chain management for the white wine industry for warehouses using neural networks." Chauhan and Yadav (Yadav et al., 2017b, 2020m) "proposed a stock model for commodity spoilage where demand depends on two stocks and stocks using a genetic algorithm." "Provide a car inventory system for inflation based on demand and inventory with a two-way distribution center using a genetic algorithm." Yadav et al. (Yadav & Swami, 2019b; Yadav et al., 2017c, 2020a, 2020d, 2020e, 2020g) "A method for calculating the reliability of the LIFO stock model with bearings in the chemical industry." "Ensuring the management of the supply chain of electronic components for the development of the electronics industry in warehouses and the impact on the environment using the particle swarm optimization algorithm." "FIFO in Electrical Component Industry Green Supply Chain Inventory Model with Distribution Centers Using Particle Swarm Optimization." "LIFO in Automotive Components Industry Green Supply Chain Inventory Model with Bearings using Differential Evolution." "FIFO & LIFO in the Industry Green Supply Chain Inventory Model for Hazardous Substance Components with Storage using Simulated Annealing." "Health inventory control systems for blood bank storage with reliability applications using a genetic algorithm." Sana (2015, 2020) "Price competition between green and non-green products in the context of a socially responsible retail and consumer services business magazine." "An EOQ model for stochastic demand for limited storage capacity." Moghdani et al. (2020) "Fuzzy model for economic production quantity with multiple items and multiple deliveries." Haseli et al. (2020) "Basic criterion for the multi-criteria decision-making method and its applications." Ameri et al. (2019) "Self-assessment of parallel network systems with intuitionistic fuzzy data: a case study." Birjandi et al. (2019) "Assessment and selection of the contractor when submitting a tender with incomplete information according to the MCGDM method." Gholami et al. (2018) "ABC analysis of clients using axiomatic design and incomplete estimated meaning." Jamali et al. (2018) "Hybrid Improved Cuckoo Search Algorithm and Genetic Algorithm to Solve Marko Modulated Demand."

3 Assumptions and Notations

In developing the mathematical model of the inventory of the sugar industry system, the following assumptions are made:

1. "The Demand rate $D(t)$ at time t is deterministic and taken as a ramp type function of time"

$$D(t) = \left(\frac{A_1 - 1}{C_F}\right) e^{-\left(\frac{\lambda_1 - 1}{C_F}\right)\{t-(t-T_1)H(t-T_1)\}}, \ \left(\frac{A_1 - 1}{C_F}\right) > 0, \ \left(\frac{\lambda_1 - 1}{C_F}\right) > 0$$

where $H(t - T_1) = \begin{cases} 0, & t < T_1 \\ 1, & t \geq T_1 \end{cases}$.

2. "Backlogging rate is exp $-\left(\frac{\delta_1 - 1}{C_F}(t)\right)$ when inventory of Sugar industry is in shortage.
The backlogging parameter $\left(\frac{\delta_1 - 1}{C_F}\right)$ is a positive constant".
3. "The variable rate of deterioration in both warehouse is taken as $\left(\frac{\theta_1 - 1}{C_F}\right)(t) = \left(\frac{\theta_1 - 1}{C_F}\right)t$
where $0 < \left(\frac{\theta_1 - 1}{C_F}\right) << 1$ and only applied to on hand inventory of Sugar industry".

"In addition, the following notations are used throughout this paper"

$\left[\overset{\text{Fifo}}{\underset{\text{ow}}{\text{I}}}(t)\right]$ = "The inventory level of Sugar industry in OW at any time t."

$\left[\overset{\text{Fifo}}{\underset{\text{rw}}{\text{I}}}(t)\right]$ = "The inventory level of Sugar industry in RW at any time t."

$\left(\frac{R_1 - 1}{C_F}\right)$ = "Inflation rate."

Q = "The ordering quantity per cycle."

T = "Planning horizon."

F_1 = "The holding cost of Sugar industry per unit per unit time in OW."

F_2 = "The holding cost of Sugar industry per unit per unit time in RW," where $F_1 < F_2$.

F_d = "The deterioration cost of Sugar industry per unit."

F_3 = "The shortage cost of Sugar industry per unit per unit time."

F_4 = "The opportunity cost of Sugar industry due to lost sales."

F^1 = "The replenishment cost of Sugar industry per order."

C_F = "The FIFO cost of Sugar industry per unit."

4 Formulation and Solution of the Model

"The inventory of the levels of the sugar industry in EV is determined by the following differential equations":

$$\frac{d\left[\overset{\text{Fifo}}{\underset{\text{ow}}{I}}(t)\right]}{dt} = -\left(\frac{\theta_1 - 1}{C_F}\right)(t)\left[\overset{\text{Fifo}}{\mathrm{I}}(t)\right], \quad 0 \le t < T_1 \tag{1}$$

$$\frac{d\left[\overset{\text{Fifo}}{\underset{\text{ow}}{\mathrm{I}}}(t)\right]}{dt} + \left(\frac{\theta_1 - 1}{C_F}\right)(t)\left[\overset{\text{Fifo}}{\mathrm{I}}(t)\right] = -\left(\frac{A_1 - 1}{C_F}\right)e^{-\left(\frac{\lambda_1 - 1}{C_F}\right)T_1}, \quad T_1 \le t \le T_2 \tag{2}$$

And

$$\frac{d\left[\overset{\text{Fifo}}{\underset{\text{ow}}{\mathrm{I}}}(t)\right]}{dt} = -\left(\frac{A_1 - 1}{C_F}\right)e^{-\left(\frac{\lambda_1 - 1}{C_F}\right)T_1}e^{-\left(\frac{\delta_1 - 1}{C_F}\right)t}, \quad T_2 \le t \le T_n \tag{3}$$

"With the boundary conditions,"

$$\left[\overset{\text{Fifo}}{\underset{\text{ow}}{\mathrm{I}}}(0)\right] = W \text{ and } \left[\overset{\text{Fifo}}{\mathrm{I}}(T_2)\right] = 0 \tag{4}$$

"The solutions of Eqs. (1), (2), and (3) are given by"

$$\left[\overset{\text{Fifo}}{\underset{\text{ow}}{\mathrm{I}}}(t)\right] = W\,e^{-\left(\frac{\theta_1 - 1}{C_F}\right)t^2/2}, \quad 0 \le t < T_1 \tag{5}$$

$$\left[\overset{\text{Fifo}}{\underset{\text{ow}}{\mathrm{I}}}(t)\right] = \left(\frac{A_1 - 1}{C_F}\right)e^{-\left(\frac{\lambda_1 - 1}{C_F}\right)T_1}\left\{\begin{array}{l}(T_2 - t)\\ +\dfrac{\left(\frac{\theta_1 - 1}{C_F}\right)(T_2^3 - t^3)}{6}\end{array}\right\}e^{-\left(\frac{\theta_1 - 1}{C_F}\right)t^2/2}, \quad T_1 \le t \le T_2 \tag{6}$$

And

$$\left[\overset{\text{Fifo}}{\underset{\text{ow}}{\mathrm{I}}}(t)\right] = \frac{\left(\frac{A_1 - 1}{C_F}\right)}{\left(\frac{\delta_1 - 1}{C_F}\right)}e^{\left[-\left(\frac{\lambda_1 - 1}{C_F}\right)T_1\right]}\left\{\begin{array}{l}e^{\left[-\left(\frac{\delta_1 - 1}{C_F}\right)t\right]}\\ -e^{\left[-\left(\frac{\delta_1 - 1}{C_F}\right)T_2\right]}\end{array}\right\}, \quad T_2 \le t \le T_n \tag{7}$$

"The inventory of Sugar industry level at RW is governed by the following differential equations":

$$\frac{d\left[\overset{\text{Fifo}}{\underset{\text{rw}}{\mathrm{I}}}(t)\right]}{dt} + \left(\frac{\theta_1 - 1}{C_F}\right)(t)\left[\overset{\text{Fifo}}{\mathrm{I}}(t)\right] = -\left(\frac{A_1 - 1}{C_F}\right)e^{-\left(\frac{\lambda_1 - 1}{C_F}\right)t}, \quad 0 \le t < T_1 \tag{8}$$

"With the boundary condition $\left[\overset{\text{Fifo}}{\underset{\text{rw}}{\mathrm{I}}}(0)\right] = 0$, the solution of Eq. (8) is"

$$\left[\overset{\text{Fifo}}{\underset{\text{rw}}{\mathrm{I}}}(t)\right] = \left(\frac{A_1 - 1}{C_F}\right)\left\{\begin{array}{l}(T_1 - t) - \frac{\left(\frac{\lambda_1 - 1}{C_F}\right)}{2}(T_1^2 - t^2) \\ + \frac{\left(\frac{\theta_1 - 1}{C_F}\right)}{6}(T_2^3 - t^3)\end{array}\right\} e^{\left[-\left(\frac{\theta_1 - 1}{C_F}\right)t^2/2\right]}, \quad T_1 \le t \le T_2 \tag{9}$$

"Due to continuity of $\left[\overset{\text{Fifo}}{\underset{\text{ow}}{\mathrm{I}}}(t)\right]$ at point $t = T_1$, it follows from Eqs. (5) and (6), one has"

$$W\,e^{-\left(\frac{\theta_1 - 1}{C_F}\right)T_1^2/2} = \left(\frac{A_1 - 1}{C_F}\right)e^{\left[-\left(\frac{\lambda_1 - 1}{C_F}\right)T_1\right]}\left\{\begin{array}{l}(T_2 - T_1) \\ + \frac{\left(\frac{\theta_1 - 1}{C_F}\right)(T_2^3 - T_1^3)}{6}\end{array}\right\} e^{\left[-\left(\frac{\theta_1 - 1}{C_F}\right)T_1^2/2\right]}$$

$$W = \left(\frac{A_1 - 1}{C_F}\right)e^{\left[-\left(\frac{\lambda_1 - 1}{C_F}\right)T_1\right]}\left\{\begin{array}{l}(T_2 - T_1) \\ + \frac{\left(\frac{\theta_1 - 1}{C_F}\right)(T_2^3 - T_1^3)}{6}\end{array}\right\} \tag{10}$$

"The total average cost consists of following elements":

(i) "Ordering cost per cycle" $= F^1$ (11)

(ii) "Holding cost per cycle (C_{HO}) in OW"

$$C_{HO} = F_1\left[\int_0^{T_1}\left[\overset{\text{Fifo}}{\underset{\text{ow}}{\mathrm{I}}}(t)\right]e^{-\left(\frac{R_1 - 1}{C_F}\right)t}dt + \int_{T_1}^{T_2}\left[\overset{\text{Fifo}}{\underset{\text{ow}}{\mathrm{I}}}(t)\right]e^{-\left(\frac{R_1 - 1}{C_F}\right)(T_1 + t)}dt\right]$$

$$C_{\mathrm{HO}} = F_1 \left\{ \begin{array}{l} W\left(\begin{array}{l} T_1 - \dfrac{\left(\frac{R_1-1}{C_F}\right)T_1^2}{2} \\ -\dfrac{\left(\frac{\theta_1-1}{C_F}\right)T_1^3}{6} \end{array} \right) \\ +\left(\dfrac{A_1-1}{C_F}\right) e^{\left[-\left(\frac{\lambda_1-1}{C_F}\right)\left(T_1+\left(\frac{R_1-1}{C_F}\right)\right)\right]} \left\{ \begin{array}{l} \dfrac{T_2^2}{2} - \dfrac{\left(\frac{R_1-1}{C_F}\right)T_2^3}{6} \\ +\dfrac{\left(\frac{\theta_1-1}{C_F}\right)T_2^4}{12} \\ -\dfrac{\left(\frac{R_1-1}{C_F}\right)\left(\frac{\theta_1-1}{C_F}\right)}{20}T_2^5 \\ -\dfrac{T_1}{2}(2T_2 - T_1) \\ -\dfrac{\left(\frac{\theta_1-1}{C_F}\right)T_1}{24}\left(4T_2^3 - T_1^3\right) \\ +\dfrac{\left(\frac{R_1-1}{C_F}\right)T_1^2}{6}(3T_2 - 2T_1) \\ +\dfrac{\left(\frac{R_1-1}{C_F}\right)\left(\frac{\theta_1-1}{C_F}\right)T_1^2}{30}\left(5T_2^3 - 3T_1^3\right) \\ +\dfrac{\left(\frac{\theta_1-1}{C_F}\right)T_1^3}{24}(4T_2 - 3T_1) \end{array} \right\} \end{array} \right\} \tag{12}$$

(iii) "Holding cost per cycle (C_{HR})" in RW

$$C_{\mathrm{HR}} = F_2\left[\int_0^{T_1}\left[\underset{\mathrm{rw}}{\overset{\mathrm{Fifo}}{\mathrm{I}}}(t)\right]e^{-\left(\frac{R_1-1}{C_F}\right)t}\,\mathrm{d}t\right]$$

$$C_{\mathrm{HR}} = F_2\left(\frac{A_1-1}{C_F}\right)\left[\begin{array}{l} \dfrac{T_1^2}{2} \\ -\dfrac{\left(3\left(\frac{\lambda_1-1}{C_F}\right)+\left(\frac{R_1-1}{C_F}\right)\right)}{6}T_1^3 \\ +\left(\dfrac{\left(\frac{\theta_1-1}{C_F}\right)}{12}+\dfrac{\left(\frac{\lambda_1-1}{C_F}\right)\left(\frac{R_1-1}{C_F}\right)}{8}\right)T_1^4 \\ -\left(\begin{array}{l} \dfrac{\left(\frac{R_1-1}{C_F}\right)\left(\frac{\theta_1-1}{C_F}\right)}{20} \\ -\dfrac{\left(\frac{\lambda_1-1}{C_F}\right)\left(\frac{\theta_1-1}{C_F}\right)}{30} \end{array} \right)T_1^5 \end{array} \right] \tag{13}$$

(iv) "Cost of deteriorated units per cycle" (C_{D})

$$= F_{\mathrm{d}}\left[\begin{array}{l} \int\limits_{0}^{T_1}\left(\frac{\theta_1-1}{C_{\mathrm{F}}}\right)t\left[\overset{\mathrm{Fifo}}{\underset{\mathrm{rw}}{\mathrm{I}}}(t)\right]\mathrm{e}^{-\left(\frac{R_1-1}{C_{\mathrm{F}}}\right)t}\mathrm{d}t \\ +\int\limits_{0}^{T_1}\left(\frac{\theta_1-1}{C_{\mathrm{F}}}\right)t\left[\overset{\mathrm{Fifo}}{\underset{\mathrm{ow}}{\mathrm{I}}}(t)\right]\mathrm{e}^{-\left(\frac{R_1-1}{C_{\mathrm{F}}}\right)t}\mathrm{d}t \\ +\int\limits_{T_1}^{T_2}\left(\frac{\theta_1-1}{C_{\mathrm{F}}}\right)t\left[\overset{\mathrm{Fifo}}{\underset{\mathrm{ow}}{\mathrm{I}}}(t)\right]\mathrm{e}^{-\left(\frac{R_1-1}{C_{\mathrm{F}}}\right)(t+T_1)}\mathrm{d}t \end{array}\right]$$

$$= F_{\mathrm{d}}\left(\frac{\theta_1-1}{C_{\mathrm{F}}}\right)\left[\begin{array}{l} \left\{\begin{array}{l} \left(\frac{A_1-1}{C_{\mathrm{F}}}\right)\frac{1}{6}T_1^3-\left(\begin{array}{l}\frac{\left(\frac{\lambda_1-1}{C_{\mathrm{F}}}\right)}{4}\\+\frac{\left(\frac{R_1-1}{C_{\mathrm{F}}}\right)}{12}\end{array}\right)T_1^4 \\ +\left(\begin{array}{l}\frac{\left(\frac{\theta_1-1}{C_{\mathrm{F}}}\right)}{40}\\+\frac{\left(\frac{R_1-1}{C_{\mathrm{F}}}\right)\left(\frac{\lambda_1-1}{C_{\mathrm{F}}}\right)}{15}\end{array}\right)T_1^5 \\ -\left(\begin{array}{l}\frac{\left(\frac{R_1-1}{C_{\mathrm{F}}}\right)\left(\frac{\theta_1-1}{C_{\mathrm{F}}}\right)}{36}\\-\frac{\left(\frac{\lambda_1-1}{C_{\mathrm{F}}}\right)\left(\frac{\theta_1-1}{C_{\mathrm{F}}}\right)}{24}\end{array}\right)T_1^6 \end{array}\right\}+W\left(\frac{T_1^2}{2}-\frac{\left(\frac{R_1-1}{C_{\mathrm{F}}}\right)T_1^3}{3}\,\frac{\left(\frac{\theta_1-1}{C_{\mathrm{F}}}\right)T_1^4}{8}\right)+ \\ \left(\frac{A_1-1}{C_{\mathrm{F}}}\right)\mathrm{e}^{-T_1\left(\left(\frac{\lambda_1-1}{C_{\mathrm{F}}}\right)+\left(\frac{R_1-1}{C_{\mathrm{F}}}\right)\right)}\left[\begin{array}{l} \frac{T_2^3}{6}-\frac{\left(\frac{R_1-1}{C_{\mathrm{F}}}\right)T_2^4}{12} \\ +\frac{\left(\frac{\theta_1-1}{C_{\mathrm{F}}}\right)T_2^5}{40} \\ -\frac{\left(\frac{R_1-1}{C_{\mathrm{F}}}\right)\left(\frac{\theta_1-1}{C_{\mathrm{F}}}\right)T_2^6}{36} \\ -\frac{T_1^2}{6}(3T_2-2T_1) \\ -\frac{\left(\frac{\theta_1-1}{C_{\mathrm{F}}}\right)T_1^2}{60}(5T_2^3-2T_1^3) \\ -\frac{\left(\frac{R_1-1}{C_{\mathrm{F}}}\right)T_1^3}{12}(4T_2-3T_1) \\ -\frac{\left(\frac{R_1-1}{C_{\mathrm{F}}}\right)\left(\frac{\theta_1-1}{C_{\mathrm{F}}}\right)T_1^3}{36}(2T_2^3-T_1^3) \\ -\frac{\left(\frac{\theta_1-1}{C_{\mathrm{F}}}\right)T_1^4}{40}(5T_2-4T_1) \end{array}\right] \end{array}\right] \tag{14}$$

(v) "Shortage cost per cycle" (C_{s})

$$= F_3\left[\int_{T_2}^{T_n} -\left[\begin{matrix}\text{Fifo}\\ \mathrm{I}\\ \text{ow}\end{matrix}(t)\right]\mathrm{e}^{-\left(\frac{R_1-1}{C_F}\right)(T_2+t)}\mathrm{d}t\right]$$

$$= \frac{-\left(\frac{A_1-1}{C_F}\right)F_3\mathrm{e}^{\left[-\left\{\begin{matrix}\left(\frac{R_1-1}{C_F}\right)T_2\\ +\left(\frac{\lambda_1-1}{C_F}\right)T_1\end{matrix}\right\}\right]}}{\left(\frac{\delta_1-1}{C_F}\right)}\left[\begin{matrix}\int_{T_2}^{T_n}\mathrm{e}^{\left[-\left\{\left(\frac{R_1-1}{C_F}\right)+\left(\frac{\delta_1-1}{C_F}\right)\right\}t\right]}\mathrm{d}t\\ -\mathrm{e}^{\left[-\left(\frac{\delta_1-1}{C_F}\right)T_2\right]}\int_{T_2}^{T_n}\mathrm{e}^{-\left(\frac{R_1-1}{C_F}\right)t}\mathrm{d}t\end{matrix}\right]$$

$$= \left[\frac{\left(\frac{A_1-1}{C_F}\right)F_3\mathrm{e}^{\left[-\left\{\begin{matrix}\left(\frac{R_1-1}{C_F}\right)T_2\\ +\left(\frac{\lambda_1-1}{C_F}\right)T_1\end{matrix}\right\}\right]}}{\left[\left(\frac{\delta_1-1}{C_F}\right)\left(\frac{R_1-1}{C_F}\right)\left\{\left(\frac{\delta_1-1}{C_F}\right)+\left(\frac{R_1-1}{C_F}\right)\right\}\right]}\left\{\begin{matrix}\left(\frac{\delta_1-1}{C_F}\right)\mathrm{e}^{\left[-\left\{\begin{matrix}\left(\frac{\delta_1-1}{C_F}\right)\\ +\left(\frac{R_1-1}{C_F}\right)\end{matrix}\right\}T_2\right]}+\\ \mathrm{e}^{\left[-\left(\frac{R_1-1}{C_F}\right)T_n\right]}\left\{\begin{matrix}\left(\frac{R_1-1}{C_F}\right)\mathrm{e}^{\left[-\left(\frac{\delta_1-1}{C_F}\right)T_n\right]}\\ -\left\{\begin{matrix}\left(\frac{\delta_1-1}{C_F}\right)\\ +\left(\frac{R_1-1}{C_F}\right)\end{matrix}\right\}\mathrm{e}^{\left[-\left(\frac{\delta_1-1}{C_F}\right)T_2\right]}\end{matrix}\right\}\end{matrix}\right\}\right] \tag{15}$$

(vi) "Opportunity cost due to lost sales per cycle" (C_0)

$$= F_4\int_{T_2}^{T_n}\left[\left(\frac{A_1-1}{C_F}\right)\left\{1-\mathrm{e}^{-\left(\frac{\delta_1-1}{C_F}\right)t}\right\}\left\{\mathrm{e}^{-\left(\frac{\lambda_1-1}{C_F}\right)T_1}\mathrm{e}^{-\left(\frac{R_1-1}{C_F}\right)(T_2+t)}\right\}\right]\mathrm{d}t$$

$$= \left[\frac{F_4\left(\frac{A_1-1}{C_F}\right)\mathrm{e}^{\left[-\left\{\begin{matrix}\left(\frac{\lambda_1-1}{C_F}\right)T_1\\ +\left(\frac{R_1-1}{C_F}\right)T_2\end{matrix}\right\}\right]}}{\left(\frac{R_1-1}{C_F}\right)\left\{\begin{matrix}\left(\frac{\delta_1-1}{C_F}\right)\\ +\left(\frac{R_1-1}{C_F}\right)\end{matrix}\right\}}\left\{\begin{matrix}\mathrm{e}^{\left[-\left(\frac{R_1-1}{C_F}\right)T_2\right]}\left\{\left\{\begin{matrix}\left(\frac{\delta_1-1}{C_F}\right)\\ +\left(\frac{R_1-1}{C_F}\right)\end{matrix}\right\}-\left(\frac{R_1-1}{C_F}\right)\mathrm{e}^{\left[-\left(\frac{\delta_1-1}{C_F}\right)T_2\right]}\right\}\\ -\mathrm{e}^{\left[-\left(\frac{R_1-1}{C_F}\right)T_n\right]}\left\{\left\{\begin{matrix}\left(\frac{\delta_1-1}{C_F}\right)\\ +\left(\frac{R_1-1}{C_F}\right)\end{matrix}\right\}-\left(\frac{R_1-1}{C_F}\right)\mathrm{e}^{\left[-\left(\frac{\delta_1-1}{C_F}\right)T_n\right]}\right\}\end{matrix}\right\}\right] \tag{16}$$

"Therefore, the total average cost per unit time of our model is obtained as follows"

$$\mathrm{TC}^{(T_2,T_n)} = \frac{1}{T_n}\left[\begin{matrix}\text{Ordering cost+}\\ \text{Holding cost in OW+}\\ \text{Holding cost in RW +}\\ \text{Deterioration cost+}\\ \text{Shortage cost+}\\ \text{Opportunity cost}\end{matrix}\right] \tag{17}$$

5 Evolutionary Algorithms

This is a population-based algorithm and consider a population size of M.

The population matrix can be shown as

$$\Upsilon^{c}_{m,i} = \left[\Upsilon^{c}_{m,1}, \Upsilon^{c}_{m,2}, \Upsilon^{c}_{m,3}, \ldots \Upsilon^{c}_{m,L}\right]$$

where c is the generation and $m = 1, 2, 3 \ldots M$.

(1) **Initial Population**

"Initial population is generated randomly between upper lower and upper bound"

$$\Upsilon_{m,i} = \Upsilon^{u}_{m,i} + \text{rand}(\,) * \left(\Upsilon^{v}_{m,i} - \Upsilon^{u}_{m,i}\right)$$

"Where Υ^{u}_{m} is the lower bound of the variable Υ_i".

"Where Υ^{v}_{m} is the lower bound of the variable Υ_i".

(2) **Mutation**

"From each parameter vector, select three other vectors Υ^{c}_{r1m}, Υ^{c}_{r2m} and Υ^{c}_{r3m} randomly".

"Add the weighted difference of two of the vectors to the third"

$$\eta^{c+1}_{m} = \Upsilon^{c}_{r1m} + G\left[\Upsilon^{c}_{r2m} - \Upsilon^{c}_{r3m}\right]$$

$$m = 1, 2, 3 \ldots M$$

"η^{c+1}_{m} is called donor vector."

"G generally taken between 0 and 1".

(3) **Recombination**

"A trial vector $u^{c+1}_{m,i}$ is developed from the target vector $\Upsilon^{c}_{m,i}$ and the donor vector" $\eta^{c+1}_{m,i}$

$$u^{c+1}_{m,i} = \left\{\begin{array}{ll} \eta^{c+1}_{m,i} & \text{if rand}(\,) \le C_{\text{p}} \text{ or } i = I_{\text{rand}} \;\; i = 1, 2, 3 \ldots L \text{ and} \\ \Upsilon^{c}_{m,i} & \text{if rand}(\,) \le C_{\text{p}} \text{ or } i = I_{\text{rand}} \;\; m = 1, 2, 3 \ldots M \end{array}\right\}$$

"C_{p} is the recombination probability."

"I_{rand} is an integer random number between $(1, L)$."

(4) **Selection**

"The target vector $\Upsilon^{c}_{m,i}$ is compared with the trial vector $u^{c+1}_{m,i}$, and the one with the lowest function value is selected for the next generation"

$$\Upsilon_m^{c+1} = \begin{Bmatrix} u_{m,i}^{c+1} \text{ if } f\left(u_{m,i}^{c+1}\right) < f\left(\Upsilon_{m,i}^{c}\right) \\ \Upsilon_m^{g} \text{ otherwise} \end{Bmatrix}$$

$$m = 1, 2, 3 \ldots M$$

6 Numerical Illustration

"To illustrate the model numerically, the following parameter values are considered."

$A_1 = 590$ units, $F^1 =$ Rs. 109 per order, $R_1 = 0.05$ unit, $\lambda_1 = 0.29$ unit, $\theta_0 = 0.0029$ unit, $T_1 = 0.2$ year, $\delta_0 = 0.1$ unit, $T_n = 1$ year, $F_1 =$ Rs. 3.9 per unit per year, $F_2 =$ Rs. 10.9 per unit, $F_3 =$ Rs. 12.9 per unit per year, $F_4 =$ Rs. 4.9 per unit, $\mathrm{TC}^{(T_2, T_n)} =$ Rs. 158.115354 per year.

7 Sensitivity Analysis

See Tables 1 and 2.

8 Conclusion

This study contains some useful bodybuilding information that can be combined with the knowledge of the sugar industry. Reducing the producer's time and the shortage in the sugar market in real life are natural. This mode helps to detect shortages in the sugar industry. In many cases, customers have been frustrated with the delivery time and may have to wait a long time to make their first choice when using the advanced program. In general, the waiting period for the next oil is the most important factor in deciding whether to accept a fish stove. Consumer willingness to wait late during the waiting period reduces the waiting time when using a different evolution cover. Thus, in this chapter, the sugar industry list has been abandoned and reorganized, but the previous percentage is seen as reducing the amount of time spent waiting for some recovery using the existing evolution system. This measure is considered to be a major factor in reducing the amount of time required for each control and is also stable. Since most manufacturers agree that inflation has no effect on the sugar industry plans, the consequences of the increase in other types of sugar products using different products are not considered. Thus, from a financial point of view, the sugar industry is sowing in equity and will be added to other resources in accordance with the company's budget. Therefore, it is important to look at the pricing patterns on the product properties of sugar companies using a variety of different brands.

Table 1 Sensitivity analysis in relation to all rates

A_1	T_1	T_2	T_n	$TC^{(T_2, T_n)}$
558	7.49688	74.8980	84.6898	640,800
608	7.58756	75.5790	85.0507	647,858
758	7.55006	79.7847	86.5888	658,940
458	7.44778	78.0978	87.4559	674,865
F^1	T_1	T_2	T_n	$TC^{(T_2, T_n)}$
8.55	7.46488	69.4764	88.6867	647,476
8.60	7.45465	66.6486	79.4780	648,950
8.75	7.48868	59.8867	74.7748	667,695
8.45	7.48785	76.4487	87.6679	678,776
F^1	T_1	T_2	T_n	$TC^{(T_2, T_n)}$
8.55	7.46488	69.4764	88.6867	647,476
8.60	7.45465	66.6486	79.4780	648,950
8.75	7.48868	59.8867	74.7748	667,695
8.45	7.48785	76.4487	87.6679	678,776
θ_0	T_1	T_2	T_n	$TC^{(T_2, T_n)}$
688	7.47468	56.6869	44.6606	677,576
668	7.47459	56.6604	44.6787	677,566
858	7.47477	56.5964	44.7056	677,778
96	7.47486	56.7678	44.6778	677,678
λ_1	T_1	T_2	T_n	$TC^{(T_2, T_n)}$
678	7.47605	57.0777	67.6067	678,686
708	7.47785	57.7866	67.0670	678,844
778	7.47967	57.9477	68.8675	640,867
668	7.47764	56.7848	65.0649	676,875
θ_0	T_1	T_2	T_n	$TC^{(T_2, T_n)}$
688	7.47468	56.6869	44.6606	677,576
668	7.47459	56.6604	44.6787	677,566
858	7.47477	56.5964	44.7056	677,778
96	7.47486	56.7678	44.6778	677,678
C_F	T_1	T_2	T_n	$TC^{(T_2, T_n)}$
8.778	7.56077	78.6887	98.7087	658,770
8.978	7.56968	84.4808	99.7488	666,740
6.488	7.77079	98.8567	686.8780	786,688
8.448	7.47687	67.8097	77.0706	664,866
F_1	T_1	T_2	T_n	$TC^{(T_2, T_n)}$

(continued)

Table 1 (continued)

A_1	T_1	T_2	T_n	$\mathrm{TC}^{(T_2, T_n)}$
8658	7.59686	57.9587	55.6058	640,688
8808	7.70547	55.8478	56.0768	646,667
6658	7.08070	58.7766	58.6698	649,574
8758	7.75049	58.7789	57.8999	674,868
F_2	T_1	T_2	T_n	$\mathrm{TC}^{(T_2, T_n)}$
68	7.46764	69.6488	88.9680	647,077
78	7.45096	66.9546	79.9066	648,606
98	7.48078	60.4577	75.6674	668,955
58	7.48546	76.6848	86.9845	678,789
F_3	T_1	T_2	T_n	$\mathrm{TC}^{(T_2, T_n)}$
86.8	7.77876	74.7006	46.7956	646,706
90.8	7.68886	75.8804	48.4778	646,798
886.8	7.06749	79.9776	54.0750	659,476
67.8	7.5958	78.0809	48.9746	676,788
F_4	T_1	T_2	T_n	$\mathrm{TC}^{(T_2, T_n)}$
0.0848	7.48566	78.0670	46.8878	677,746
0.0858	7.49444	69.5888	40.6887	670,488
0.0898	7.58704	66.6776	76.0787	666,777
0.0888	7.46888	74.6988	46.7690	646,686

Table 2 Sensitivity analyses with differential evolution rate

Function	Algorithm	Best	Worst	Mean	Standard deviation
A_1	DE	0.80608	84.0900	64.6098	040,800
F^1	DE	0.86488	89.4664	60.6806	043,436
λ_1	DE	0.86466	80.6060	64.0498	046,604
θ_0	DE	0.86468	60.6809	84.0600	036,860
C_F	DE	0.86608	63.0333	83.6066	038,080
F_1	DE	0.80063	68.6083	80.6003	030,630
F_2	DE	0.80608	84.0900	64.6098	040,800
F_3	DE	0.86488	89.4664	60.6806	043,436
F_4	DE	0.86466	80.6060	64.0498	046,604

Therefore, this idea is accepted in this mode. Comparison of the model showed that the time to keep up with the sugar industry products increases with the increase in fish stocks in the early stages, while the sugar industry declines with increasing losses and inflation. The assets of the first sugar industry are reduced by inflation and inflation rate, while the volume of the sugar industry is increased by the increase in evolution lag parliament. The rate of change continues to increase with the increase in the number of human casualties and decreases with the increase in the degree of variability. The required mode can proceed in different ways. For example, we can extend this decision-making process to different marketing products. We can also extend the mod by using other specific settings such as cash flow, sugar savings, and others can also change the time using a different evolution strategy.

References

Ameri, Z., Sana, S. S., & Sheikh, R. (2019). Self-assessment of parallel network systems with intuitionist fuzzy data: A case study. *Soft Computing, 23*(23), 12821–12832.

Birjandi, A. K., Akhyani, F., Sheikh, R., & Sana, S. S. (2019). Evaluation and selecting the contractor in bidding with incomplete information using MCGDM method. *Soft Computing, 23*(20), 10569–10585.

Gholami, A., Sheikh, R., Mizani, N., & Sana, S. S. (2018). ABC analysis of the customers using axiomatic design and incomplete rough set. *RAIRO-Operations Research, 52*(4–5), 1219–1232.

Haseli, G., Sheikh, R., & Sana, S. S. (2020). Base-criterion on multi-criteria decision-making method and its applications. *International Journal of Management Science and Engineering Management, 15*(2), 79–88.

Jamali, G., Sana, S. S., & Moghdani, R. (2018). Hybrid improved cuckoo search algorithm and genetic algorithm for solving Markov modulated demand. *RAIRO-Operations Research, 52*(2), 473–497.

Moghdani, R., Sana, S. S., & Shahbandarzadeh, H. (2020). Multi-item fuzzy economic production quantity model with multiple deliveries. *Soft Computing, 24*(14), 10363–10387.

Sana, S. S. (2015). An EOQ model for stochastic demand for limited capacity of own warehouse. *Annals of Operations Research, 233*(1), 383–399.

Sana, S. S. (2020). Price competition between green and non-green products under corporate social responsible firm. *Journal of Retailing and Consumer Services, 55*, 102118.

Yadav, A. S., Abid, M., Bansal, S., Tyagi, S. L., & Kumar, T. (2020a). FIFO & LOFO in green supply chain inventory model of hazardous substance components industry with storage using simulated annealing. *Advances in Mathematics: Scientific Journal, 9*(7), 5127–5132.

Yadav, A. S., Ahlawat, N., Agarwal, S., Pandey, T., & Anupam Swami, A. (2020b). Red wine industry of supply chain management for distribution center using neural networks. *Test Engraining & Management, 83*, 11215–11222.

Yadav, A. S., Ahlawat, N., Dubey, R., Pandey, G., & Swami, A. (2020c). Pulp and paper industry inventory control for storage with wastewater treatment and inorganic composition using genetic algorithm (ELD problem). *Test Engraining & Management, 83*, 15508–15517.

Yadav, A. S., Ahlawat, N., Sharma, N., Swami, A., & Navyata. (2020d). Healthcare systems of inventory control for blood bank storage with reliability applications using genetic algorithm. *Advances in Mathematics: Scientific Journal, 9*(7), 5133–5142.

Yadav, A. S., Bansal, K. K., Shivani, Agarwal, S., & Vanaja, R. (2020e). FIFO in green supply chain inventory model of electrical components industry with distribution centres using particle swarm optimization. *Advances in Mathematics: Scientific Journal, 9*(7), 5115–5120.

Yadav, A. S., Dubey, R., Pandey, G., Ahlawat, N., & Swami, A. (2020f). Distillery industry inventory control for storage with wastewater treatment & logistics using particle swarm optimization. *Test Engraining & Management, 83*, 15362–15370.

Yadav, A. S., Kumar, A., Agarwal, P., Kumar, T., & Vanaja, R. (2020g). LOFO in green supply chain inventory model of auto-components industry with warehouses using differential evolution. *Advances in Mathematics: Scientific Journal, 9*(7), 5121–5126.

Yadav, A. S., Kumar, J., Malik, M., & Pandey, T. (2019). Supply chain of chemical industry for warehouse with distribution centres using artificial bee colony algorithm. *International Journal of Engineering and Advanced Technology, 8*(2S2), 14–19.

Yadav, A. S., Mahapatra, R. P., Sharma, S., & Swami, A. (2017a). An inflationary inventory model for deteriorating items under two storage systems. *International Journal of Economic Research, 14*(9).

Yadav, A. S., Mishra, R., Kumar, S., & Yadav, S. (2016). Multi objective optimization for electronic component inventory model & deteriorating items with two-warehouse using genetic algorithm. *International Journal of Control Theory and Applications, 9*(2).

Yadav, A. S., Navyata, Sharma, N., Ahlawat, N., & Swami, A. (2020h). Reliability consideration costing method for LOFO inventory model with chemical industry warehouse. *International Journal of Advanced Trends in Computer Science and Engineering, 9*(1), 403–408.

Yadav, A. S., Pandey, P., Ahlawat, N., Dubey, R., & Swami, A. (2020i). Wine industry inventory control for storage with wastewater treatment and pollution load using ant colony optimization algorithm. *Test Engraining & Management, 83*, 15528–15535.

Yadav, A. S., Pandey, T., Ahlawat, N., Agarwal, S., & Swami, A. (2020j). Rose wine industry of supply chain management for storage using genetic algorithm. *Test Engraining & Management, 83*, 11223–11230.

Yadav, A. S., Selva, N. S., & Tandon, A. (2020k). Medicine manufacturing industries supply chain management for block chain application using artificial neural networks. *International Journal of Advanced Science and Technology, 29*(8s), 1294–1301.

Yadav, A. S., & Swami, A. (2018a). A partial backlogging production-inventory lot-size model with time-varying holding cost and Weibull deterioration. *International Journal of Procurement Management, 11*(5).

Yadav, A. S., & Swami, A. (2018b). Integrated supply chain model for deteriorating items with linear stock dependent demand under imprecise and inflationary environment. *International Journal of Procurement Management, 11*(6).

Yadav, A. S., & Swami, A. (2019a). A volume flexible two-warehouse model with fluctuating demand and holding cost under inflation. *International Journal of Procurement Management, 12*(4), 441–456.

Yadav, A. S., & Swami, A. (2019b). An inventory model for non-instantaneous deteriorating items with variable holding cost under two-storage. *International Journal of Procurement Management, 12*(6), 690–710.

Yadav, A. S., Swami, A., Ahlawat, N., Bhatt, D., & Kher, G. (2020l). Electronic components supply chain management of electronic industrial development for warehouse and its impact on the environment using particle swarm optimization algorithm. In *Optimization and inventory management* (pp. 427–445).

Yadav, A. S., Swami, A., Kher, G., & Kumar, S. (2017b). Supply chain inventory model for two warehouses with soft computing optimization. *International Journal of Applied Business and Economic Research, 15*(4).

Yadav, A. S., Tandon, A., & Selva, N. S. (2020m). National blood bank centre supply chain management for blockchain application using genetic algorithm. *International Journal of Advanced Science and Technology, 29*(8s), 1318–1324.

Yadav, A. S., Taygi, B., Sharma, S., & Swami, A. (2017c). Effect of inflation on a two-warehouse inventory model for deteriorating items with time varying demand and shortages. *International Journal of Procurement Management, 10*(6).

A Stackelberg Game Approach in Supply Chain for Imperfect Quality Items with Learning Effect in Fuzzy Environment

Rita Yadav, Mandeep Mittal, Navneet Kumar Lamba, and Mahesh Kumar Jayaswal

Abstract In recent decades, researchers have effectively worked on seeking optimal policies under supply chain management for attaining practical and powerful outcomes. This paper studies supply chain model for imperfect quality items in which demand depends upon the buyer's price and marketing cost. The buyer segregates the defective items from supplied lot by seller and sell them at discounted price. In today's scenario, learning effect methodology has become a promotional tool in supply chain management. It impacts profit or loss of the members of the supply chain. The rapid change in the life cycle of product makes the parameters of the supply chain models more and more uncertain. Fuzzy analysis becomes a powerful tool to deal such type of vague or uncertain parameters in computing form. It examines the better assessment and performance of imprecise parameters. Keeping in view, some supply chain models for imperfect quality items have been developed by considering learning effect under fuzzy environment. A non-cooperative Stackelberg game theoretic approach is used to find the optimal decision variables and optimum profit of the supply chain members in fuzzy environment. Various numerical results with sensitivity analysis have been explained to justify the model.

Keywords Learning curve · Fuzzy system · Imperfect quality items · Non-cooperative games · Supply chain · Game theory

1 Introduction

Supply chain management is primarily related to the integration of activities and process between and within the organization. To analyze the interaction between

R. Yadav · M. K. Jayaswal (✉)
Department of Mathematics and Statistics, Banasthali Vidyapith, Banasthali, Rajasthan, India

M. Mittal
Amity Institute of Applied Sciences, Amity University Uttar Pradesh (AUUP), Noida, Uttar Pradesh, India

N. K. Lamba
Department of Mathematics, S.L.P.M., Mandhal, R.T.M. Nagpur University, Nagpur, India

N. H. Shah and M. Mittal (eds.), *Soft Computing in Inventory Management*, Inventory Optimization, https://doi.org/10.1007/978-981-16-2156-7_7

the members of the supply chain, the theory of non-cooperative Stackelberg game is preferred and used to study supply chain connected problems. There have been many researchers/academicians involve in working of the mathematical model implementing the learning curve. Some researches like Wright (1936), Baloff (1966), Cunningham (1980), and Argote et al. (1990) have contributed their work in the field of learning and forgetting curves by discussing the mathematical behavior of learning theory. Salameh et al. (1993) developed production inventory model (limited manufactured stock form) to optimize the cost with the outcome of human knowledge by taking the variable demand rate and learning with respect to time. Jaber and Bonney (1996) discovered and discussed a comparative study of the theory of learning and forgetting and also focused analytically different types of models.

Salameh and Jaber (2000) explored EOQ model for defective items with an inspection process at the buyer's end. These items may occur due to any reasons. Further, Eroglu and Ozdemir (2007) stretched the model of Salameh and Jaber (2000) by permitting shortages. Jaber and Bonney (2003) developed mathematical model which focused on reducing the setup time, eliminating rework and increasing production capacity with the help of learning curve. Jaber et al. (2008) deliberated the EOQ model in which they discussed that by using the concept of the learning curve, the percentage of defective items per batch decreased. Khan et al. (2010) minimized the production cost and maximized the production in their EOQ model for defective items by letting learning in screening process. Anzanello and Fogliatto (2011) advised the mathematical forms with their applications of learning curves models. Konstantaras et al. (2012) established a model to maximize production by allowing shortages for the imperfect items with an inspection as learning. Jaber et al. (2013) considered a manufacture stock model with "learning and forgetting" theory in manufacture. Game theory is a competent tool to balance the coordination among the players like seller and buyer in supply chain industry. Jayaswal et al. (2019) established an inventory model for imperfect quality items with permission delay under learning effect. Mittal et al. (2017) proposed an inventory model for price and demand are time depended under inflation.

Many times, there is ups and downs in the market. So it becomes necessary and useful for business to use fuzzy number to get best strategy. Wei and Zhao (2013) discussed three supply chain models in which expected profit is determined by fuzzy game theory. Soleimani (2016) analyzed manufacturer–leader Stackelberg game in which manufacturing cost and demand of customer are precise in nature. Optimum value of whole sale price and buyer's price are obtained by game theoretic approach. Patro et al. (2017) investigated two models crisp as well as fuzzy EOQ models with imperfect quality items (proportionate discount items) under learning effect in a finite time horizon. The optimal order lot size is determined to maximize the total profit where the defective items follow a learning curve and the demand rate assumed as triangle fuzzy number. Chavoshlou et al. (2019) developed three players (government, manufacture, and customer) green supply chain optimization model under fuzzy environment. Optimal strategies are obtained by Nash equilibrium game, and positive effects of fuzzy game model over non-fuzzy game model are discussed.

Some researchers like Abad and Jaggi (2003) have developed supply chain model in which the seller endorsed credit period to the buyer (payer) by cooperative and non-cooperative game theoretical structure. Esmaeili et al. (2009) also developed supply chain models by the game theoretical approach (cooperative and non-cooperative) in which demand is influenced by both the selling cost and marketing expenditure cost. Yadav et al. (2020) developed supply chain models for defective items with learning effect by Stackelberg non-cooperative approach. None of the researchers have developed such model under fuzzy environment, where demand is sensitive to selling rate and marketing expenditure charges of the buyer. To obtain their optimal policies, the fuzzy set theory is adopted to solve these fuzzy models. Meanwhile, fuzzy analysis is a commanding tool that deals with the information which arises from computational awareness and perception. Therefore, we consider the correlation between one buyer and one seller in a fuzzy decision-marking environment, where the parameters of the models can be forecasted and expressed as the triangular fuzzy variables.

Fuzzy theory basically comprises the process to find out the proper range for indistinct items in a vague/imprecise environment for smooth coordination between players of supply chain. In this paper, ordering cost of the buyer and setup cost of the seller are imprecise in nature. The total optimal profit in fuzzy environment is defuzzified with the help of the centroid method. In this paper, two-level supply chain models under fuzzy environment with the learning effect have been developed. The non-cooperative game theoretic approaches have been discussed in which demand is influenced by the marketing expenditure/promotional cost and selling price of the player, purchaser. Seller-Stackelberg and Buyer-Stackelberg, two different game approaches, have been discussed.

In this paper, impact of learning curve (LC) curve is shown on the different parameters of the supply chain. In this paper, learning curve is assumed to be in the form of $p(n) = a/\left(g + s^{bn}\right)$, where a, b and $g > 0$ are the active parameters, and $p(n)$ is the percentage defective per batch n, whereas n is the cumulative number of lots.

2 Notations

Seller's decision variables

c_{b} Seller's selling price ($/unit)

Buyer's decision variables

M Marketing cost (promotional price) ($/unit)
p_{b} Buyer's selling price ($/unit)
y_n Order quantity (in units) in nth batch, where $n \geq 1$

Parameters

A_b	Buyer's ordering cost ($/order)
A_s	Seller's ordering cost ($/order)
H_b	Inventory cost ($/unit/time)
I	Percent of inventory's carrying cost ($/unit)
$p(n)$	Defective percentage of items/products per batch (n) in y_n (units)
C	Seller's purchasing cost ($/unit)
c_s	Cost of defective value items per unit ($year) ($c_s < c_b$)
β	Marketing expenditure (promotional) elasticity of demand ($0 < \beta < 1,\ \beta + 1 < e$)
e	Price elasticity of the marketing demand ($e > 1$)
D	Annual demand rate (unit/year) $= kp_b^{-e}M^{\beta}$
λ	Screening rate decided by the buyer in units per unit of time ($D < \lambda$)
s_c	Cost to screen the product ($/units)
t_n	Time taken to screen a lot for imperfect items, $t_n = y_n/\lambda$ (years)
k	Scaling constant for the promoting demand ($k > 0$)
$\widetilde{A_b}$	Fuzzy ordering cost of the buyer ($/order)
$\widetilde{A_s}$	Fuzzy ordering cost of the seller ($/order)
$\mathrm{TP}_b^c(p_b, M, y_n)$	Buyer's profit function
$\mathrm{TP}_s^c(c_b)$	Seller's profit function
$\mathrm{TP}_{b^*}^c(p_b, M, y_n)$	Fuzzy buyer's profit
$\mathrm{TP}_{s^*}^c(c_b)$	Fuzzy seller's profit
T_n	Cycle length/span of the buyer (in years), $T_n = y_n(1 - p(n))/D$
T_n^*	Cycle length/span of the seller (in years), $T_n^* = y_n/D$
T_n^{**}	Cycle length/span of the Stackelberg models (in years), $T_n^{**} = \mathrm{Max}(T_n, T_n^*)$

2.1 Assumptions

1. Marketing demand is considered as a function of p_b and M.
2. Planning horizon is assumed as infinite.
3. No shortages acceptable (the demand is fulfilled).
4. Demand and screening follows at the same time and ($D < \lambda$).
5. Holding/inventory cost is not reflected for the seller as a lot-to-lot strategy rule have been considered.
6. The defective percentage items follow the Wright's curve (assumed) and the worth of the good product is assumed to be more than that of the imperfect quality items.
7. The number of imperfect items present in each batch is assumed by learning curve $p(n) = \frac{a}{g+s^{bn}}$, b is the learning rate, where a, b and $g > 0$ are the effective parameters, n is the cumulative number of lots or shipment, and $p(n)$ is the percentage defective per batch n.

8. The buyer's ordering cost and seller's setup cost are imprecise in nature.
9. Defuzzify the total profit function by the triangular method.

2.2 Some Definitions

Fuzzification

Fuzzification is a function which assigns input of a set to some degree of membership. The degree of membership may lie within the closed interval [0, 1]. If interval value is 1, then the value completely belongs to the fuzzy set. If its value is 0, then value does not belong to the given fuzzy set and if value lie between 0 and 1, that signifies the degree of vagueness or uncertainty that the given value belong in the set. Fuzzy environment process tries to solve the problems with a rough/imprecise data that makes it possible to obtain a group of exact conclusions.

Defuzzification: If $\check{A} = (a_1, a_2, a_3)$ is triangular fuzzy number then centroid method for defuzzification is defined as $C\left(\check{A}\right) = \frac{a_1+a_2+a_3}{3}$.

3 Mathematical Crisp Models

3.1 Buyer's Model

The objective of the present model is to optimize the buyer's price, marketing cost, and the ordered quantity with the corresponding profit for the retailer with the learning effect.

Buyer's profit = Sales income − purchasing cost − screening cost − marketing expenditure cost − ordering cost − holding cost

$$\begin{aligned}\mathrm{TP_b}(p_\mathrm{b}, M, y_n) &= p_\mathrm{b}(1-p(n))y_n + c_\mathrm{s}p(n)y_n - c_\mathrm{b}y_n - s_\mathrm{c}y_n \\ &\quad - My_n - A_\mathrm{b} - \left(\frac{Q(1-p(n))T_1}{2} + \frac{p(n)Q^2}{\lambda}\right)H_\mathrm{b}\end{aligned}$$

Put $T_n = \frac{(1-p(n))y_n}{D}$, $t = \frac{y_n}{\lambda}$, $H_\mathrm{b} = Ic_\mathrm{b}$ then buyer's profit is given by

$$\begin{aligned}\mathrm{TP_b}(p_\mathrm{b}, M, y_n) &= p_\mathrm{b}(1-p(n))y_n + c_\mathrm{s}p(n)y_n - c_\mathrm{b}y_n - My_n - s_\mathrm{c}y_n \\ &\quad - A_\mathrm{b} - \left(\frac{y_n^2(1-p(n))^2}{2D} + \frac{p(n)y_n^2}{\lambda}\right)Ic_\mathrm{b}\end{aligned}$$

We assumed that the demand function is $D = kp_\mathrm{b}^{-e}M^{\beta}$.

Buyer's profit per cycle is given by

$$\mathrm{TP}_{\mathrm{b}}^{c}(p_{\mathrm{b}}, M, y_n) = \left[\frac{\mathrm{TP}_{\mathrm{b}}(p_{\mathrm{b}}, M, y_n)}{T_n}\right]$$

$$\frac{D}{(1-p(n))y_n}[p_{\mathrm{b}}(1-p(n))y_n + c_{\mathrm{s}}p(n)y_n - c_{\mathrm{b}}y_n$$

$$-My_n - s_{\mathrm{c}}y_n - A_{\mathrm{b}} - \left(\frac{y_n^2(1-p(n))^2}{2D} + \frac{p(n)y_n^2}{\lambda}\right)Ic_{\mathrm{b}}\Bigg]$$

$$= p_{\mathrm{b}}D + \frac{1}{(1-p(n))}\Bigg[c_{\mathrm{s}}p(n)D - c_{\mathrm{b}}D - MD - s_{\mathrm{c}}D - \frac{A_{\mathrm{b}}D}{y_n}$$

$$-\left(\frac{y_n(1-p(n))^2}{2} + \frac{p(n)y_nD}{\lambda}\right)Ic_{\mathrm{b}}\Bigg]$$

$$\mathrm{TP}_{\mathrm{b}}^{c}(p_{\mathrm{b}}, M, y_n) = kp_{\mathrm{b}}^{-e+1}M^{\beta} + \frac{kp_{\mathrm{b}}^{-e}M^{\beta}}{(1-p(n))}\Bigg[c_{\mathrm{s}}p(n) - c_{\mathrm{b}} - s_{\mathrm{c}} - M - \frac{A_{\mathrm{b}}}{y_n}$$

$$-\frac{p(n)y_n}{\lambda}Ic_{\mathrm{b}}\Bigg] - \left(\frac{y_n(1-p(n))^2}{2(1-p(n))}Ic_{\mathrm{b}}\right) \tag{1}$$

The buyer's goal is to find optimal values for order quantity y_n, selling price, p_{b}, marketing expenditure cost, M, such that his profit becomes maximum.

For this, we equate first derivative of Eq. (1) with respect to p_{b} to zero. $\frac{\partial[\mathrm{TP}_{\mathrm{b}}^{c}(p_{\mathrm{b}}, M, y_n)]}{\partial p_{\mathrm{b}}} = 0$, yields

$$p_{\mathrm{b}} = \frac{e}{(e-1)(1-p(n))}\left[M + c_{\mathrm{b}} + s_c - c_{\mathrm{s}}p(n) + \frac{A_{\mathrm{b}}}{y_n} + \frac{Ic_{\mathrm{b}}p(n)y_n}{\lambda}\right] \tag{2}$$

The buyer's profit $\left[\mathrm{TP}_{\mathrm{b}}^{c}(p_{\mathrm{b}}, M, y_n)\right]$ is pseudoconcave with respect to p_{b} for constants M and y_n (Yadav et al. 2018).

Substituting the value of p_{b} into Eq. (1) and then subsequent equation is

$$\left[\mathrm{TP}_{\mathrm{b}}^{c}(p_{\mathrm{b}}(M), M, y_n(M))\right] = \frac{K}{e}\Bigg[\frac{e}{(e-1)(1-p(n))}\Bigg(M + c_{\mathrm{b}} + s_{\mathrm{c}} + \frac{A_{\mathrm{b}}}{y_n}$$

$$+\frac{p(n)y_nIc_{\mathrm{b}}}{\lambda} - c_{\mathrm{s}}p(n)\Bigg)\Bigg]^{-e+1}M^{\beta} - \left(\frac{y_n(1-p(n))^2}{2(1-p(n))}Ic_{\mathrm{b}}\right) \tag{3}$$

Taking differentiation of Eq. (3) w.r.t. M, we get

$$M = \frac{\beta}{(e-\beta-1)}\left[c_{\mathrm{b}} + s_{\mathrm{c}} + \frac{A_{\mathrm{b}}}{y_n} + \frac{Ic_{\mathrm{b}}p(n)y_n}{\lambda} - c_{\mathrm{s}}p(n)\right] \tag{4}$$

The buyer's profit, $\left[\mathrm{TP}_{\mathrm{b}}^{c}(p_{\mathrm{b}}(M), M, y_n(M))\right]$, is concave with respect to M for constant y_n (Yadav et al. 2018).

Substituting the value of Eq. (4) into Eq. (2), we get

$$p_b = \frac{e}{(e-\beta-1)(1-p(n))}\left[c_b + s_c + \frac{A_b}{y_n} + \frac{Ic_b p(n) y_n}{\lambda} - c_s p(n)\right] \tag{5}$$

$$\begin{aligned}\left[\mathrm{TP}^c(y_n)\right] &= k\left(\frac{e}{(e-\beta-1)(1-p(n))}\left[c_b + s_c + \frac{A_b}{y_n} + \frac{Ic_b p(n) y_n}{\lambda} - c_s p(n)\right]\right)^{-e} \\ &\left(\frac{\beta}{(e-\beta-1)}\left[c_b + s_c + \frac{A_b}{y_n} + \frac{Ic_b p(n) y_n}{\lambda} - c_s p(n)\right]\right)^{\beta} \\ &\left\{\left(\frac{e}{(e-\beta-1)(1-p(n))}\left[c_b + s_c + \frac{A_b}{y_n} + \frac{Ic_b p(n) y_n}{\lambda} - c_s p(n)\right]\right)\right. \\ &+ \frac{1}{(1-p(n))}\left[c_s p(n) - s_c - c_b - \left(\frac{\beta}{(e-\beta-1)}\left[c_b + s_c + \frac{A_b}{y_n}\right.\right.\right. \\ &\left.\left.\left.+ \frac{Ic_b p(n) y_n}{\lambda} - c_s p(n)\right]\right) - \frac{A_b}{y_n} - \frac{p(n) y_n}{\lambda} Ic_b - \frac{y_n\left[(1-p(n))^2\right]}{2} Ic_b\right]\right\}\end{aligned} \tag{6}$$

The first-order condition of Eq. (6) w.r.t. y_n finds the constraints as follows:

$$\begin{aligned}&y_n^2 Ic_b\left((1-p(n))^2\right)\lambda + 2Dp(n) = 2D\lambda, \quad \text{i.e.} \\ &y_n^2 Ic_b\left((1-p(n))^2\right)\lambda = 2ke^{-e}\beta^{\beta}\left(\left[c_b + s_c + \frac{A_b}{y_n} + \frac{Ic_b p(n) y_n}{\lambda} - c_s p(n)\right]\right)^{\beta-e} \\ &\quad (e-\beta-1)^{e-\beta}(1-p(n))^{e}\left(\lambda A_b - y_n^2 p(n)\right)\end{aligned} \tag{7}$$

It is quite difficult to prove the concavity of the above total profit function defined in Eq. (6) analytically.

Thus, buyer's total profit $\left[\mathrm{TP}_b^c(y_n)\right]$ defined in Eq. (6) is concave function with respect to order quantity is shown with the help of the graph (Fig. 1).

Fig. 1 Plot of buyer's profit function with respect to order quantity

3.2 Seller's Model

Seller's yield = Sales revenue − purchasing cost − ordering cost

$$\mathrm{TP_s}(c_\mathrm{b}) = c_\mathrm{b} y_n - C y_n - A_\mathrm{s}$$

Seller's cycle length, $T_n^* = \frac{y_n}{D}$.

Seller's profit per cycle is given by,

$$\mathrm{TP_s^c}(c_\mathrm{b}) = \frac{D}{y_n}(c_\mathrm{b} y_n - C y_n - A_\mathrm{s})$$
$$= k p_\mathrm{b}^{-e} M^\beta \left(c_\mathrm{b} - C - \frac{A_\mathrm{s}}{y_n} \right) \tag{8}$$

Seller's plan is to achieve his net profit, by finding the optimal value of selling price, c_b.

Seller's profit is zero at $c_{\mathrm{b}_0} = C + \frac{A_\mathrm{s}}{y_n}$.

Since the seller always would prefer to have positive profit,

$c_{\mathrm{b}_0} > C + \frac{A_\mathrm{s}}{y_n}$, let

$$\boldsymbol{c_b} = F c_{\mathrm{b}_0} = F\left(C + \frac{A_\mathrm{s}}{y_n} \right) \quad \text{for some, } F > 1 \tag{9}$$

i.e., the optimal value for c_b obtained through negotiation by seller and buyer.

3.3 The Non-cooperative Stackelberg Game Theory Approach

The Stackelberg non-cooperative game considers two players. Among them, one player is recognized as dominant player and takes the advantage of making the first move/travel and other player acts as follower, making their best probable move serially using preceding available information.

3.3.1 The Seller-Stackelberg Model

In this model, seller is treated as dominant player. The seller's objective is to find his yield on the basis of buyer's decision variables. The problem is,

$$\text{Max} \ \left(\mathrm{TP_s^c}(c_\mathrm{b}) \right)$$

$$\mathrm{TP}_{\mathrm{s}}^{c}(c_{\mathrm{b}}) = \frac{D}{y_n}(c_{\mathrm{b}} y_n - C y_n - A_{\mathrm{s}})$$
$$= k p_{\mathrm{b}}^{-e} M^{\beta}\left(c_{\mathrm{b}} - C - \frac{A_{\mathrm{s}}}{y_n}\right) \tag{10}$$

Subject to

$$M = \frac{\beta}{(e-\beta-1)}\left[c_{\mathrm{b}} + s_{\mathrm{c}} + \frac{A_{\mathrm{b}}}{y_n} + \frac{I c_{\mathrm{b}} p(n) y_n}{\lambda} - c_{\mathrm{s}} p(n)\right] \tag{11}$$

$$p_{\mathrm{b}} = \frac{e}{(e-\beta-1)(1-p(n))}\left[c_{\mathrm{b}} + s_{\mathrm{c}} + \frac{A_{\mathrm{b}}}{y_n} + \frac{I c_{\mathrm{b}} p(n) y_n}{\lambda} - c_{\mathrm{s}} p(n)\right] \tag{12}$$

Constraints

$$y_n^2 I c_{\mathrm{b}}\left((1-p(n))^2\right)\lambda = 2ke^{-e}\beta^{\beta}\left(\left[c_{\mathrm{b}} + s_{\mathrm{c}} + \frac{A_{\mathrm{b}}}{y_n} + \frac{I c_{\mathrm{b}} p(n) y_n}{\lambda} - c_{\mathrm{s}} p(n)\right]\right)^{\beta-e}$$
$$(e-\beta-1)^{e-\beta}(1-p(n))^{e}\left(\lambda A_{\mathrm{b}} - y_n^2 p(n)\right) \tag{13}$$

Cycle length, $T_n^{**} = \max\left(T_n, T_n^{*}\right)$.

By using Eqs. (11) and (12) and the constraints (13) in Eq. (10), the subsequent equation can be resolved using software Mathematica 9.0.

3.3.2 The Buyer-Stackelberg Model

$$\mathrm{Max}\left[\mathrm{TP}_{\mathrm{b}}^{c}(p_{\mathrm{b}}, M, y_n)\right] = k p_{\mathrm{b}}^{-e+1} M^{\beta} + \frac{k p_{\mathrm{b}}^{-e} M^{\beta}}{(1-p(n))}\left[c_{\mathrm{s}} p(n) - c_{\mathrm{b}} - s_{\mathrm{c}} - M - \frac{A_{\mathrm{b}}}{y_n}\right.$$
$$\left. - \frac{p(n) y_n}{\lambda} I c_{\mathrm{b}}\right] - \left(\frac{y_n (1-p(n))^2}{2(1-p(n))} I c_{\mathrm{b}}\right) \tag{14}$$

Subject to

$$\text{At } c_{\mathrm{b}_0} = F\left(C + \frac{A_{\mathrm{s}}}{y_n}\right) \tag{15}$$

By using Eq. (15) on Eq. (14), the resultant nonlinear equation can be explained using software Mathematica 9.0.

4 Mathematical Fuzzy Model

In this section, different mathematical models such as buyer's fuzzy model, seller's fuzzy model, seller-Stackelberg fuzzy model, and buyer's Stackelberg fuzzy model with learning effect under fuzzy environment have been explained.

4.1 Buyer's Fuzzy Model

The objective of the present model is to optimize the buyer's price, marketing cost, and the ordered quantity with the corresponding profit for the retailer with learning effect under fuzzy environment.

Let us assume that due to uncertainty existing in parameters, the inventory model is in fuzzy environment. Also, we have assumed that the parameters $\widetilde{A}_{\mathrm{b}} = (A_{\mathrm{b}1}, A_{\mathrm{b}2}, A_{\mathrm{b}3})$, $\widetilde{A}_{\mathrm{s}} = (A_{\mathrm{s}1}, A_{\mathrm{s}2}, A_{\mathrm{s}3})$ are triangular fuzzy numbers, then the entire profit per unit time in fuzzy environment is in each model.

Buyer's total profit per cycle in fuzzy environment

$$\mathrm{TP}^{c}_{\mathrm{b}^*}(p_{\mathrm{b}}, M, y_n) = kp_{\mathrm{b}}^{-e+1}M^{\beta} + \frac{kp_{\mathrm{b}}^{-e}M^{\beta}}{(1-p(n))} \left[c_{\mathrm{s}}p(n) - c_{\mathrm{b}} - s_{\mathrm{c}} - M - \frac{\widetilde{A}_{\mathrm{b}}}{y_n} - \frac{p(n)y_n}{\lambda}Ic_{\mathrm{b}}\right] - \left(\frac{y_n(1-p(n))^2}{2(1-p(n))}Ic_{\mathrm{b}}\right) \quad (16)$$

$$\mathrm{TP}^{c}_{\mathrm{b}1}(p_{\mathrm{b}}, M, y_n) = kp_{\mathrm{b}}^{-e+1}M^{\beta} + \frac{kp_{\mathrm{b}}^{-e}M^{\beta}}{(1-p(n))} \left[c_{\mathrm{s}}p(n) - c_{\mathrm{b}} - s_{\mathrm{c}} - M - \frac{A_{\mathrm{b}1}}{y_n} - \frac{p(n)y_n}{\lambda}Ic_{\mathrm{b}}\right] - \left(\frac{y_n(1-p(n))^2}{2(1-p(n))}Ic_{\mathrm{b}}\right) \quad (17)$$

$$\mathrm{TP}^{c}_{\mathrm{b}2}(p_{\mathrm{b}}, M, y_n) = kp_{\mathrm{b}}^{-e+1}M^{\beta} + \frac{kp_{\mathrm{b}}^{-e}M^{\beta}}{(1-p(n))} \left[c_{\mathrm{s}}p(n) - c_{\mathrm{b}} - s_{\mathrm{c}} - M - \frac{A_{\mathrm{b}2}}{y_n} - \frac{p(n)y_n}{\lambda}Ic_{\mathrm{b}}\right] - \left(\frac{y_n(1-p(n))^2}{2(1-p(n))}Ic_{\mathrm{b}}\right) \quad (18)$$

$$\mathrm{TP}^{c}_{\mathrm{b}3}(p_{\mathrm{b}}, M, y_n) = kp_{\mathrm{b}}^{-e+1}M^{\beta} + \frac{kp_{\mathrm{b}}^{-e}M^{\beta}}{(1-p(n))} \left[c_{\mathrm{s}}p(n) - c_{\mathrm{b}} - s_{\mathrm{c}} - M - \frac{A_{\mathrm{b}3}}{y_n} - \frac{p(n)y_n}{\lambda}Ic_{\mathrm{b}}\right]$$

$$-\left(\frac{y_n(1-p(n))^2}{2(1-p(n))}Ic_b\right) \tag{19}$$

Now we defuzzify the entire profit per unit time by centroid method

$$\mathrm{TP}^c_{b*}(p_b, M, y_n) = \frac{\mathrm{TP}^c_{b1}(p_b, M, y_n) + \mathrm{TP}^c_{b2}(p_b, M, y_n) + \mathrm{TP}^c_{b3}(p_b, M, y_n)}{3} \tag{20}$$

Substituting the values from Eqs. (17), (18), and (19) in Eq. (20), we get

$$\begin{aligned}
\mathrm{TP}^c_{b}\cdot(p_b, M, y_n) = \frac{1}{3}\Bigg\{& kp_b^{-e+1}M^\beta + \frac{kp_b^{-e}M^\beta}{(1-p(n))} \\
&\left[c_s p(n) - c_b - s_c - M - \frac{A_{b1}}{y_n} - \frac{p(n)y_n}{\lambda}Ic_b\right] - \left(\frac{y_n(1-p(n))^2}{2(1-p(n))}Ic_b\right) \\
&+ kp_b^{-e+1}M^\beta + \frac{kp_b^{-e}M^\beta}{(1-p(n))}\left[c_s p(n) - c_b - s_c - M - \frac{A_{b2}}{y_n} - \frac{p(n)y_n}{\lambda}Ic_b\right] \\
&- \left(\frac{y_n(1-p(n))^2}{2(1-p(n))}Ic_b\right) + kp_b^{-e+1}M^\beta + \frac{kp_b^{-e}M^\beta}{(1-p(n))} \\
&\left[c_s p(n) - c_b - s_c - M - \frac{A_{b3}}{y_n} - \frac{p(n)y_n}{\lambda}Ic_b\right] - \left(\frac{y_n(1-p(n))^2}{2(1-p(n))}Ic_b\right)\Bigg\}
\end{aligned}$$

$$\begin{aligned}
\mathrm{TP}^c_{b*}(p_b, M, y_n) = &\frac{(A_{b1}+A_{b2}+A_{b3})}{3}\left(\frac{kp_b^{-e}M^\beta}{(1-p(n))y_n}\right) \\
&+ \Bigg[kp_b^{-e+1}M^\beta + \frac{kp_b^{-e}M^\beta}{(1-p(n))}[c_s p(n) - c_b \\
&- s_c - M - \frac{p(n)y_n}{\lambda}Ic_b\Big] - \left(\frac{y_n(1-p(n))^2}{2(1-p(n))}Ic_b\right)\Bigg]
\end{aligned} \tag{21}$$

Now, our objective is to find the optimal values of three decision variables p_b, M, and y_n to optimize the profit function $\mathrm{TP}^c_{b*}(p_b, M, y_n)$. The first-order condition of Eq. (21) w.r.t. p_b and M, we have

$$M = \frac{\beta}{(e-\beta-1)}\left[c_b + s_c + \frac{(A_{b1}+A_{b2}+A_{b3})}{3y_n} + \frac{Ic_b p(n)y_n}{\lambda} - c_s p(n)\right] \tag{22}$$

$$p_b = \frac{e}{(e-\beta-1)(1-p(n))}\left[c_b + s_c + \frac{(A_{b1}+A_{b2}+A_{b3})}{3y_n} + \frac{Ic_b p(n)y_n}{\lambda} - c_s p(n)\right] \tag{23}$$

The total buyer's fuzzy profit is pseudoconcave with respect to p_b and M (Yadav et al., 2018).

Substituting the values of p_b and M in Eq. (21), we get

$$\left[\mathrm{TP}^c_{b*}(y_n)\right] = k\left(\frac{e}{(e-\beta-1)(1-p(n))}\left[c_b + s_c + \frac{(A_{b1}+A_{b2}+A_{b3})}{3y_n}\right.\right.$$

$$+\frac{Ic_b p(n) y_n}{\lambda} - c_s p(n)\Big]\Big)^{-e}\Bigg(\frac{\beta}{(e-\beta-1)}\Big[c_b + s_c + \frac{(A_{b1}+A_{b2}+A_{b3})}{3y_n}$$
$$+\frac{Ic_b p(n) y_n}{\lambda} - c_s p(n)\Big]\Big)^{\beta}\Bigg\{\Bigg(\frac{e}{(e-\beta-1)(1-p(n))}[c_b + s_c$$
$$+\frac{(A_{b1}+A_{b2}+A_{b3})}{3y_n} + \frac{Ic_b p(n) y_n}{\lambda} - c_s p(n)\Big]\Big) + \frac{1}{(1-p(n))}[c_s p(n) - s_c$$
$$-c_b - \Bigg(\frac{\beta}{(e-\beta-1)}\Big[c_b + s_c + \frac{(A_{b1}+A_{b2}+A_{b3})}{3y_n} + \frac{Ic_b p(n) y_n}{\lambda} - c_s p(n)\Big]\Bigg)$$
$$-\frac{(A_{b1}+A_{b2}+A_{b3})}{3y_n} - \frac{p(n) y_n}{\lambda} Ic_b - \frac{y_n\big[(1-p(n))^2\big]}{2} Ic_b\Big]\Bigg\} \quad (24)$$

The first-order condition of Eq. (24) w.r.t. y_n, we find the constraints as follows:

$$y_n^2 Ic_b\big((1-p(n))^2\big)\lambda + 2Dp(n) = 2D\lambda, \quad \text{i.e.}$$

$$y_n^2 Ic_b\big((1-p(n))^2\big)\lambda = 2ke^{-e}\beta^{\beta}\Bigg(\Big[c_b + s_c + \frac{(A_{b1}+A_{b2}+A_{b3})}{3y_n}$$
$$+\frac{Ic_b p(n) y_n}{\lambda} - c_s p(n)\Big]\Bigg)^{\beta-e}(e-\beta-1)^{e-\beta}$$
$$(1-p(n))^{e}\left(\frac{\lambda}{3}(A_{b1}+A_{b2}+A_{b3}) - y_n^2 p(n)\right)$$

Thus, total fuzzy profit $\big[\mathrm{TP}^{c}_{b^*}(y_n)\big]$ defined in Eq. (24) is concave function with respect to order quantity which is shown analytically with the help of the graph (Fig. 2).

Fig. 2 Plot of fuzzy buyer's profit function with respect to order quantity

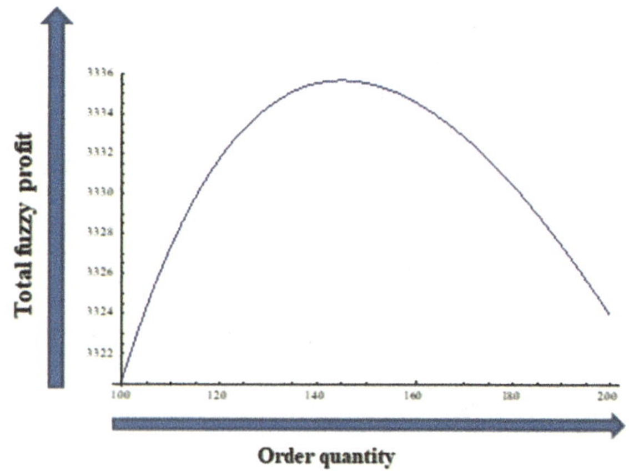

4.2 Seller's Fuzzy Model

The objective of the present model is to optimize the seller's price with the corresponding profit for the seller with learning effect under fuzzy environment.

Seller's total profit per cycle in fuzzy environment is given by

$$\mathrm{TP}^{c}_{s*}(c_b) = kp_b^{-e}M^{\beta}\left(c_b - C - \frac{\widetilde{A}_s}{y_n}\right) \quad (25)$$

$$\mathrm{TP}^{c}_{s1}(c_b) = kp_b^{-e}M^{\beta}\left(c_b - C - \frac{A_{s1}}{y_n}\right) \quad (26)$$

$$\mathrm{TP}^{c}_{s2}(c_b) = kp_b^{-e}M^{\beta}\left(c_b - C - \frac{A_{s2}}{y_n}\right) \quad (27)$$

$$\mathrm{TP}^{c}_{s3}(c_b) = kp_b^{-e}M^{\beta}\left(c_b - C - \frac{A_{s3}}{y_n}\right) \quad (28)$$

Now we defuzzify the entire profit per unit time by centroid method

$$\mathrm{TP}^{c}_{s*}(c_b) = \frac{\mathrm{TP}^{c}_{s1}(c_b) + \mathrm{TP}^{c}_{s2}(c_b) + \mathrm{TP}^{c}_{s3}(c_b)}{3} \quad (29)$$

Substituting the values from Eqs. (26), (27), and (28) in Eq. (25), we get

$$\mathrm{TP}^{c}_{s*}(c_b) = \left\{\frac{kp_b^{-e}M^{\beta}\left(c_b - C - \frac{A_{s1}}{y_n}\right) + kp_b^{-e}M^{\beta}\left(c_b - C - \frac{A_{s2}}{y_n}\right) + kp_b^{-e}M^{\beta}\left(c_b - C - \frac{A_{s3}}{y_n}\right)}{3}\right\}$$

$$= \frac{kp_b^{-e}M^{\beta}}{3y_n}(A_{s1} + A_{s2} + A_{s3}) + kp_b^{-e}M^{\beta}(c_b - C) \quad (30)$$

4.3 Seller's Stackelberg Fuzzy Model

Seller is the dominant player. The seller's main aim is to find his profit on the basis of given buyer's decision variables. The problem is,

$$\text{Max } \mathrm{TP}^{c}_{s*}(c_b) = \frac{kp_b^{-e}M^{\beta}}{3y_n}(A_{s1} + A_{s2} + A_{s3}) + kp_b^{-e}M^{\beta}(c_b - C) \quad (31)$$

Subject to

$$M = \frac{\beta}{(e - \beta - 1)}\left[c_b + s_c + \frac{(A_{b1} + A_{b2} + A_{b3})}{3y_n} + \frac{Ic_b p(n) y_n}{\lambda} - c_s p(n)\right] \quad (32)$$

$$p_{\mathrm{b}} = \frac{e}{(e-\beta-1)(1-p(n))}\left[c_{\mathrm{b}} + s_{\mathrm{c}} + \frac{(A_{\mathrm{b}1}+A_{\mathrm{b}2}+A_{\mathrm{b}3})}{3y_n} + \frac{Ic_{\mathrm{b}}p(n)y_n}{\lambda} - c_{\mathrm{s}}p(n)\right] \tag{33}$$

Constraints

$$\begin{aligned} y_n^2 Ic_{\mathrm{b}}((1-p(n))^2)\lambda &= 2ke^{-e}\beta^{\beta}\left(\left[c_{\mathrm{b}} + s_{\mathrm{c}} + \frac{(A_{\mathrm{b}1}+A_{\mathrm{b}2}+A_{\mathrm{b}3})}{3y_n}\right.\right. \\ &\left.\left.+\frac{Ic_{\mathrm{b}}p(n)y_n}{\lambda} - c_{\mathrm{s}}p(n)\right]\right)^{\beta-e}(e-\beta-1)^{e-\beta} \\ &(1-p(n))^e\left(\lambda\frac{(A_{\mathrm{b}1}+A_{\mathrm{b}2}+A_{\mathrm{b}3})}{3} - y_n^2 p(n)\right) \end{aligned} \tag{34}$$

4.4 The Buyer's Stackelberg Fuzzy Model

The buyer is the dominant player. The buyer's main aim is to find his profit on the basis of given seller's decision variables. The problem is,

$$\begin{aligned} \text{Max } \mathrm{TP}^c_{\mathrm{b}*}(p_{\mathrm{b}}, M, y_n) &= \frac{(A_{\mathrm{b}1}+A_{\mathrm{b}2}+A_{\mathrm{b}3})}{3}\left(\frac{kp_{\mathrm{b}}^{-e}M^{\beta}}{(1-p(n))y_n}\right) \\ &+\left[kp_{\mathrm{b}}^{-e+1}M^{\beta} + \frac{kp_{\mathrm{b}}^{-e}M^{\beta}}{(1-p(n))}\left[c_{\mathrm{s}}p(n) - c_{\mathrm{b}} - s_{\mathrm{c}} - M - \frac{p(n)y_n}{\lambda}Ic_{\mathrm{b}}\right]\right. \\ &\left.-\left(\frac{y_n(1-p(n))^2}{2(1-p(n))}Ic_{\mathrm{b}}\right)\right] \end{aligned} \tag{35}$$

Subject to

$$\text{At } c_{\mathrm{b}_0} = F\left(C + \frac{(A_{\mathrm{s}1}+A_{\mathrm{s}2}+A_{\mathrm{s}3})}{3y_n}\right) \tag{36}$$

5 Numerical Examples

Example 1

The seller-Stackelberg game model is shown in the given example which shows the effect of learning on the decision variables. Input parameters are taken from two papers Esmaeili et al. (2009) and Jaber et al. (2008), $C = \$1.5$ units, $A_{\mathrm{b}} = \$38$, $A_{\mathrm{s}} = \$40$, $k = 36{,}080$, $F = 1.8$, $\lambda = 175{,}200$ unit/year, $c_{\mathrm{s}} = \$3.5$, $\beta = Le$, $e = 1.7$, $L = 0.088$, $Sc = \$0.035$, $I = 0.38$, $F = 1.8$, $a = 40$, $b =$

1.8, $n = 5$, $g = 999$, $s = 2.99$, $p(n) = 0.0019$. Equation (13) gives the results, $y_n = 138$ units and $c_b = \$4.291$. Equations (11) and (12) produce the results, $p_b = \$14.227$ and $M = \$1.252$. The seller's profit, $\mathrm{TP}_s^c = \$1023.08$ and the buyer's profit, $\mathrm{TP}_b^c = \$3309.80$.

Example 2

The buyer-Stackelberg game model is shown in the given example which shows the effect of learning on the decision variables. We consider the values of all parameters are same as defined in Example 1 except $c_s = 2.5$. Equation (14) gives the results, $p_b = \$9.280$, $M = \$0.817$, and $y_n = 413$ units. Equation (15) generates the results, $c_b = \$2.874$. Seller's profit, $\mathrm{TP}_s^c = \$1013.11$ and buyer's profit, $\mathrm{TP}_b^c = \$4103.86$.

Fuzzy Numerical Example 3

Effect of learning on the decision variables in fuzzy seller-Stackelberg game model is shown in the given example. Input parameters are taken from two papers Esmaeili et al. (2009) and Jaber et al. (2008), $C = \$1.5$ units, $\widetilde{A}_b = (35, 40, 45)$, $\widetilde{A}_s = (45, 50, 55)$, $k = 36{,}080$, $F = 1.8$, $\lambda = 175{,}200$ unit/year, $c_s = \$3.5$, $\beta = Le$, $e = 1.7$, $L = 0.088$, $Sc = \$0.035$, $I = 0.38$, $F = 1.8$, $a = 40$, $b = 1.8$, $n = 5$, $g = 999$, $s = 2.99$, $p(n) = 0.0019$. Equation (34) gives the results, $y_n = 141$ units and $c_b = \$4.320$. Equations (32) and (33) produce the results, $p_b = \$14.345$ and $M = \$1.263$. Fuzzy seller's profit, $\mathrm{TP}_{s*}^c = \$999.50$ and fuzzy buyer's profit, $\mathrm{TP}_{b*}^c = \$3291.34$.

Fuzzy Numerical Example 4

Effect of learning on the decision variables in fuzzy buyer-Stackelberg game model is shown in the given example. We consider the values of all parameters are same as defined in Example 1 except $c_s = 2.5$. Equation (35) gives the results, $p_b = \$9.357$, $M = \$0.824$, and $y_n = 446$ units and Eq. (36) generates the results, $c_b = \$2.902$. Fuzzy seller's profit, $\mathrm{TP}_{s*}^c = \$ = \$1009.72$ and fuzzy buyer's profit, $\mathrm{TP}_{b*}^c = \$4063.70$.

Results indicate that the high seller's selling price results the more gain in the profit to the seller in seller Stackelberg model. Result shows that seller got higher profit when he is leader and less when he is follower, whereas results also show that higher profit gained by the purchaser shows that he is better off in the second model. In both the cases, buyer got more profit as compared to the player seller due to the learning effect.

In case of fuzzy environment, result shows that buyer is more benefited when he is leader but seller got more in case of follower. When we compare crisp model example with fuzzy example, we conclude that both the players obtain less profit in fuzzy as compared to crisp model example.

6 Sensitivity Analysis

In this section, sensitivity analysis is carry out on the basis of key factors/parameters to estimate the strength of the model. This part shows the effect of learning rate on the different decision variables and profit of the players.

6.1 *Effect of Learning on the Player's Profit*

Seller-Stackelberg

See Table 1.

Buyer-Stackelberg

See Table 2.

Table 1 Effect of learning rate on the parameter p_b, M, Q, C_b, $[TP_s^c]$ and $[TP_b^c]$ with learning rate $b = 1.8$

No. of shipment n	Defective percent in per lot $p(n)$	Order quantity $y(n)$	Selling price of the seller C_b	Selling price of the buyer p_b	Marketing expenditure M	Buyer profit $[TP_b^c]$	Seller profit $[TP_s^c]$
1	0.0397	153	4.064	13.545	1.147	3382.30	1010.13
2	0.0381	152	4.074	13.576	1.152	3378.80	1010.66
3	0.0291	149	4.127	13.740	1.177	3360.79	1013.53
4	0.0107	142	4.237	14.069	1.228	3325.97	1019.83
5	0.0019	138	4.291	14.227	1.252	3309.80	1023.08

Table 2 Effect of learning rate on the parameter p_b, M, Q, C_b, $[TP_s^c]$ and $[TP_b^c]$ with learning rate $b = 1.8$

No. of shipment n	Defective percent in per lot $p(n)$	Order quantity $y(n)$	Selling price of the seller C_b	Selling price of the buyer p_b	Marketing expenditure M	Buyer profit $[TP_b^c]$	Seller profit $[TP_s^c]$
1	0.0397	427	2.868	9.3134	0.789	4072.04	999.648
2	0.0381	426	2.869	9.3118	0.790	4073.49	1000.24
3	0.0291	423	2.870	9.303	0.797	4081.05	1003.59
4	0.0107	416	2.873	9.287	0.810	4096.44	1010.08
5	0.0019	413	2.874	9.280	0.817	4103.86	1013.11

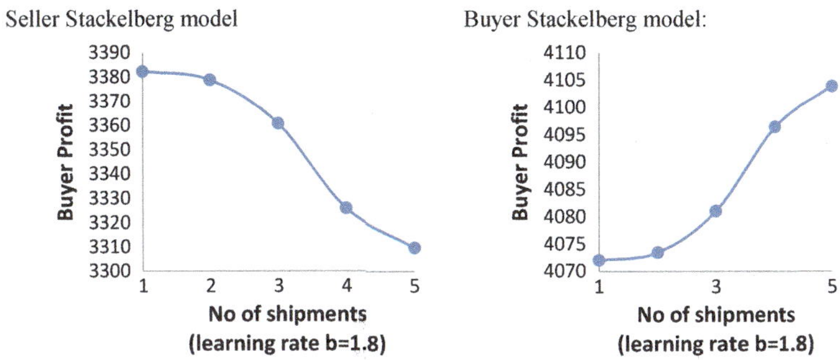

Fig. 3 Effect of shipments on buyer's profit

Effect of no. of shipments and learning rate on buyer's profit in both Stackelberg models (Fig. 3).

6.2 *Fuzzy Seller-Stackelberg*

See Table 3.

Fuzzy Buyer-Stackelberg

See Table 4.

Fuzzy Seller-Stackelberg

See Table 5.

Fuzzy Buyer-Stackelberg

See Table 6.

Table 3 Effect of learning rate on the parameter p_b, M, Q, C_b, $[TP_s^c]$ and $[TP_b^c]$ in fuzzy environment ($A_b = 40$, $A_s = 50$, learning rate $b = 1.8$)

No. of shipment n	Defective percent in per lot $p(n)$	Order quantity $y(n)$	Selling price of the seller C_b	Selling price of the buyer p_b	Marketing expenditure M	Fuzzy buyer profit $[TP_b^c]$	Fuzzy seller profit $[TP_s^c]$
1	0.0397	155	4.092	13.690	1.1599	3359.38	982.49
2	0.0381	154	4.102	13.701	1.1629	3359.26	982.98
3	0.0291	151	4.156	13.862	1.187	3341.51	985.66
4	0.0107	144	4.266	14.189	1.238	3307.24	991.54
5	0.0019	141	4.320	14.345	1.263	3291.34	999.50

Table 4 Effect of learning rate on the parameter $p_b, M, Q, C_b, [TP_s^c]$ and $[TP_b^c]$ in fuzzy environment ($A_b = 40, A_s = 50$, learning rate $b = 1.8$)

No. of shipment n	Defective percent in per lot $p(n)$	Order quantity $y(n)$	Selling price of the seller C_b	Selling price of the buyer p_b	Marketing expenditure M	Fuzzy buyer profit $[TP_b^c]$	Fuzzy seller profit $[TP_s^c]$
1	0.0397	461	2.895	9.392	0.796	4032.22	995.93
2	0.0381	460	2.896	9.389	0.797	4033.65	996.61
3	0.0291	457	2.897	9.381	0.804	4041.14	999.90
4	0.0107	450	2.900	9.365	0.817	4056.36	1006.41
5	0.0019	446	2.902	9.357	0.824	4063.70	1009.72

Table 5 Effect of learning rate on the parameter $p_b, M, Q, C_b, [TP_s^c]$ and $[TP_b^c]$ in fuzzy environment ($A_b = 50, A_s = 60$, learning rate $b = 1.8$)

No. of shipment n	Defective percent in per lot $p(n)$	Order quantity $y(n)$	Selling price of the seller C_b	Selling price of the buyer p_b	Marketing expenditure M	Fuzzy buyer profit $[TP_b^c]$	Fuzzy seller profit $[TP_s^c]$
1	0.0397	173	4.092	13.768	1.166	3335.32	960.14
2	0.0381	172	4.102	13.801	1.171	3331.97	960.60
3	0.0291	168	4.156	13.965	1.196	3314.41	963.13
4	0.0107	160	4.265	14.295	1.247	3280.54	968.70
5	0.0019	156	4.319	14.455	1.273	4264.76	971.59

Table 6 Effect of learning rate on the parameter $p_b, M, Q, C_b, [TP_s^c]$ and $[TP_b^c]$ in fuzzy environment ($A_b = 50, A_s = 60$, learning rate $b = 1.8$)

No. of shipment n	Defective percent in per lot $p(n)$	Order quantity $y(n)$	Selling price of the seller C_b	Selling price of the buyer p_b	Marketing expenditure M	Fuzzy buyer profit $[TP_b^c]$	Fuzzy seller profit $[TP_s^c]$
1	0.0397	504	2.914	9.493	0.804	3982.57	985.96
2	0.0381	503	2.915	9.491	0.806	3983.98	986.62
3	0.0291	500	2.916	9.483	0.812	3991.38	989.74
4	0.0107	492	2.920	9.466	0.826	4006.41	996.46
5	0.0019	488	2.921	9.458	0.833	4013.67	999.69

Table 7 Effect of learning rate on the parameter p_b, M, Q, C_b, $[TP_s^c]$ and $[TP_b^c]$ in fuzzy environment ($A_b = 60$, $A_s = 70$, learning rate $b = 1.8$)

No. of shipment n	Defective percent in per lot $p(n)$	Order quantity $y(n)$	Selling price of the seller C_b	Selling price of the buyer p_b	Marketing expenditure M	Fuzzy buyer profit $[TP_b^c]$	Fuzzy seller profit $[TP_s^c]$
1	0.0397	188	4.093	13.868	1.175	3310.39	939.63
2	0.0381	187	4.103	13.900	1.179	3307.05	940.07
3	0.0291	182	4.156	14.068	1.205	3289.78	942.46
4	0.0107	174	4.265	14.368	1.254	3260.09	947.75
5	0.0019	170	4.318	14.553	1.281	3240.75	950.49

Table 8 Effect of learning rate on the parameter p_b, M, Q, C_b, $[TP_s^c]$ and $[TP_b^c]$ in fuzzy environment ($A_b = 60$, $A_s = 70$, learning rate $b = 1.8$)

No. of shipment n	Defective percent in per lot $p(n)$	Order quantity $y(n)$	Selling price of the seller C_b	Selling price of the buyer p_b	Marketing expenditure M	Fuzzy buyer profit $[TP_b^c]$	Fuzzy seller profit $[TP_s^c]$
1	0.0397	543	2.932	9.587	0.812	3937.22	976.85
2	0.0381	542	2.932	9.585	0.816	3938.61	977.61
3	0.0291	538	2.934	9.577	0.820	3945.92	980.74
4	0.0107	529	2.938	9.559	0.834	3960.78	987.73
5	0.0019	525	2.940	9.552	0.841	3967.95	990.81

Fuzzy Seller-Stackelberg

See Table 7.

Fuzzy Buyer-Stackelberg

See Table 8.

7 Observations

Following are the observations

(a) Results indicate from example 1 and example 2 that both the players are better off when they are leader and they got less profit when they are follower.
(b) Numerical example shows that seller profit and buyer profit obtained in seller-Stackelberg model and buyer-Stackelberg model are more as compared to obtained in fuzzy Stackelberg model.

(c) Figure 3 concludes that as number of shipments increases with a given learning rate at $b = 1.8$, buyer profit decreases in seller-Stackelberg model, whereas, Fig. 3 illustrates that buyer profit and seller profit increase as number of shipments increases with same learning rate in buyer-Stackelberg model.
(d) Data from Table 3 designate that seller-Stackelberg model under fuzzy environment as shipment increases in numbers, the buyer's profit decreases whereas seller's profit increases. This means that seller get benefitted in case of headship position.
(e) Data from Table 4 indicate that in buyer-Stackelberg model under fuzzy environment as shipment increases in numbers, the buyer's profit and seller's profit increases. This means both the players get benefitted in fuzzy environment.

8 Conclusions

Two-level supply chain models have been established for imperfect quality items under fuzzy environment with learning effect environment The effect of learning and fuzziness is shown on the players' optimal policies. Buyer's price, marketing expenditure cost, and order quantity and corresponding profit of players of supply chain are optimized. The learning impact on the calculation of gains or losses of the supply chain has been shown in the sensitivity analysis and numerical example. Results show that due to learning effect, buyer's gain is more than the seller in both the model. Both the players get benefitted in case of leadership position. It is shown from the result that seller's profit and buyer's profit obtained in mathematical crisp model is more that obtained in fuzzy model. A future extension to present model can be assume a stochastic learning curve instead of deterministic. This model can be extended by considering the idea of shortages and trade credit period.

References

Abad, P. L., & Jaggi, C. K. (2003). A joint approach for setting unit price and the length of the credit period for a seller when end demand is price sensitive. *International Journal of Production Economics, 83*, 115–122.

Anzanello, M. J., & Fogliatto, F. S. (2011). Learning curve models and applications: Literature review and research directions. *International Journal of Industrial Ergonomics, 41*, 573–583.

Argote, L., Beckman, S. L., & Eppe, D. (1990). The persistence and transfer of learning in industrial settings. *Management Science, 36*, 140–154.

Baloff, N. (1966). The learning curve: Some controversial issues. *Journal of Industrial Economics, 14*, 275–282.

Chavoshlou, A. S., Khamseh, A. A., & Naderi, B. (2019). An optimization model of three-player payoff based on fuzzy game theory in green supply chain. *Computers & Industrial Engineering, 128*, 782–794.

Cunningham, J. A. (1980). Management: Using the learning curve as a management tool: The learning curve can help in preparing cost reduction programs, pricing forecasts, and product development goals. *IEEE Spectrum, 17*, 45–48.

Eroglu, A., & Ozdemr, G. (2007). An economic order quantity model with defective items and shortages. *International Journal of Production Economics, 106*, 544–549.

Esmaeili, M., Abad, P. L., & Aryanezhad, M. B. (2009). Seller-buyer relationship when end demand is sensitive to price and promotion. *Asia-Pacific Journal of Operational Research, 26*, 605–621.

Jaber, M. Y., & Bonney, M. (1996). Production breaks and the learning curve: The forgetting phenomenon. *Applied Mathematical Modelling, 2*, 162–169.

Jaber, M. Y., & Bonney, M. (2003). Lot sizing with learning and forgetting inset-ups and in product quality. *International Journal of Production Economics, 83*, 95–111.

Jaber, M. Y., Givi, Z. S., & Neumann, W. P. (2013). Incorporating human fatigue and recovery into the learning–forgetting process. *Applied Mathematical Modelling, 37*, 7287–7299.

Jaber, M. Y., Goyal, S. K., & Imran, M. (2008). Economic production quantity model for items with imperfect quality subject to learning effects. *International Journal of Production Economics, 115*, 143–150.

Jayaswal, M. K., Sangal, I., Mittal, M., & Malik, S. (2019). Effects of learning on retailer ordering policy for imperfect quality items with trade credit financing. *Uncertain Supply Chain Management, 7*, 49–62.

Khan, M., Jaber, M. Y., & Wahab, M. I. M. (2010). Economic order quantity model for items with imperfect quality with learning in inspection. *International Journal of Production Economics, 124*, 87–96.

Konstantaras, I., Skouri, K., & Jaber, M. Y. (2012). Inventory models for imperfect quality items with shortages and learning in inspection. *Applied Mathematical Modelling, 36*, 5334–5343.

Mittal, M., Khanna, A., & Jaggi, C. K. (2017). Retailer's ordering policy for deteriorating imperfect quality items when demand and price are time-dependent under inflationary conditions and permissible delay in payments. International Journal of Procurement Management, 10(4), 461–494. https://doi.org/10.1504/IJPM.2017.085037

Patro, R., Acharya, M., Nayak, M. M., & Patnaik, S. (2017). A fuzzy imperfect quality inventory model with proportionate discount under learning effect. *International Journal of Intelligent Enterprise, 4*, 303–327.

Salameh, M. K., Abdul-Malak, M. A. U., & Jaber, M. Y. (1993). Mathematical modelling of the effect of human learning in the finite production inventory model. *Applied Mathematical Modelling, 17*, 613–615.

Salameh, M. K., & Jaber, M. Y. (2000). Economic production quantity model for items with imperfect quality. *International Journal of Production Economics, 64*, 59–64.

Soleimani, F. (2016). Optimal pricing decisions in a fuzzy dual-channel supply chain. *Soft Computing, 20*, 689–696.

Wei, J., & Zhao, J. (2013). Reverse channel decisions for a fuzzy closed-loop supply chain. *Applied Mathematical Modelling, 37*, 1502–1513.

Wright, T. P. (1936). Factors affecting the cost of airplanes. *Journal of the Aeronautical Sciences, 3*, 122–128.

Yadav, R., Mahesh, K. J., Mittal, M., Pareek, S., & Sangal, S. (2020). A game theoretic approach: Impact of learning on the optimal ordering policies for imperfect quality items. *Revista Investigacion Operacional, 41*, 200–213.

Yadav, R., Pareek, S., & Mittal, M. (2018). Supply chain models with imperfect quality items when end demand is sensitive to price and marketing expenditure. *International Journal RAIRO-Operations Research, 52*, 725–742.

An Analytic and Genetic Algorithm Approach to Optimize Integrated Production-Inventory Model Under Time-Varying Demand

Isha Talati, Poonam Mishra, and Azharuddin Shaikh

Abstract This paper addresses the cost minimization problem of an integrated production-inventory model which has optimized by analytical method and evolutionary algorithm. We have formulated our model for items that deteriorate with respect to time and follow Weibull distribution. For controlling deterioration rate, we have used preservation technology. Further, we assumed that ordering cost is lot size dependent. Classical optimization methods demonstrate a number of difficulties when faced with complex problems. Moreover, most of the classical optimization methods do not have the global perspective and often get converged to a locally optimum solution. Genetic algorithm (GA) is an adaptive heuristic search algorithm based on the evolutionary ideas of natural selection and genetics. In this model, we optimized our model by gradient-based analytical method and GA in integrated as well as independent scenario. Numerical example is carried out. Sensitivity of different inventory parameters is carried out. The results of the proposed model help researchers to think about optimizing their complex problems using different evolutionary search algorithm.

Keywords Integrated inventory · Weibull distribution · Time-dependent demand · Genetic algorithm · Lot size-dependent ordering cost · Preservation technology

MSC 90B05 · 90B85 · 90C26

I. Talati (✉)
Department of Engineering and Physical Sciences, Institute of Advanced Research, Koba Institutional Area, Gandhinagar 382426, India

P. Mishra
Department of Mathematics, School of Technology, Pandit Deendayal Petroleum University, Raisan, Gandhinagar 382007, India

A. Shaikh
Institute of Management, Nirma University, Sarkhej-Gandhinagar Highway, Ahmedabad 382481, India

N. H. Shah and M. Mittal (eds.), *Soft Computing in Inventory Management*, Inventory Optimization, https://doi.org/10.1007/978-981-16-2156-7_8

1 Introduction

For survival and growth of business, proper coordination and communication among supply chain players place an important role in this competitive atmosphere. Firstly, Goyal (1976) formulated an integrated model for single supplier and single customers. Banerjee (1986) made an appropriate price adjustment and obtained joint order so that it is beneficial to both parties. Chung and CÃardenas-BarrÃşn (2013) generated model for deteriorating items for stock dependent demand with two-level trade credits. Chung et al. (2014) extended previous model for exponentially deteriorating items. Shah (2015) derived model with two-level trade credits for items deteriorate constantly. Further, Shah et al. (2015) extended this model by taking price sensitive and time-dependent demand.

Most of the inventory researchers have used constant rate demand. But in the real world, demand is not always constant. It may vary with time. Donaldson (1977) obtained the fundamental result in EOQ model with time-varying linear demand over a known and finite time horizon. Dave and Patel (1981) extended model for deteriorating items. Further, Wee and Wang (1999) considered time varying demand and developed a variable production policy. Mishra and Singh (2011) had taken into account time-dependent holding cost and formulated an inventory model under shortages. Mishra (2013) extended model for time-varying deterioration.

Deterioration is the process in which the items loses its utility and become useless. In classical EOQ model, researcher considered inventory depletes due to demand only. But in the real world, inventory is not only reduce due to demand but also reduced due to deterioration. In earlier literature, Ghare and Schrader (1963) developed model for items those deteriorates exponential. Firstly, Philip and Covert (1973) formulated model for time-dependent deteriorating items which follow Weibill distribution. Further, Philip (1974) generalized this model. Manna and Chaudhuri (2001) derived inventory model under shortages for time-dependent deteriorating items. Bakker et al. (2012) gave up to date review of inventory models for deteriorating items. To reduce deterioration rate, different researcher used preservation technology. Mishra (2013) used preservation technology for time-dependent deteriorating items that follow Weibull Distribution. Chang (2013) used preservation technology for non-instantaneous deteriorating items. Singh and Rathore (2015) extended that model under shortages. Mishra and Talati (2018) derived integrated inventory model and used preservation technology under quantity discount scenario. Mahapatra et al. (2019) formulated inventory model for deteriorating items under fuzzy environment.

In last decades, to optimize the inventory models, researchers used different heuristic search algorithms like ant colony, swarm intelligence and genetic algorithm. Genetic algorithm describes a set of techniques inspired by natural selection like inheritance, mutation, selection and crossover. This technique requires fitness function and genetic representation of solution domain. In each generation, it uses fitness function to select global optimum. This process terminates when the satisfactory fitness level has been reached. Goldberg (1989) used GA for optimization. Then, different researchers like Murata et al. (1996), Goren et al. (2008), Radhakrishnan et al. (2009, 2010), Narmadha et al. (2010), Woarawichai et al. (2012), Mishra and Talati (2015), Talati and Mishra (2019), Alejo-Reyes et al. (2021) used heuristic search algorithm for optimized their models.

2 Notations and Assumptions

2.1 Notations

2.1.1 Inventory Parameters for Manufacturer

$D(t)$	Time-dependent demand
P	Production rate
a	Fix fraction of demand
γ	Salvage cost/unit ($)
h_m	Holding cost/unit/annum
A_m	Set-up costs ($)
TC_m	Total cost for manufacturer
T	The length of cycle time (Decision variable)
b_1	Deteriorating cost/unit ($)
Q_m	Inventory level for manufacturer
ξ_1	Preservation technology cost for manufacturer that reduce deterioration rate in order to preserve the product $\xi_1 > 0$
$\theta(t)$	Deterioration rate at t, where $\theta(t) = \alpha\beta t^{\beta}$
m	Reduce deteriorating rate
τ_P	Resultant deterioration rate $\tau_P = \theta(t) - m$

2.1.2 Inventory Parameters for Retailer

Q_r	Retailer's order
$C_0 Q_r^{\eta}$	Ordering Cost/cycle $(0 < \eta < 1)$
C_0	Fixed ordering cost, η (Decision variable)
ξ_2	Preservation technology cost for manufacturer that reduce deterioration rate in order to preserve the product $\xi_2 > 0$
γ	Salvage value associated with deteriorated items
TC_r	Total cost for retailer

2.2 Assumptions

1. In present model, we have considered two-echelon supply chain model (single manufacturer and single retailer) for single item.
2. Demand is time dependent $D(t) = a + bt; a, b > 0$.
3. Replenishment rate is infinite.
4. Lead time is zero.
5. Shortages are not allowed.
6. Constant production rate is considered. $P > D(t)$.
7. Ordering cost is lot size dependent.
8. The inventory deteriorate with respect to time and follow Weibull distribution $\theta(t) = \alpha\beta t^{\beta}$
   where α is shape parameter $0 < \alpha < 1$, and β is scale parameter $\beta \geq 1$.
9. Preservation technologies are used for reducing the deterioration rate.
10. The salvage value $\gamma, 0 \leq \gamma \leq 1$ is associated to deteriorated units.

3 Model Formulation

3.1 Manufacturer's Total Cost

Here, we considered production dominates demand. Due to preservation technology, the rate of change of inventory during period [0,T] is shown in Fig. 1.

Thus, the on-hand inventory for manufacturer is generated by the following differential equation

$$\frac{\mathrm{d}Q_{\mathrm{m}}}{\mathrm{d}t} + \tau_{\mathrm{P}} Q_{\mathrm{m}} = P - D(t); \quad 0 \leq t \leq T \tag{1}$$

Solving Eq. (1) using boundary condition $Q_{\mathrm{m}}(0) = 0$ and $Q_{\mathrm{m}}(T) = Q_{\mathrm{m}}$

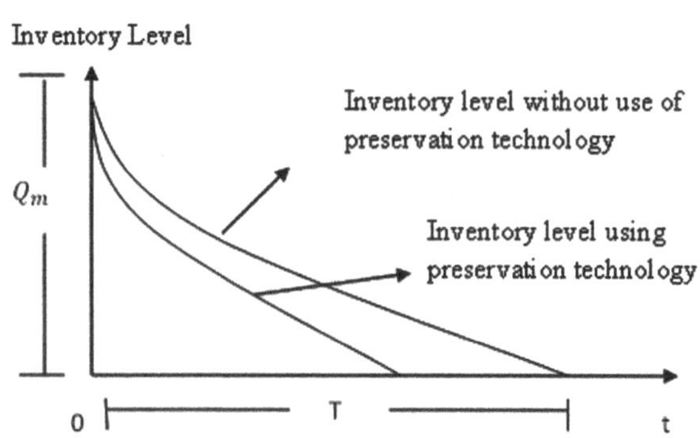

Fig. 1 Inventory level for manufacturer. *Source* own

$$Q_m(t) = \left((P-a)t\left(1+\frac{\alpha t^\beta}{\beta+1}\right) - (Pm+b-ma)t^2\left(\frac{1}{2}+\frac{\alpha t^\beta}{\beta+2}\right) - mbt^3\left(\frac{1}{3}+\frac{\alpha t^\beta}{\beta+3}\right)\right)(1-\alpha t^\beta + mt - m\alpha t^{\beta+1})$$

So total quantity by manufacturer per cycle is $Q_m(T) = Q_m$.

Basic Costs

1. Set-up cost

$$SC_m = A_m \tag{2}$$

2. Inventory holding cost per unit is given by

$$HC_m = h_m \int_0^T Q_m(t)\,dt \tag{3}$$

3. Now number of deteriorating units during cycle time T

$$DE_1(T) = Q_m - aT - \frac{(bT^2)}{2} \tag{4}$$

4. Deteriorating cost is given by

$$DC_m = b_1 DE_1(T) \tag{5}$$

5. Salvage value is given by

$$SV_m = \gamma DE_1(T) \tag{6}$$

6. Preservation cost is given by

$$PC_m = \xi_1 \tag{7}$$

Thus, the total cost of manufacturer is

$$TC_m(T) = SC_m + HC_m + DC_m - SV_m + PC_m \tag{8}$$

3.2 *Retailer's Total Cost*

Retailer's on-hand inventory depletes with time-dependent demand and deterioration under preservation technology. The rate of change of inventory level due to preservation technology is shown in Fig. 2. So the governing differential equation describes the inventory level at instantaneous time t which is given by

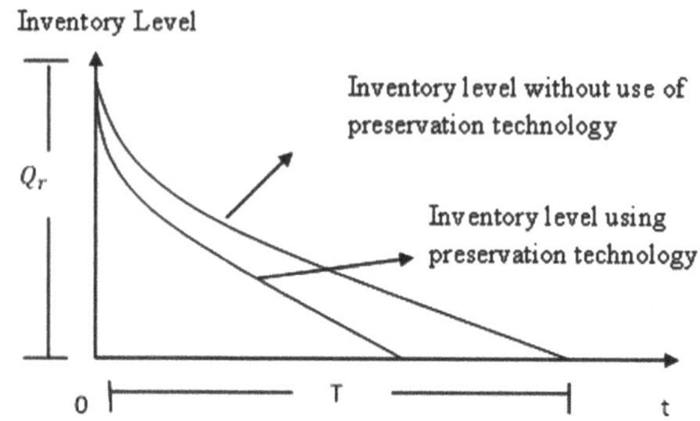

Fig. 2 Inventory level for retailer. *Source* own

$$\frac{dQ_r}{dt} + \tau_P Q_r = -D(t); \quad 0 \le t \le T \tag{9}$$

Solving Eq. (9) using boundary condition $Q_r(T) = 0$ and $Q_m(0) = Q_r$, we get

$$\begin{aligned} Q_r(t) = &\Big[a(T-t) + \frac{b}{2}(T^2 - t^2) + \frac{\alpha a}{\beta+1}(T^{\beta+2} - t^{\beta+2}) - \frac{ma}{2}(T^2 - t^2) \\ &- \frac{mb}{3}(T^3 - t^3) - \frac{\alpha a}{\beta+2}(T^{\beta+2} - t^{\beta+2}) - \frac{m\alpha b}{\beta+3}(T^{\beta+3} - t^{\beta+3})\Big] \\ &[1 - \alpha t^\beta + mt - m\alpha t^{\beta+1}] \end{aligned} \tag{10}$$

∴ Total quantity purchase by retailer per cycle is

$$\begin{aligned} Q_r = Q_r(0) = &\Big[a(T) + \frac{b}{2}(T^2) + \frac{\alpha a}{\beta+1}(T^{\beta+2}) - \frac{ma}{2}(T^2) - \frac{mb}{3}(T^3) \\ &- \frac{\alpha a}{\beta+2}(T^{\beta+2}) - \frac{m\alpha b}{\beta+3}(T^{\beta+3})\Big] \end{aligned} \tag{11}$$

Basic costs associated with retailer total cost are

1. Ordering cost is lot size dependent

$$OC_r = C_0 Q_r^\eta \tag{12}$$

2. Holding cost per unit is given by

$$HC_r = h_r \int_0^T Q_r(t)dt \tag{13}$$

3. Total number of deteriorating units during cycle time T

$$\mathrm{DE}_2(T) = Q_\mathrm{r} - aT - \frac{(bT^2)}{2} \tag{14}$$

4. The deteriorating cost per time unit is

$$\mathrm{DC}_\mathrm{r} = b_1 \mathrm{DE}_2(T) \tag{15}$$

5. Salvage value per time unit is

$$\mathrm{SV}_\mathrm{r} = \gamma \mathrm{DE}_2(T) \tag{16}$$

6. Preservation cost is given by

$$\mathrm{PC}_\mathrm{r} = \xi_2 \tag{17}$$

The total cost for retailer is by

$$\mathrm{TC}_\mathrm{r} = \mathrm{OC}_\mathrm{r} + \mathrm{HC}_\mathrm{r} + \mathrm{DC}_\mathrm{r} + \mathrm{PC}_\mathrm{r} - \mathrm{SV}_\mathrm{r} \tag{18}$$

3.3 *Joint Total Cost*

Total cost for the inventory system is

$$\mathrm{TC} = \mathrm{TC}_\mathrm{m} + \mathrm{TC}_\mathrm{r} \tag{19}$$

4 Computational Algorithm

4.1 *Analytical Approach*

- Set all parameters value in the mathematical model except decision variables.
- Find optimum T using TC_m.
- Used optimal T and Q_m to find total cost for manufacturer.
- Optimized T and η simultaneously from TC_r.
- Used optimal T, η and Q_r and obtain total cost for retailer.
- Find optimal T and η from system total cost.
- Used optimal T, η and optimal quantity and calculate total system cost.

4.2 Genetic Algorithm Approach

- Set all parameters value in the fitness function except decision variables.
- Start G.A. with an initial population of 20 chromosomes.
- On the basis of their fitness score rank the chromosomes.
- Chromosomes with good fitness score will enter in mating pool.
- Perform stochastic uniform crossover for reproduction. We have considered crossover fraction is 0.8 and each generation is 2-Elites.
- On the basis of their fitness value, rank all members and select members for new generation.
- Perform step (iii) and step (iv) till absolute difference between two successive members is 10^{-5}.

5 Numerical Example and Sensitivity Analysis

5.1 Numerical Example

Consider one integrated production-inventory system with $P = 500,\ a = 400,\ m = 0.5, b = 2,\ \alpha = 0.5,\ \beta = 2,\ h_{\mathrm{m}} = 0.2,\ \xi_1 = 500\$,\ \xi_2 = 500\$,\ h_{\mathrm{r}} = 0.2,\ C_0 = 2000,\ A_{\mathrm{m}} = 2000.$
We have optimized this using analytical method by MAPLE18; we get some computational results those are shown in Table 1.

Here, in independent decision, the convexity of the function is given below
For manufacturer

$$\frac{\mathrm{d}^2\mathrm{TC}_{\mathrm{m}}}{\mathrm{d}T^2}|_{(T=T^*)} = 2808.527238 \geq 0$$

Table 1 Computational results obtained by analytical approach

Optimal	Independent scenario	Integrated scenario
Cycle time (year)	0.02501172258	0.02501546196
η	0.08506027179	0.03756340374
Lot size	25	25
Total cost	Independent scenario	Integrated scenario
Manufacturer ($)	1972.520628	1499.249742
Retailer ($)	2499.997751	2400.999625
System ($)	4471.518379	3900.24567

Source own

Table 2 Computational results obtained by using genetic algorithm

	Independent scenario	Integrated scenario
Iterations	51 and 190	84
Optimal	Independent scenario	Integrated scenario
Cycle time (year)	0.02	0.02
η	0.05	0.05
Lot size	32	34
Total cost	Independent scenario	Integrated scenario
Manufacturer ($)	1963.6	1452.21
Retailer ($)	2288.41	1241.23
System ($)	3952.01	2893.44

Source own

For retailer

$$\begin{vmatrix} \frac{\partial^2 \mathrm{TC_r}}{\partial \eta^2} & \frac{\partial^2 \mathrm{TC_r}}{\partial \eta \partial T} \\ \frac{\partial^2 \mathrm{TC_r}}{\partial \eta \partial T} & \frac{\partial^2 \mathrm{TC_r}}{\partial T^2} \end{vmatrix} = 5.545177044479552 \times 10^2 > 0$$

and

$$\frac{\partial^2 \mathrm{TC_r}}{\partial T^2} = 8.256 \times 10^2 \geq 0$$

For integrated

$$\begin{vmatrix} \frac{\partial^2 \mathrm{TC_r}}{\partial \eta^2} & \frac{\partial^2 \mathrm{TC_r}}{\partial \eta \partial T} \\ \frac{\partial^2 \mathrm{TC_r}}{\partial \eta \partial T} & \frac{\partial^2 \mathrm{TC_r}}{\partial T^2} \end{vmatrix} = 5.26352 \times 10^2 > 0$$

and

$$\frac{\partial^2 \mathrm{TC_r}}{\partial T^2} = 0.8039621 \times 10^3 \geq 0$$

Above example is also optimized by genetic algorithm using MATLAB16a. Computational results obtain by genetic algorithm are shown in Table 2. For independent decision, genetic algorithm took 51 for manufacturer, 190 for retailer and 84 for integrated system. Best fitness plot of manufacturer, retailer and the system is shown in Figs. 3, 4 and 5, respectively.

The sensitivity analysis for the above example is carried out to check the behaviour of inventory and supply chain parameters related to total cost in joint decision by varying inventory parameters as −20, −10, 10 and 20%. The computational results is shown in Table 3.

The results obtained in Table 3 can be summarized as follows:

- As inventory parameters $a,\ b,\ \alpha,\ h_{\mathrm{m}}$ increase, integrated total cost decreases.
- As inventory parameters $m,\ \beta,\ h_{\mathrm{r}}$ increase, integrated total cost increases.

Table 3 Sensitivity analysis for inventory and supply chain parameters

Parameters	Change	Generations	Integrated total cost
	−20%	80	2893.4422220173033
	−10%	80	2893.440313935822
a	0	51	2893.4402274468635
	10%	75	2893.44014557451607
	20%	51	2893.4400680390536
	−20%	108	2893.3983955247295
	−10%	149	2893.4191946532046
m	0	51	2893.4401874468635
	10%	51	2893.4623950272157
	20%	89	2893.4846156768504
	−20%	86	2893.449783693166
	−10%	76	2893.4425591065487
b	0	51	2893.4401874468635
	10%	138	2893.439330496022
	20%	135	2893.4398683311897
	−20%	120	2893.4448207696682
	−10%	51	2893.442330496022
α	0	51	2893.4401874468635
	10%	58	2893.44006788676355
	20%	167	2893.44002539623709
	−20%	75	2893.4341786444675
	−10%	74	2893.4388061031786
β	0	51	2893.4401874468635
	10%	90	2893.440616458528
	20%	79	2893.4407451316824
	−20%	117	2893.4431508922
	−10%	51	2893.4407278538433
h_{m}	0	51	2893.4401874468635
	10%	72	2893.44002016096947
	20%	74	2893.4402023774837
	−20%	51	2893.4401554573037
	−10%	114	2893.44016537294647
h_{r}	0	51	2893.4401874468635
	10%	112	2893.4402036655782
	20%	51	2893.4402194364234

Source own

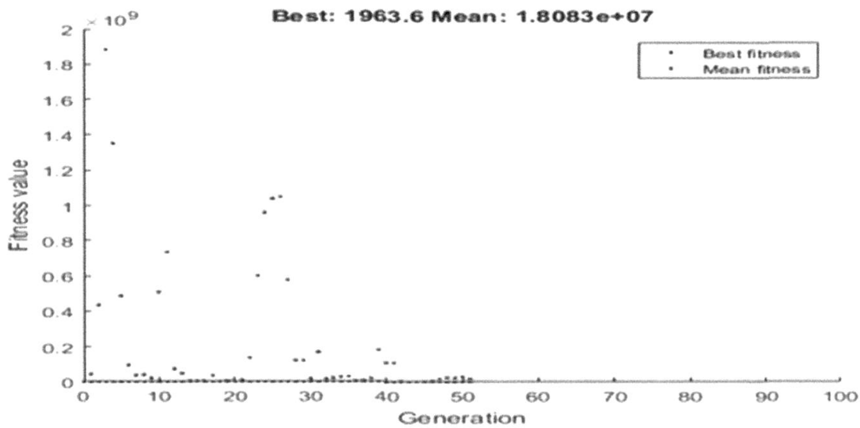

Fig. 3 Best fitness solution for manufacturer total cost. *Source* own

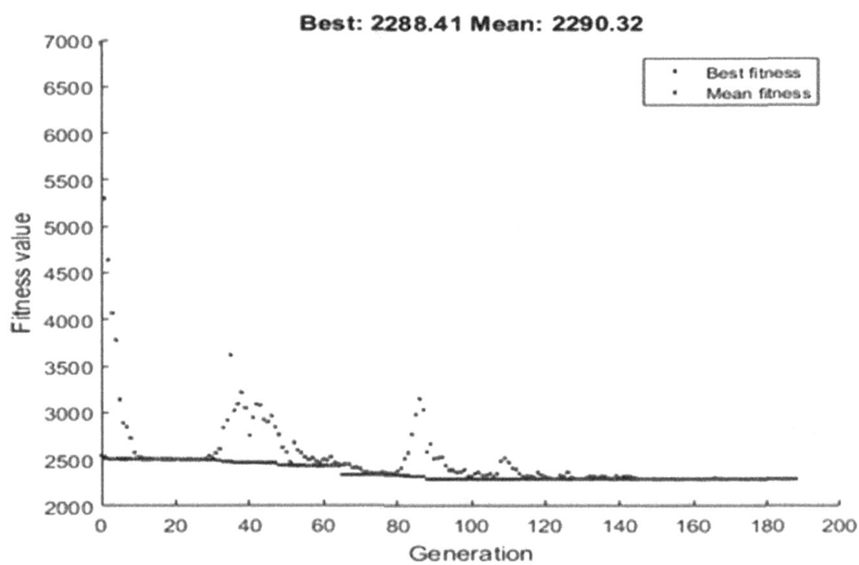

Fig. 4 Best fitness solution for retailer total cost. *Source* own

6 Conclusion

Supply chain management has required models and processes which can find a solution in a fast and efficient way. For comparison purposes, we have found a solution for the same numerical example using gradient-based analytical method and genetic algorithm. Complexity is explained mathematically for analytical techniques and graphically for genetic algorithms. It is shown that the decision taken in an integrated scenario reduces the cost compared to the decision in an isolated scenario

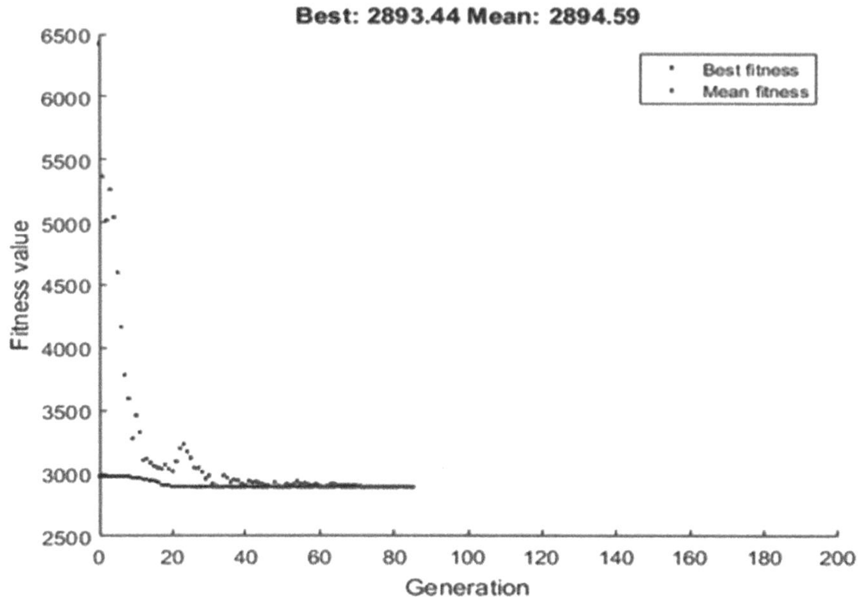

Fig. 5 Best fitness solution for system. *Source* own

in both techniques. Results clearly show that in our model, evolutionary algorithm provides global minimum while the analytical method fails. Future research may be extended into more realistic situations like shortages, random demand and inflation. Additionally, genetic algorithms can be modified to find solutions in a very efficient manner.

References

Alejo-Reyes, A., Mendoza, A., & Olivares-Benitez, E. (2021). A heuristic method for the supplier selection and order quantity allocation problem. *Applied Mathematical Modelling*, *90*, 1130–1142.

Bakker, M., Reizebos, J., & Teunter, R. H. (2012). Review of inventory system with deterioration since 2001. *European Journal of Operational Research*, *221*(2), 275–284.

Banerjee, A. (1986). A joint economic-lot-size model for purchaser and vendor. *Decision Sciences*, *17*(3), 292–311.

Chang, Y. (2013). The effect of preservation technology investment on a non instantaneous deteriorating inventory model. *Omega*, *41*, 872–880.

Chung, K. J., & Cardenas-Barron, L. E. (2013). The simplified solution procedure for deteriorating items under stock-dependent demand and two-level trade-credit in the supply chain management. *Applied Mathematical Modelling*, *37*(7), 4653–4660.

Chung, K. J., Cardenas-Barron, L. E., & Ting, P. S. (2014). An inventory model with non-instantaneous receipt and exponentially deteriorating items for an integrated three layer supply chain system under two levels of trade credit. *International Journal of Production Economics*, *155*, 310–317.

Dave, U., & Patel, L. K. (1981). (T, Si) policy inventory model for deteriorating items with time proposal demand. *Journal of Operational Research Society*, *32*, 137–142.
Donaldson, W. A. (1977). Inventory replenishment policy for a linear trend in demand—An analytical solution. *Operation Research Quarterly*, *28*(3), 663–670.
Ghare, P. M., & Schrader, G. P. (1963). A model for an exponentially decaying inventory. *Journal of Industrial Engineering*, *14*(5), 238–243.
Goldberg, D. E. (1989). *Genetic algorithms in search, optimization and machine learning*. Addison-Wesley.
Goren, G. H., Tunali, S., & Jans, R. (2008). A review of applications of genetic algorithms in lot sizing. *Journal of Intelligent Manufacturing*.
Goyal, S. K. (1976). An integrated inventory model for a single supplier-single customer problem. *International Journal of Production Research*, *15*(1), 107–111.
Mahapatra, A. S., Sarkar, B., Mahapatra, M. S., Soni, H. N., & Mazumder, S. K. (2019). Development of a fuzzy economic order quantity model of deteriorating items with promotional effort and learning in fuzziness with a finite time horizon. *Inventions*, *4*, 36.
Manna, S. K., & Chaudhuri, K. S. (2001). An economic order quantity model for deteriorating items with time-dependent deterioration rate, demand rate, unit production cost and shortages. *International Journal of Production Research*, *32*(8), 1003–1009.
Mishra, P., & Talati, I. (2015). A genetic algorithm approach for an inventory model when ordering cost is lot size dependent. *International Journal of Latest Technology in Engineering, Management & Applied Science*, *4*(2), 92–97.
Mishra, P., & Talati, I. (2018). Quantity discount for integrated supply chain model with back order and controllable deterioration rate. *Yogoslav Journal of Operation Research*, *28*(3), 355–369.
Mishra, V. K. (2013). Deteriorating inventory model using preservation technology with salvage value and shortages. *APEM Journal*, *8*(3), 185–192.
Mishra, V. K., & Singh, L. S. (2011). Deteriorating inventory model for time dependent demand and holding cost with partial backlogging. *International Journal of Management Science and Engineering Management*, *6*(4), 267–271.
Mishra, V. K., Singh, L. S., & Kumar, R. (2013). An inventory model for deteriorating items with time dependent demand and time varying holding cost under partial backlogging. *International Journal of Industrial Engineering*, *9*(4), 1–5.
Murata, T., Ishibuchi, H., & Tanaka, H. (1996). Multi objective algorithm and its applications to flow shop scheduling. *Computers & Industrial Engineering*, *30*(4), 954–968.
Narmadha, S., Selladurai, V., & Sathish, G. (2010). Multiproduct inventory optimization using uniform crossover genetic algorithm. *IJCSIS*, *7*(1), 170–179.
Philip, G. C. (1974). A generalized EOQ model for items with Weibull distribution. *AIIE Transactions*, *6*(2), 159–162.
Philip, G. C., & Covert, R. P. (1973). An EOQ model for items with Weibull distribution deterioration. *AIIE Transactions*, *5*(4), 323–326.
Radhakrishnan, P., Prasad, V. M., & Jeyanthi, N. (2009). Inventory optimization in supply chain management using genetic algorithm. *International Journal of Computer Science and Network Security*, *9*(1), 33–40.
Radhakrishnan, P., Prasad, V. M., & Jeyanthi, N. (2010). Design of genetic algorithm based supply chain inventory optimization with lead time. *International Journal of Computer Science and Network Security*, *10*(3), 1820–1826.
Shah, N. H. (2015). Manufacturer-retailer inventory model for deteriorating items with price-sensitive credit-linked demand under two-level trade credit financing and profit sharing contract. *Cogent Engineering*, *2*(1).
Shah, N. H., Shah, D. B., & Patel, D. G. (2015). Optimal pricing and ordering policies for inventory system with two-level trade credits under price-sensitive trended demand. *International Journal of Applied and Computational Mathematics*, *1*(1), 101–110.
Singh, S., & Rathore, H. (2015). Optimal payment policy with preservation technology investment and shortages under trade credit. *Indian Journal of Science and Technology*, *8*(S7), 203–212.

Talati, I., & Mishra, P. (2019). Optimal production integrated inventory model with quadratic demand for deteriorating items under inflation using genetic algorithm. *Investigacion Operacional*, *40*(3).

Wee, H. M., & Wang, W. T. (1999). A variable production scheduling policy for deteriorating items with time varying demand. *Computers & Operations Research*, *26*(3), 237–254.

Woarawichai, C., Kuruvit, K., & Vashirawongpinyo, P. (2012). Applying genetic algorithms for inventory lot-sizing problem with supplier selection under storage capacity. *Constraints*, *9*(1), 18–23.

Sustainable Inventory Model with Carbon Emission Dependent Demand Under Different Carbon Emission Policies

Shikha Yadav, Farah Siddiqui, and Aditi Khanna

Abstract Sustainability issues, such as GHG discharges and harmful waste are admissible concerns in the world. Consumer consciousness towards the environment is an effective motivator for the firms to adopt various alternatives, e.g., swap gears, redesigning kits and transportation modes, and using environmentally friendly products to reduce carbon emissions. Moreover, the growing GHG emissions, influence the demand of eco-friendly products significantly, hence emission-sensitive demand is considered. The major sources of carbon emissions are transportation and inventory holding. Thus, the present research aims to contribute to the existing literature by developing a sustainable model with environmental sensitive demand under two different carbon policies—"Carbon tax and Cap-and-trade mechanism". The objective of the article is to optimize the order quantity by minimizing the annual cost and carbon emissions. Further, a comparative analysis of "carbon tax and cap-and-trade mechanism" has been established. Numerical examples and sensitivity analysis are performed to elucidate the model. Findings recommend that the "carbon cap-and-trade mechanism" is favorable for the decision-maker and also helps to mitigate the carbon discharges.

Keywords Carbon emission · Carbon emission dependent demand · Environmental regulations · Carbon tax · Cap-and-trade · Transportation

MSC 90B05 · 13P25 · 90B06

1 Introduction

Global warming caused by GHG emissions is becoming a worldwide concern at present. The worsening environment not only affected society badly but also has an intensive impact on environmental sustainability.

S. Yadav · F. Siddiqui · A. Khanna (✉)
Department of Operational Research, University of Delhi, Delhi 110007, India

N. H. Shah and M. Mittal (eds.), *Soft Computing in Inventory Management*, Inventory Optimization, https://doi.org/10.1007/978-981-16-2156-7_9

Developing an inventory system to relieve the environment from GHG emissions is an important concern in the present day. Generally, demand for the product is considered constant or a demand varies in terms of different parameters such as price, time, etc. but currently, the sustainability notion is quite matured. The eco-friendly products positively encourage the demand, further, due to growing GHG emissions, the demand is significantly affected by the carbon discharges, hence emission-sensitive demand is much more practical nowadays. Chen et al. (2013) studied a carbon-controlled EOQ model along with the constant demand. Hovelaque and Bironneau (2015) discussed an EOQ model with carbon reliant demand. Juxia (2016) proposed a price and emission-reliant supply chain model. Li (2016) explored the price and emission-sensitive model for the integrated scenario. Pang et al. (2018) studied the model which is reliant on carbon trading and customer receptiveness. Rani et al. (2019) discussed a model for a deteriorating item that is reliant on emissions. Tang et al. (2020) discussed a sustainable integrated model for transportation management under carbon policies.

Transportation is a significant source of GHG emissions. Transhipments of products may arise many environmental issues; e.g., air emissions, fuel consumption and depletion of natural resources, etc. To protect public health, efficient transportation arrangement has been taken into consideration to reduce transportation cost and environmental damages. Sarkar et al. (2016) studied the significance of flexible and static transhipment costs to mitigate emissions. Salehi et al. (2017) explored the green transportation scheduling with the trade-off amongst the transhipment and carbon discharges. Darma Wangsa and Wee (2018) proposed a collaborative study with stochastic demand. Mosca et al. (2019) reviewed the literature of integrated transportation inventory models and highlighted the research gaps with current and emerging industry practices. Hota et al. (2020) discussed the impact of flexible transportation on the supply chain.

As per global concern, sustainability has been fascinating the society to mitigate the ecological footprint. Government and non-governmental organizations have been introducing some policies, rules, and regulations to mitigate the impact of carbon discharges e.g., the development of renewable sources, encouraging the use of natural fuels, and eco-friendly objects. Two popular policies are "carbon taxes and carbon cap-and-trade" mechanism among the other carbon policies. Metcalf (2009) discussed the different market strategies to regulate carbon emanations. He et al. (2015) defined "Under the cap-and-trade mechanism, firms initially obtain a pre-determined amount of carbon allowances (carbon quotas) from the government agencies and the total carbon emissions generated at a certain period should be lower than the carbon quotas. Firms could buy/sell carbon allowances in the carbon trading market when they have lack/surplus allowances where allowance price is determined by the trading market". Singh and Weninger (2017) studied transaction charges and feature irreversibility under carbon trading mechanism. Wang et al. (2018) explored the firm's strategies to lessen the discharges under the cap-and-trade mechanism. Mishra et al. (2020a) discussed a waste control model for a sustainable supply chain.

Initially, the USA has executed a tax policy on carbon, Ghosh et al. (2018) defined "carbon tax" as a toll that imposes on carbon discharges; it is a form of carbon pricing. The returns made by the tax would then be applied to a payroll tax rebate of revenues to taxpayers. Datta (2017) addressed the impact of the carbon tax on a sustainable model. Ma et al. (2018) proposed the optimal pricing strategies on a model with tax. Halat and Hafezalkotob (2019) studied different carbon strategies for the multi-echelon model. Khanna and Yadav (2020) discussed the comparison amongst the carbon policies with price-sensitive demand on an inventory system. Mishra et al. (2020b) discussed a scenario to regulate the carbon discharges under different carbon policies. Yadav and Khanna (2021) proposed a sustainable inventory model for perishable products with expiration date under carbon tax policy. A carbon tax can reduce emissions very efficiently and effectively.

Research gap and our contribution

The notion of this study is to fulfill the gap by formulating a model that considers the impact of carbon emissions on inventory policy by taking environmentally sensitive demand under two different carbon policies. Due to the growing GHG emissions, the effect of carbon emissions on the demand is increasing significantly, hence firms have more focused and responsive towards the environmentally-friendly products which strongly influence their customers. Therefore, carbon emission-dependent demand is much more appropriate in this current scenario. Also, transportation cost is taken into consideration in terms of fixed and variable transportation cost. Further, while managing inventory systems it is accepted that carbon-emissions are caused due to transshipment and inventory holding. Thus, two diverse carbon policies i.e., "carbon-tax and cap-and-trade mechanism" has been implemented to support the environment in order to lessen the carbon discharges. The objective of the study is to minimize the annual cost by improving the optimal order quantity. The present research is organized in the given manner: Sect. 2 gives the notation and assumptions: Sect. 3 presents the mathematical model: Sect. 4 gives the solution procedure: numerical and sensitivity analysis has been illustrated by Sects. 5 and 6. Finally, Sect. 7 summarizes the conclusion and future directions.

2 Assumptions and Notations

Assumptions

1. The carbon emission dependent demand, $D(Q) = \alpha - \beta(\mathrm{CE}(Q))$. Here $\alpha > 0$ and $0 < \beta < 1$ is scale and shape parameter, and both are positive known constants.
2. Infinite time horizon with zero lead-time.
3. Emissions of carbon are caused due to transportation and inventory holding.
4. Transportation cost:
   $A_T = A_0 + A_1(Q)$
   where A_0 is a fixed cost and A_1 is a variable cost.
5. One type of transportation mode is used.

Notations

The notations that are used while modeling are listed in Table 1.

3 Mathematical Model

Due to the growing environmental concerns, environmental regulations have become more stringent by the governments, which motivates the firms to pay more attention towards sustainability. As consumer's awareness of the environment increases the demand for environmental friendly products has been raised significantly. Thus, the environmental sensitive demand has been taken into consideration to support sustainability positively. The motive of the article is to lessen the carbon emanations by implementing a "Carbon tax and Cap-and-trade mechanism". The vital elements of carbon emanations are transportation and inventory holding. Thus, the purpose of the models is to minimize the total cost so as to get the optimal order quantity.

Table 1 Notations

Symbol	Description
Decision variable	
Q	Order quantity in a cycle (units)
Parameters	
$D(Q)$	Carbon emission dependent demand (units/time)
K	Cost of ordering ($/order)
C	Purchase cost ($/unit)
h	Inventory carrying cost ($/unit)
A_0	Fixed transportation cost ($)
A_1	Variable transportation cost ($)
A_T	Transportation cost ($)
A_C	Carbon emission due to transportation (kg/unit)
h_C	Carbon emission due to inventory holding (kg/unit)
z	Emissions quota of carbon per unit time (kg)
C_P	Quota price of carbon ($/kg)
w	Tax charged on carbon ($/kg)
TC_1	Total cost per unit time with a "cap-and-trade" ($/time)
TC_2	Total cost per unit time with "carbon emissions tax" ($/time)

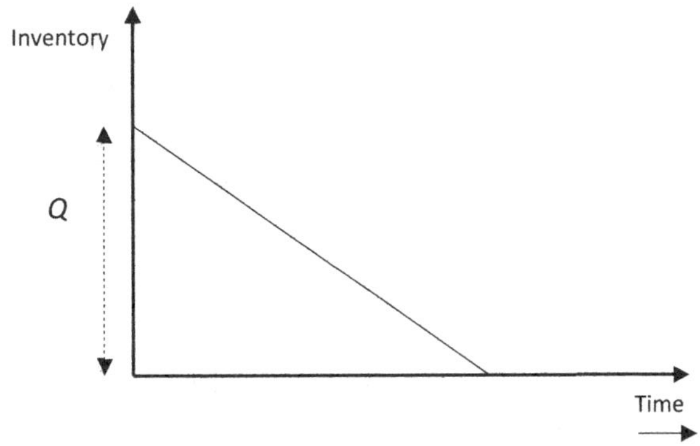

Fig. 1 Graphical representation of the inventory scenario

Using the given assumptions; The proposed scenario is depicted in Fig. 1. The cycle begins at time zero with inventory Q and reduces continuously due to demand. Finally, the inventory exhausts with time.

The carbon emission dependent demand *D(Q)*, is:

$$D(Q) = \alpha - \beta(\mathrm{CE}(Q)) \tag{1}$$

The carbon emission in transportation and inventory holding is as follows:

$$\mathrm{CE} = A_c\left(\frac{D}{Q}\right) + h_c\left(\frac{Q}{2}\right) \tag{2}$$

After using "Eq. (2)" in "Eq. (1)"

$$D(Q) = \left(\frac{Q * ((2 * \alpha) - (\beta * h_C * Q))}{2(Q + (\beta * A_C))}\right) \tag{3}$$

Ordering cost:

Within a certain time period, the retailer orders the new products with an ordering cost is:

$$\mathrm{OC} = K \tag{4}$$

Holding cost:

Proper storage of products is required to control their spoilage/deterioration. Thus the retailer incurs the inventory holding cost for the maintenance of products in stock. It is calculated for the proposed model as:

$$\mathrm{HC} = \left(h * \left(\frac{Q}{2}\right)\right) \tag{5}$$

Purchase cost:

The cost of the material depends on the order quantity purchased during the cycle and the per-unit cost of the material. The purchase cost is:

$$\mathrm{PC} = C \times Q \tag{6}$$

Transportation Cost:

The retailer incurs a transportation cost due to the delivery of goods. As both the quantity of the container and the distance is flexible so fixed and the variable transportation cost is taken. Thus, the cost is:

$$A_{\mathrm{T}} = A_0 + A_1(Q) \tag{7}$$

Due to the transportation and inventory holding carbon emissions are produced in the environment. A "carbon tax and carbon cap-and-trade" is levied on carbon emission in a form of carbon pricing so as to keep a check and control the carbon emanations.

Thus, "carbon emission cost under emission tax policy and the cap-and-trade mechanism" is given as:

Carbon emission cost in transportation and inventory holding under carbon tax is:

$$\mathrm{Tax}^{\mathrm{c}} = w(\mathrm{CE}) = w\left(A_{\mathrm{c}}\left(\frac{D}{Q}\right) + h_{\mathrm{c}}\left(\frac{Q}{2}\right)\right) \tag{8}$$

Carbon emission cost in transportation and inventory holding under cap-and-trade mechanism is:

$$\mathrm{Cap}^{\mathrm{c}} = C_{\mathrm{p}}(\mathrm{CE} - z) = C_{\mathrm{P}}\left(\left(A_{\mathrm{c}}\left(\frac{D}{Q}\right) + h_{\mathrm{c}}\left(\frac{Q}{2}\right)\right) - z\right) \tag{9}$$

Case 1. Cap-and-trade

"Total cost per unit time due to cap-and-trade is":

"Total cost = ordering cost + holding cost + purchase cost + transportation cost + cap-and-trade cost"

$$\begin{aligned}\mathrm{TC}_1(Q) = &\left(\left(\left(\frac{Q}{2}\right) * \left(h + \left(C_{\mathrm{p}} * h_{\mathrm{c}}\right)\right)\right) - \left(C_{\mathrm{p}} * z\right)\right.\\ &\left.+\left(\frac{\left((Q * A_1) + (Q * C) + K + A_0 + \left(C_p * A_c\right)\right) * ((2 * \alpha) - (\beta * h_c * Q))}{2(Q + (\beta * A_c))}\right)\right)\end{aligned} \tag{10}$$

Case 2. Carbon tax

"Total cost per unit time due to the carbon tax is":

"Total cost = ordering cost + holding cost + purchase cost + transportation cost + carbon tax cost"

$$\mathrm{TC}_2(Q) = \left(\left(\left(\frac{Q}{2}\right) * (h + (w * h_c))\right) + \left(\frac{((Q * A_1) + (Q * C) + K + A_0 + (w * A_c)) * ((2 * \alpha) - (\beta * h_c * Q))}{2(Q + (\beta * A_c))}\right)\right) \tag{11}$$

4 Solution Procedure

The optimality of "the order quantity (Q)" is given below:

Case 1. Carbon cap-and-trade:

Now, the necessary condition for the optimality of the total cost function is:

$$\frac{\partial \mathrm{TC}_1(Q)}{\partial Q} = 0$$

$$\frac{\partial \mathrm{TC}_1(Q)}{\partial Q} = \frac{2\alpha(A_1 + C) - \beta h_c}{2(Q + \beta A_c)} + \frac{\beta h_c Q - 2\alpha\left(A_1 Q + CQ + C_p A_c + A_0 + K\right)}{2(Q + \beta A_c)^2} + \frac{C_p h_c + h}{2} \tag{12}$$

The optimal value of Q^*

$$Q^* = \pm \frac{\sqrt{\begin{array}{l}\left(-2\alpha\beta C_p A_c h_c - 2\alpha\beta h A_c\right)A_1 + \left(\beta^2 C_p A_c h_c^2\right) \\ + \left(\left(2\alpha C_p^2 - 2\alpha\beta C C_p + \beta^2 h\right)A_c \right. \\ \left. + (2\alpha A_0 + 2\alpha K)C_p\right)h_c + \left(2\alpha h C_p - 2\alpha\beta C h\right)A_c \\ + 2\alpha h A_0 + 2\alpha h K\end{array}} + \beta C_p A_c h_c + \beta h A_c}{(C_p h_c + h)} \tag{13}$$

The sufficiency condition for the optimality of the total cost is:

$$\frac{\partial^2 \mathrm{TC}_1(Q)}{\partial Q^2} \geq 0$$

$$\frac{\partial^2 \mathrm{TC}_1(Q)}{\partial Q^2} = \frac{2\alpha\left(A_1 Q + CQ + C_p A_c + A_0 + k\right) - \beta h_c Q}{(Q + \beta A_c)^3} - \frac{2\alpha(A_1 + C) - \beta h_c}{(Q + \beta A_c)^2} \tag{14}$$

Case 2: Carbon tax:

Now, the necessary condition for the optimality of the total cost function is:

$$\frac{\partial \mathrm{TC}_2(Q)}{\partial Q} = 0$$

$$\frac{\partial \mathrm{TC}_2(Q)}{\partial Q} = \frac{2\alpha(A_1 + C) - \beta h_c}{2(Q + \beta A_c)} - \frac{2\alpha(A_1 Q + CQ + wA_c + A_0 + K) - \beta h_c Q}{2(Q + \beta A_c)^2} + \frac{wh_c + h}{2} \tag{15}$$

The optimal value of Q^* is

$$Q^* = \pm \frac{\sqrt{\begin{array}{l}(-2\alpha\beta w A_c h_c - 2\alpha\beta h A_c)A_1 + \left(\beta^2 w A_c h_c^2\right) \\ + \left(-2\alpha A_c w^2 + (-2\alpha\beta C A_c + 2\alpha A_0 + 2\alpha K)w + \beta^2 h A_c\right)h_c + \beta w A_c h_c + \beta h A_c \\ + (2\alpha h w h_c - 2\alpha\beta C h)A_c + 2\alpha h A_0 + 2\alpha h K\end{array}}}{(C_p h_c + h)} \tag{16}$$

The sufficiency condition for the total cost is:

$$\frac{\partial^2 \mathrm{TC}_2(Q)}{\partial Q^2} \geq 0$$

$$\frac{\partial^2 \mathrm{TC}_2(Q)}{\partial Q^2} = \frac{2\beta h_c - 4\alpha(A_1 + C)}{2(Q + \beta A_c)^2} + \frac{2\alpha(QA_1 + CQ + A_c w + A_0 + K) - \beta h_c Q}{(Q + \beta A_c)^3} \tag{17}$$

Further, Fig. 2 establishes the optimality of the Cap-and-trade case by the graphical method with the help of Mathematica.

5 Numerical Examples

Example 1: Carbon cap-and-trade case:

For numerical illustration, the data values have been taken as:

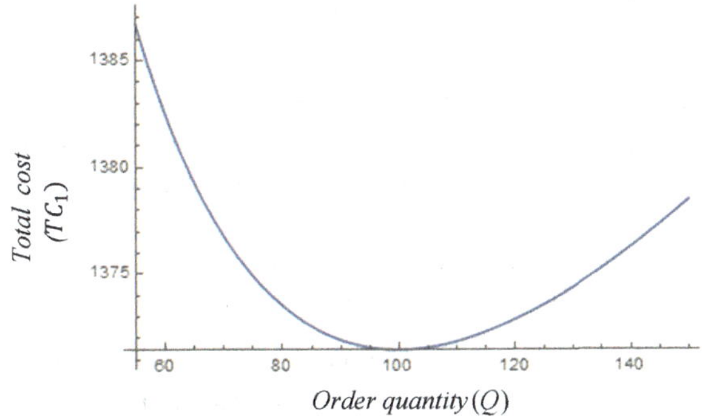

Fig. 2 Graphical representation of the convexity

Parameters	Parameters
$K = \$20/\text{order}$ $C = \$12/\text{unit}$ $h = \$2/\text{unit}$ $A_0 = 25\ (\$)$ $A_1 = 1\ (\$)$ $A_c = 0.5(\text{kg/unit})$	$\alpha = 100$ $\beta = 0.6$ $h_c = 0.2(\text{kg/unit})$ $C_P = 2(\$/\text{kg})$ $z = 5(\text{kg})$
The optimal results are:	
Total cost $TC_1 = \$1371.456$	Order quantity $Q = 99.827$units

Example 2: Carbon tax case: For numerical illustration, the data values have been taken as:

Parameters	Parameters
$K = \$20/\text{order}$ $C = \$12/\text{unit}$ $h = \$2/\text{unit}$ $A_0 = 25\ (\$)$ $A_1 = 1\ (\$)$	$\alpha = 100$ $\beta = 0.6$ $h_c = 0.2(\text{kg/unit})$ $A_c = 0.5(\text{kg/unit})$ $w = 3(\$/\text{kg})$
The optimal results are:	
Total cost $TC_2 = \$1391.428$	Order quantity $Q = 99.219$ units

From the above results, one can easily see that the total cost is lower in the "carbon cap-and-trade" case than that of the "carbon tax" case. Hence "carbon cap-and-trade mechanism" is favorable to implement for the decision-maker.

6 Sensitivity Analysis

In this section, sensitivity analysis for on key model parameters (α, β, A_0, A_1, h, C_P, z) for the carbon "cap-and-trade" case has been performed, based on which the change in the values of decision variable and total cost is analyzed. The results are recorded in Table 2.

Observations and discussion:

The following insights have been discussed based on Table 2:

- With an increase in demand parameter, (α) one can boost the demand, and hence the order size increases which leads to high cost.
- When the emission-sensitive parameter (β) of demand rises the total cost and order quantity decreases as the parameter has an adverse effect on demand.
- When the fixed (A_0) and variable (A_1) transportation cost increases the order quantity also increases which results in a higher cost.
- A higher holding cost (h) indicates improved storage conditions, which will eventually lead to higher costs.
- An increase in carbon price (C_p) contributes to increasing the total cost component.
- An increase in carbon quota (z) has an adverse effect on the total cost.
- An increase in parameters (α), (A_0), (A_1) increases the carbon emission whereas the increase in (β), (h), (C_P) will decrease the carbon emissions.

7 Conclusion

Carbon emission is an inevitable topic in today's world, due to the growing GHG emissions, the influence of carbon discharges on the demand is increasing significantly. With health and environment-conscious consumers, the demand for environmentally-friendly products is rising rapidly. In this paper, a cost-minimization model with carbon emission-dependent demand with transportation cost under two different carbon policies is developed. Further to support green inventory reduction of carbon emissions in various processes viz. transportation and inventory holding. In addition, a comparative analysis of "carbon tax and cap-and-trade" is implemented to mitigate carbon emissions. Numerical and sensitivity analysis are executed for structuring the model features. Some important observations are made from numerical and sensitivity analysis. The key findings of the paper are concluded as:

- For higher holding costs, it is preferable to order small lots in order to manage the inventory effectively.
- Transportation cost has an adverse effect on carbon discharges but the total cost increases.
- The carbon discharge declines with an increase in the carbon price.
- "Carbon tax policy and Cap-and-trade mechanism" is an effective tool for green inventory systems and a cleaner environment.

Table 2 Sensitivity analysis of the key parameters

Parameters		Q	CE	TC
α	80	89.259	9.342	1102.578
	90	94.69	9.912	1237.14
	100	99.828	10.452	1371.456
	110	104.714	10.965	1505.56
	120	109.383	11.455	1639.482
β	0.4	159.312	16.204	1396.782
	0.5	119.218	12.305	1384.71
	0.6	99.828	10.452	1371.456
	0.7	87.918	9.334	1356.347
	0.8	159.312	16.204	1337.78
A_0	23	97.42	10.223	1369.553
	24	98.631	10.338	1370.511
	25	99.828	10.452	1371.456
	26	101.01	10.564	1372.389
	27	102.178	10.675	1373.31
A_1	0.5	96.605	10.146	1324.544
	0.75	98.174	10.295	1348.011
	1	99.827	10.452	1371.456
	1.5	103.422	10.794	1418.27
	1.75	105.382	10.981	1441.636
h	1	–	–	–
	1.5	157.082	15.995	1340.933
	2	99.828	10.452	1371.456
	2.5	78.976	8.498	1393.503
	3	67.352	7.444	1411.679
C_P	1	113.727	11.781	1365.386
	1.5	106.061	11.046	1368.586
	2	99.828	10.452	1371.456
	2.5	94.632	9.96	1374.055
	3	90.216	9.544	1376.428
z	3	99.828	10.452	1375.456
	4	99.828	10.452	1373.456
	5	99.828	10.452	1371.456
	6	99.828	10.452	1369.456
	7	99.828	10.452	1367.456

- Comparative analysis suggests that the "Cap-and-trade mechanism is better than the Carbon tax policy".

The developed model can be explored in numerous ways, a valuable contribution would be made by executing deterioration, vendor–buyer coordination, multiple shipments. Time and storage cost-dependent demand would be another dimension that can be explored.

Acknowledgements The authors deeply appreciate the editor and the anonymous reviewers for their valuable comments and suggestions to improve the quality of the chapter. The corresponding author would like to thank the University of Delhi, Delhi for funding this work through the Faculty Research Programme (FRP) of the IoE scheme under the grant number IoE/FRP/PCMS/2020/27.

Conflicts of Interest On behalf of all authors, the corresponding author states that there is no conflict of interest.

References

Chen, X., Benjaafar, S., & Elomri, A. (2013). The carbon-constrained EOQ. *Operations Research Letters, 41*, 172–179.

Darma Wangsa, I., & Wee, H. M. (2018). An integrated vendor–buyer inventory model with transportation cost and stochastic demand. *International Journal of Systems Science: Operations & Logistics, 5*, 295–309.

Datta, T. K. (2017). Effect of green technology investment on a production-inventory system with carbon tax. *Advances in Operations Research*

Ghosh, A., Sarmah, S. P., & Jha, J. K. (2018). Collaborative model for a two-echelon supply chain with uncertain demand under carbon tax policy. *Sādhanā, 43*, 144.

Halat, K., & Hafezalkotob, A. (2019). Modeling carbon regulation policies in inventory decisions of a multi-stage green supply chain: A game theory approach. *Computers & Industrial Engineering, 128*, 807–830.

He, P., Zhang, W., Xu, X., & Bian, Y. (2015). Production lot-sizing and carbon emissions under cap-and-trade and carbon tax regulations. *Journal of Cleaner Production, 103*, 241–248.

Hota, S. K., Sarkar, B., & Ghosh, S. K. (2020). Effects of unequal lot size and variable transportation in unreliable supply chain management. *Mathematics, 8*, 357.

Hovelaque, V., & Bironneau, L. (2015). The carbon-constrained EOQ model with carbon emission dependent demand. *International Journal of Production Economics, 164*, 285–291.

Juxia, H. (2016). Two-Echelon supply chain decision model with price-and-carbon-emission dependent demand. *International Business and Management*, 12.

Khanna, A., & Yadav, S. (2020). Effect of carbon-tax and cap-and-trade mechanism on an inventory system with price-sensitive demand and preservation technology investment. *Yugoslav Journal of Operations Research, 30*, 361–380.

Li, L. (2016). Coordination contracts for two-echelon supply chain with price-and-carbon-emission dependent demand. *Modern Economy, 7*, 606.

Ma, X., Ji, P., Ho, W., & Yang, C.-H. (2018). Optimal procurement decision with a carbon tax for the manufacturing industry. *Computers and Operations Research, 89*, 360–368.

Metcalf, G. E. (2009). Market-based policy options to control US greenhouse gas emissions. *Journal of Economic Perspectives, 23*, 5–27.

Mishra, M., Hota, S. K., Ghosh, S. K., Sarkar, B. (2020a). Controlling waste and carbon emission for a sustainable closed-loop supply chain management under a cap-and-trade strategy. *Mathematics, 8*, 466.

Mishra, U., Wu, J.-Z., Sarkar, B. (2020b). A sustainable production-inventory model for a controllable carbon emissions rate under shortages. *Journal of Cleaner Production, 256*, 120268.

Mosca, A., Vidyarthi, N., Satir, A. (2019). Integrated transportation–inventory models: A review. *Operations Research Perspectives, 6*, 100101.

Pang, Q., Li, M., Yang, T., Shen, Y. (2018). Supply chain coordination with carbon trading price and consumers' environmental awareness dependent demand. *Mathematical Problems in Engineering, 2018*.

Rani, S., Ali, R., & Agarwal, A. (2019). Fuzzy inventory model for deteriorating items in a green supply chain with carbon concerned demand. *Opsearch, 56*, 91–122.

Salehi, M., Jalalian, M., & Siar, M. M. V. (2017). Green transportation scheduling with speed control: Trade-off between total transportation cost and carbon emission. *Computers & Industrial Engineering, 113*, 392–404.

Sarkar, B., Ganguly, B., Sarkar, M., & Pareek, S. (2016). Effect of variable transportation and carbon emission in a three-echelon supply chain model. *Transportation Research Part E: Logistics and Transportation Review, 91*, 112–128.

Singh, R., & Weninger, Q. (2017). Cap-and-trade under transactions costs and factor irreversibility. *Economic Theory, 64*, 357–407.

Tang, Z., Liu, X., Wang, Y., Ma, D. (2020). Integrated inventory-transportation scheduling with sustainability-dependent demand under carbon emission policies. *Discrete Dynamics in Nature and Society, 2020*.

Wang, S., Wan, L., Li, T., Luo, B., & Wang, C. (2018). Exploring the effect of cap-and-trade mechanism on firm's production planning and emission reduction strategy. *Journal of Cleaner Production, 172*, 591–601.

Yadav, S., Khanna, A. (2021). Sustainable model for perishable products with expiration date and price reliant demand under carbon tax policy. *Process Integration and Inventory Optimization for Sustainability*, 1–12.

Impact of Two Different Trade Credits Options on a Supply Chain with Joint and Independent Decision Under Trapezoidal Demand

Urmila Chaudhari, Nita H. Shah, and Mrudul Y. Jani

Abstract The traditional economic order quantity model adopts that the retailer should settle down all accounts at the time of receiving an order. In fact, allowing customers to delay payment for goods that are already delivered is a very common business practice. The supplier often offers trade credit as a promotion strategy to increase sales and decrease the on-hand inventory level. In this paper, the supply chain deals with a single supplier and a single retailer. Here, the supplier sets two trade credit options for the retailer. If the retailer settles down all the payments at the first trade credit then the supplier offers a discount on purchasing price to the retailer. But, if the retailer settles down all the payments at the time of the second credit period then the retailer will not be entitled to the discount. In this paper, the model considers price sensitive trapezoidal demand and a product with constant deterioration rate. The classical optimization is used to optimize the total profit of the supply chain with respect to selling price and cycle time and also analyzed the best scenario for the supply chain. The model is supported by numerical examples. Sensitivity analysis is done to deduce managerial insights.

Keywords Two different trade credit · Discount in purchasing price · Constant deterioration · Trapezoidal demand

1 Introduction

To boost the demand for the product, the player gives permissible delay in payment that is called trade credit. Trade credit concerns the business-to-business credit limit and has been a necessary way for trades to obtain short-term development. Buyer

U. Chaudhari (✉)
Government Polytechnic Dahod, Dahod, Gujarat 389151, India

N. H. Shah
Department of Mathematics, Gujarat University, Ahmedabad, Gujarat 380009, India

M. Y. Jani
Department of Applied Sciences, Faculty of Engineering and Technology, Parul University, Vadodara, Gujarat 391760, India

N. H. Shah and M. Mittal (eds.), *Soft Computing in Inventory Management*, Inventory Optimization, https://doi.org/10.1007/978-981-16-2156-7_10

can sell the product before paying the purchase cost of the product and can free up cash flow for other business purposes. Nowadays trade credit is the most popular tool to increase the profit of the individual. Chen et al. (2014) investigated EPQ models with up-stream full trade credit and down-stream partial trade credit for deteriorating items. Wu et al. (2016) formulated an inventory model under down-stream partial trade credit to credit-risk customers by discounted cash flow analysis for deteriorating items with maximum lifetime. Rameswari and Uthayakumar (2017) developed a model of two-level trade credit with price-dependent demand. Motlagh et al. (2018) established a concept of coordination of challenging duopolistic retailers' credit limit and controlling the manufacturer's promotional efforts. Sobhani et al. (2019) worked on a vendor–buyer inventory model which explained the working environment of the players. Tiwari et al. (2018) discussed an inventory model for joint pricing and time-dependent deteriorating items with partial backlogging under two-level partial trade credits in the supply chain. Yu (2018) gave the concept of shortage back ordering, trade credit, and decreasing Rental Conditions under the two-warehouse system.

The act or method of flattering reduced or mediocre in quality, operative, or condition is called deterioration. Raafat (1991) studied a literature survey on a deteriorating inventory model. Aggarwal and Jaggi (1995) introduced a deteriorating items model for optimal ordering policy under trade credit. Goyal and Nebebe (2000) developed a model of a single manufacturer and a single retailer system for a deteriorating item with shipment policies. Goyal and Giri (2001) established a model of the recent trend in the modeling of deteriorating stocks. Rau et al. (2003) derived an inventory model of deteriorating items for the multi-layered supply chain. Sarkar (2012) investigated an EOQ model with trade credit and time-varying deterioration rate. Bakker et al. (2012) examined the inventory system with a deterioration since 2001. Sarkar and Sarkar (2013) determined a manufacturing quantity model with probabilistic deterioration. Cai et al. (2013) discussed a dynamic tracking control to find optimal pricing policy for perishable items. Moussawi-Haidar et al. (2014) worked on the effect of deterioration with imperfect quality items. Sarkar et al. (2015) extended an inventory model with variable deterioration for fixed lifetime items and permissible delay in payment. Rabbani et al. (2015) investigated coordinated renewal and marketing strategies for non-instantaneous stock perishable item's problem. Chang et al. (2015) studied optimal estimating and ordering strategies for non-instantaneously deteriorating items under trade credit. Shah et al. (2016a, 2016b) derived supply chain inventory model of the perishable item under trade credit and price-dependent demand. Shah and Jani (2016) derived model of quadratic demand with the variable deterioration of the product. Developed an integrated production-inventory model for perishable items with the reflection of the optimal production rate and deterioration during delivery. Sarkar and Saren (2017) studied ordering and transfer policy and variable deterioration for a warehouse model. Tai (2019) established a random deteriorating item model under joint inspection. Considered the different decision in a model like pricing, replenishment, and preservation technology investment for non-instantaneous deteriorating items. Observed the impact of the two-stage deterioration of the product under capacity utilization and trade credit.

A pricing approach is a vital component of a profitable business. Pricing element directly impacts on player's profit. If the player chooses pricing strategy then it helps the player to achieve a sale, promotion of brand or product, the best profit from the markets, etc. Commonly, a player must set pricing strategy after observing a market. A pricing idea is framed taking into deliberation aspects of cost, competition and revenue objectives. Because of the importance of the pricing strategy, this article focuses on discount in purchasing cost. At the earliest, Drezner and Wesolowsky (1989) gave an idea on pricing strategy with multi-buyer. Wee and Yu (1997) considered a temporary price discount in deteriorating inventory model. After that, evaluated an inventory model on pricing, partial back ordering and quantity discount under deterioration. some interesting articles on discount pricing decisions are Viswanathan and Wang (2003), Yang (2004), Qin et al. (2007), Bykadorov et al. (2009), Chang (2013), Taleizadeh and Pentico (2014), Chua (2016), Venegas and Ventura (2017). Luo et al. (2014) and Shao et al. (2017) evaluated a model on pricing policy for an electrical vehicle. Recently, Nie and Du (2016) estimated dual-fairness coordinating system with the discount contract. Wang et al. (2018) examined lost-sales inventory systems with unit discount under procurement strategies. Khouja et al. (2019) analyzed the effect of return and price modification strategies on a retailer's Performance. Niu et al. (2019) deliberated the joint price and quality decisions considering Chinese customers.

In a traditional study of inventory management, most of the researchers consider constant demand. However, demand rarely remains fixed for an infinite planning horizon. Shah et al. (2011) studied a coordinated decision policy when demand is quadratic with two-level trade credit, observed in seasonal items. Sarkar and Mahapatra (2017) considered fuzzy inventory model with fuzzy demand. Feng et al. (2017) evaluated pricing and lot-sizing policies when demand depends on selling price, displayed the stock, and expiration date. Cheng et al. (2011) offered trapezoidal demand where demand increases linearly with time up to a certain limit and then after becomes constant during a certain period and decreases exponentially in the last phase, observed in fashion goods and electronics items. Shah et al. (2017) formulated the retailer's optimal policy for price-credit sensitive trapezoidal demand. Shah et al. (2019) examined the effect of manufacturer's innovation and retailer's promotion on trapezoidal demand. Recently, Yang (2020) studied retailer's ordering policy where demand is depending of expiration date.

Authors	Promotion strategy	Deterioration	Demand	Decision policy
Ho et al. (2008)	Cash discount and trade credit	NA	The downward sloping function of the selling price	Joint and individual
Sarkar and Saren (2017)	NA	Probabilistic	Time-price dependent	Individual
Feng et al. (2017)	NA	Maximum fixed lifetime	The exponential function of the price	Individual

(continued)

(continued)

Authors	Promotion strategy	Deterioration	Demand	Decision policy
Rameswari and Uthayakumar (2017)	Two-level trade credit	Constant	Displayed stock and selling price dependent	Individual
Shah et al. (2017)	Two-level trade credit	NA	Price sensitive trapezoidal	Individual
Yu (2018)	Trade credit	Constant	Constant	Individual
Proposed model	Discount in purchase cost and trade credit	Constant	Price sensitive trapezoidal	Joint and individual

From the study of existing research literature, one can observe that most of the researchers consider trade credit as the only promotional strategy to boost the business. However, they ignore the fact that every buyer's local objectives and requirements are different and may frequently conflict. Therefore, this model represents two different types of promotional strategies. In the first case, if the retailer is ready to pay at the end of first trade credit then he can enjoy the benefits of discount cash flow. On the other hand, if the retailer opts second credit period then he will not get the benefit of a discount on the purchase cost. Moreover, deterioration is the natural procedure which will reduce the quality of the product with time. So, the proposed model considers the deterioration rate. In addition, the demand rate of the product is price sensitive trapezoidal which is suitable for electronics and fashion industries.

The remaining of the article is structured as follow. Section 2 contains the notation and the assumptions that are used to progress model. Section 3 of the paper deals with the construction of the mathematical model of the anticipated inventory control problem. Section 4 explores the centralized and decentralized strategies. Section 5 validates the resulting two-layered supply chain inventory model with numerical examples. Section 6 provides a sensitivity analysis of the inventory parameters and also provides some managerial perceptions. Section 7 concludes the outcomes and provides a vision for future research in the field.

1.1 Notation

To develop an inventory model we need some notation and assumptions

$D(p, t)$	The demand for the product
a	Total scale demand of the product, $a > 0$
b_1	The linear rate of change of demand for the product, $0 < b_1 \leq 1$
b_2	The exponential rate of change of demand for the product, $0 < b_2 \leq 10$

(continued)

(continued)

p	The selling price of the item (\$/unit)
η	The mark-up for selling price
θ	Constant deterioration rate (in %), $0 < \theta \leq 1$
Q	Initial inventory level (per lot)
T	Cycle time (in years)
A_r	Ordering cost for the retailer (\$/lot)
h	Holding cost rate (\$/unit/year)
P_s	The purchasing cost of the product (\$/unit)
α	Supplier offers a discount on the purchasing cost (in %)
I_{er}	Rate of interest earned for the retailer (%/unit time)
M_i	Trade credit offer to the retailer by the supplier (in a year) ($i = 1, 2$)
I_{cr}	Rate of interest charged for the retailer (%/unit time)
I_{cs}	Rate of interest charged for the supplier (%/unit time)
F_{cs}	The flexibility cash rate of the supplier (/unit time/year)
A_v	Ordering cost for the vendor (\$/lot)
C	The purchasing cost of the item for the vendor (\$/unit)
$\pi_r(p, T)$	Total profit of the retailer (in \$)
$\pi_s(p, T)$	Total profit of the supplier (in \$)
$\pi_J(p, T)$	Total profit of the supply chain in the joint decision (in \$)
$\pi_I(p, T)$	Total profit of the supply chain in the independent decision (in \$)

1.2 Assumptions

1. The supply chain includes a single supplier, a single retailer, and a single constant deteriorating item.
2. The demand rate for the item is a function of selling price and time. The demand $D(p, t)$ is considered to be a trapezoidal type whose functional form is

$$D(p,t) = \begin{cases} f(t)p^{-\eta}, \ 0 \leq t \leq t_1 \\ D_0 p^{-\eta}, \quad t_1 \leq t \leq t_2 \\ g(t)p^{-\eta}, \ t \geq t_2 \end{cases} \quad \text{(Shah et al., 2019)}$$

where $f(t)$ by the linear function of t between time interval 0 to t_1 and t_1 is the time point when the increasing demand function $f(t)$ changes to constant demand D_0. $g(t)$ is the exponentially decreasing function of t between time interval 0 to t_2 and t_2 is the time point from where constant demand D_0 starts decreasing exponentially. Therefore, the demand function is

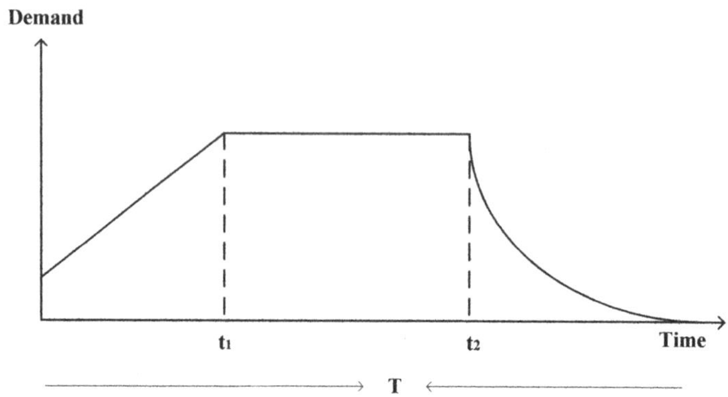

Fig. 1 Time- and price-dependent trapezoidal demand (Shah et al., 2019)

$$D(p,t) = \begin{cases} D_1(p,t),\ 0 \le t \le t_1 \\ D_2(p,t),\ t_1 \le t \le t_2 \\ D_3(p,t),\ t \ge t_2 \end{cases}.$$

where $D_1(p,t) = a(1+b_1t)p^{-\eta}$, $D_2(p,t) = a(1+b_1t_1)p^{-\eta}$, $D_3(p,t) = a(1+b_1t_1)e^{-b_2(t-t_2)}$.

3. The units in the inventory system of each player are subjected to deteriorate at a constant rate. The deteriorated units are not repaired or replaced during the cycle time (Fig. 1).
4. To haste up cash arrival and reduce the threat of cash flow shortage, the supplier offers a $\alpha\%$ discount in purchasing price if retailer settles down the account within trade credit M_1. If the retailer pays all the payments after M_1 means up to M_2 then the retailer is not entitled to discount in purchasing cost. Where $M_2 > M_1 \ge 0$.
5. During the period $[M_1, M_2]$, a cash flexibility rate, F_{cs}, is used to quantize the advantage of early cash income for the supplier (Ho et al., 2008).
6. During the credit period, the supplier suffers an interest (opportunity) loss with an annual rate I_{cs} while the retailer earns interest at an annual rate I_{er} by depositing his sales revenue in an interest-bearing account (Shah et al., 2016a, 2016b).
7. The planning horizon is infinite which will facilitate long time agreement.
8. Lead time is zero or negligible.
9. Shortages are not allowed.

2 Mathematical Model

This model basically depends on the effect of trade credit on the player's profit. The model considers the supply chain of supplier and retailer with the constant deteriorating item under the effect of two different trade credits. If the retailer pays payment up to first trade credit M_1, then retailer entitled for discount in purchasing cost. But if the retailer settled down all the payments up to second trade credit M_2 then the retailer has to pay whole purchasing cost.

2.1 Supplier's Model

Supplier's role is only of the bought-out type of business. So, there is no need to hold the product. Hence, in this model holding cost is not considered. Supplier purchasing cost per unit is $\mathrm{PC_s} = \frac{\mathrm{CQ}}{T}$. Supplier's sales revenue depends on the retailer's purchasing cost. For each unit of product, the retailer pays payment up to M_i. So, the sales revenue of the supplier is $\mathrm{SR_{si}} = \frac{Q(P_s(1-k_i\alpha))}{T}$. Where $i = 1, 2$, $k_1 = 1, k_2 = 0$.

As the supplier receives payment before or after the total diminution of inventory, the model has the following two possible scenarios, (1S) $T \le M_i$ and (2S) $T \ge M_i$, where $i = 1, 2$. For these two cases, the interest earned and opportunity cost are derived accordingly.

Scenario 1S: $T \le M_i$ (where $i = 1, 2$)

In this scenario, the supplier's opportunity loss due to offering credit limit to a retailer with the rate of I_{c2} is

$$\mathrm{OppC}_{s1i} = \frac{I_{cs}P_s(1-k_i\alpha)}{T}\left[\int_0^{t_1} D_1(p,t)\mathrm{d}t + \int_{t_1}^{t_2} D_2(p,t)\mathrm{d}t + \int_{t_2}^{T} D_3(p,t)\mathrm{d}t + Q(M_i - T)\right].$$

However, if the retailer pays at the time M_1, during $M_2 - M_1$ the supplier can use the revenue to evading a cash flow crunch or generate profits. With a cash flexibility rate f_{cs}, the interest earned during $[M_1, M_2]$ is $\mathrm{IE}_{s1i} = \frac{f_{cs}P_s(1-k_i\alpha)}{T}Q(M_2 - M_1)$.

Hence the total profit of the supplier per unit time is

$$\pi_{s1i}(p,T) = \mathrm{SR}_{si1} - \mathrm{PC_s} - \mathrm{OppC}_{s1i} + \mathrm{IE}_{s1i}$$

Scenario 2S: $M_i \le T$ (where $i = 1, 2$)

In this scenario, the supplier gets payment before the cycle time and due to trapezoidal demand three cases arise as follows

(2S.1) $M_i \le t_1 \le t_2 \le T$ (2S.2) $t_1 \le M_i \le t_2 \le T$ (2S.3) $t_1 \le t_2 \le M_i \le T$.

Case 2S.1: $M_i \le t_1 \le t_2 \le T$

In this scenario, the supplier's opportunity loss due to offering credit limit to a retailer with the rate of I_{c2} is $\mathrm{OppC}_{s2i1} = \frac{I_{cs}P_s(1-k_i\alpha)}{T}\left[\int_0^{M_i} D_1(p,t)\mathrm{d}t\right]$. The retailer pays all the payment up to M_1 and after that supplier can invest that money in other businesses.

With a cash flexibility rate f_{cs}, interest earned during $[M_i, T]$ is

$$\mathrm{IE}_{s2i1} = \frac{f_{cs}P_s(1-k_i\alpha)}{T}\left[\int_{M_i}^{t_1} tD_1(p,t)\mathrm{d}t + \int_{t_1}^{t_2} tD_2(p,t)\mathrm{d}t + \int_{t_2}^{T} tD_3(p,t)\mathrm{d}t\right].$$

Then the total profit of the supplier per unit time is $\pi_{s2i1}(p,T) = \mathrm{SR}_{si1} - \mathrm{PC}_s - \mathrm{OppC}_{s2i1} + \mathrm{IE}_{s2i1}$.

Case 2S.2: $t_1 \le M_i \le t_2 \le T$

In this scenario, the supplier's opportunity loss due to offering credit limit to a retailer with the rate of I_{c2} is $\mathrm{OppC}_{s2i2} = \frac{I_{cs}P_s(1-k_i\alpha)}{T}\left[\int_0^{t_1} D_1(p,t)\mathrm{d}t + \int_{t_1}^{M_i} D_2(p,t)\mathrm{dt}\right]$. The retailer pays all the payment up to M_1 and after that supplier can invest that money in other businesses.

With a cash flexibility rate f_{cs}, interest earned during $[M_i, T]$

$$\mathrm{IE}_{s2i2} = \frac{f_{cs}P_s(1-k_i\alpha)}{T}\left[\int_{M_i}^{t_2} tD_2(p,t)\mathrm{d}t + \int_{t_2}^{T} tD_3(p,t)\mathrm{d}t\right].$$

Then the total profit of the supplier per unit time is $\pi_{s2i2}(p,T) = \mathrm{SR}_{si1} - \mathrm{PC}_s - \mathrm{OppC}_{s2i2} + \mathrm{IE}_{s2i2}$.

Case 2S.3: $t_1 \le t_2 \le M_i \le T$

In this scenario, the supplier's opportunity loss due to offering credit limit to a retailer with the rate of I_{c2} is

$$\mathrm{OppC}_{s2i3} = \frac{I_{cs}P_s(1-k_i\alpha)}{T}\left[\int_0^{t_1} D_1(p,t)\mathrm{d}t + \int_{t_1}^{t_2} D_2(p,t)\mathrm{d}t + \int_{t_2}^{M_i} D_3(p,t)\mathrm{d}t + \int_{M_i}^{T} D_3(p,t)\mathrm{d}t\right].$$

The retailer pays all the payment up to M_1 and then after the supplier can earn money to invest in other business with a cash flexibility rate f_{cs}. Hence, an interest earned by the supplier during $[M_i, T]$ is

$$\mathrm{IE}_{s2i3} = \frac{f_{cs}P_s(1-k_i\alpha)}{T}\left[\int_{M_i}^{T} tD_3(p,t)\mathrm{d}t\right].$$

Thus, the total profit of the supplier per unit time is $\pi_{s2i3}(p, T) = SR_{si1} - PC_s - OppC_{s2i3} + IE_{s2i3}$.

The whole scenario of a supplier's total profit is summarized as follows:

The total profit earned by the supplier per unit time is $\pi_s(p, T) = \begin{cases} \pi_{s1i}(p, T), & M_i \geq T \\ \pi_{s2i}(p, T), & M_i \leq T \end{cases}$.

Where $\pi_{s2i}(p, T) = \begin{cases} \pi_{s2i1}(p, T), & M_i \leq t_1 \leq t_2 \leq T \\ \pi_{s2i2}(p, T), & t_1 \leq M_i \leq t_2 \leq T \\ \pi_{s2i3}(p, T), & t_1 \leq t_2 \leq M_i \leq T \end{cases}$.

2.2 Retailer's Model

In this section, retailer's total profit is evaluated where the retailer's inventory level at any time t during replenishment time depletes due to constant deterioration of the product and trapezoidal demand in which, the demand growths linearly during $[0, t_1]$, becomes constant between $[t_1, t_2]$, thereafter diminutions exponentially during $[t_2, T]$. The rate of change of inventory level of the retailer during the entire cycle T is given by

$\frac{dI_r(t)}{dt} + \theta I_r(t) = \begin{cases} -D_1(p, t), & 0 \leq t \leq t_1 \\ -D_2(p, t), & t_1 \leq t \leq t_2 \\ -D_3(p, t), & t_2 \leq t \leq T \end{cases}$ with boundary condition $I_r(T) = 0$.

Hence, the inventory level of the retailer is

$$I_1(t) = -\frac{ap^{-\eta}(1 + b_1 t)}{\theta} + \frac{b_1 a p^{-\eta}}{\theta^2}\left(1 - e^{\theta(t_1 - t)}\right) + a(1 + b_1 t_1)e^{\theta(t_1 - t)}\left(\begin{array}{c} -\frac{1}{\theta}\left(1 - e^{\theta(t_2 - t_1)}\right) + \frac{p^{-\eta}}{\theta} \\ \left(-\frac{p^{-\eta}e^{\theta(t_2 - t_1)}}{-b_2 + \theta} + \frac{p^{-\eta}e^{b_2(t_2 - T) + \theta(T - t)}}{-b_2 + \theta}\right) \end{array}\right), \quad 0 \leq t \leq t_1$$

$$I_2(t) = a(1 + b_1 t_1)\left(-\frac{p^{-\eta}}{\theta} + \frac{e^{\theta(t_2 - t)}p^{-\eta}}{-b_2 + \theta}\left(-1 + e^{(-b_2 + \theta)T}\right) + \frac{e^{\theta(t_2 - t)}}{\theta}\right), \quad t_1 \leq t \leq t_2 \text{ and}$$

$$I_3(t) = \frac{a(1 + b_1 t_1)p^{-\eta}}{-b_2 + \theta}\left(-e^{(t_2 - t)b_2} + e^{(t_2 - T)b_2}e^{(T - t)\theta}\right), \quad t \geq t_2.$$

Initially, inventory at the retailer is $Q = I_1(0) = -\frac{ap^{-\eta}}{\theta} + \frac{b_1 a p^{-\eta}}{\theta^2}\left(1 - e^{\theta t_1}\right) + a(1 + b_1 t_1)e^{\theta t_1}\left(\begin{array}{c} -\frac{1}{\theta}\left(1 - e^{\theta(t_2 - t_1)}\right) + \frac{p^{-\eta}}{\theta} \\ \left(-\frac{p^{-\eta}e^{\theta(t_2 - t_1)}}{-b_2 + \theta} + \frac{p^{-\eta}e^{b_2(t_2 - T) + \theta T}}{-b_2 + \theta}\right) \end{array}\right)$.

At the end of the cycle time, the retailer can earn sales revenue as follows:

$$\mathrm{SR_r} = \frac{p}{T}\left[\int_0^{t_1} D_1(p,t)\mathrm{d}t + \int_{t_1}^{t_2} D_2(p,t)\mathrm{d}t + \int_{t_2}^{T} D_3(p,t)\mathrm{d}t\right]$$

The relevant inventory costs can be calculated by considering the following components.

2.2.1 Ordering Cost

The ordering cost contains set-up cost, transportation cost, the labor cost, etc., and hence, total ordering cost per lot attained by the retailer is $\mathrm{OC_r} = \frac{A_r}{T}$ (Shah et al., 2019).

2.2.2 Purchasing Cost

In this model, the supplier offers two types of trade credits M_1 and M_2 to the retailer. If the retailer pays all the payment up to M_1 then supplier gives some discount in purchasing cost P_s to the retailer and If the retailer pays all the payment up to M_2 then the supplier is not entitled to give a discount on purchasing cost P_s. Hence the purchasing cost per unit is governed by the '$\mathrm{PC_r}$' $\mathrm{PC_r} = \frac{Q(P_s(1-k_i\alpha))}{T}$ (Ho et al., 2008), where $k_1 = 1$ and $k_2 = 0$.

2.2.3 Inventory Holding Cost

As there are no shortages, the total inventory holding cost per unit per-unit-time for perfect quality products can be defined as $\mathrm{HC_r} = \frac{h}{T}\left[\int_0^{t_1} I_1(t)\mathrm{d}t + \int_{t_1}^{t_2} I_2(t)\mathrm{d}t + \int_{t_2}^{T} I_3(t)\mathrm{d}t\right]$.

As the retailer pays payment before or after the total diminution of inventory, the model has the following two possible scenarios, (i) $T \le M_i$ and (ii) $T \ge M_i$, where $i = 1, 2$. For these two cases, the interest earned and the interest charged is derived accordingly (Fig. 2).

Scenario 1R: $T \le M_i$ (where $i = 1, 2$)

In this scenario basically, it is assumed that if the retailer pays all the payments after cycle time then $T \le M_i$ case occurs. In addition, $M_1 \le M_2$.

In this case, the retailer's payment time ends after the cycle time means inventory depleted completely, so no need to pay the interest charged for the inventory to the supplier, i.e., $\mathrm{IC}_{\mathrm{r}1i} = 0$. Instantaneously, the retailer uses the sales revenue to earn the interest rate during trade credit at the rate of 'I_{er}'. Hence interest earned by the retailer during trade credit per unit time is

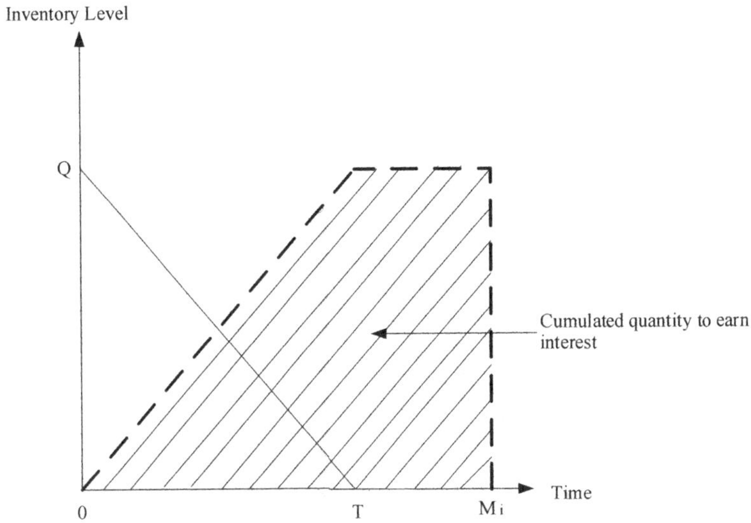

Fig. 2 Inventory level variation and loss of interest in scenario 1 (Ho et al., 2008)

$$\mathrm{IE}_{\mathrm{r}1i} = \frac{I_{\mathrm{er}}p}{T}\left[\int_0^{t_1} D_1(p,t)t\,\mathrm{d}t + \int_{t_1}^{t_2} D_2(p,t)t\,\mathrm{d}t + \int_{t_2}^{T} D_3(p,t)t\,\mathrm{d}t + Q(M_i - T)\right],$$
(where $i = 1, 2$).

Hence, the total profit achieved by the retailer per unit time is

$$\pi_{\mathrm{r}1i}(p, T) = \mathrm{SR_r} - \mathrm{OC_r} - \mathrm{HC_r} - \mathrm{PC_r} + \mathrm{IE}_{\mathrm{r}1i} - \mathrm{IC}_{\mathrm{r}1i}, \quad \text{where } i = 1, 2$$

Scenario 2R: $T \geq M_i$ (where $i = 1, 2$)

In this scenario, three cases arise due to trapezoidal demand as follows (2.1) $M_i \leq t_1 \leq t_2 \leq T$ (2.2) $t_1 \leq M_i \leq t_2 \leq T$ (2.3) $t_1 \leq t_2 \leq M_i \leq T$ (Fig. 3).

Case 2R.1: $M_i \leq t_1 \leq t_2 \leq T$

This case indicates that the retailer pays a payment on or before cycle time when inventory is depleted completely. Subsequently, in the time span when the demand of the product increases linearly, the retailer does not pay the supplier until the end of the credit period, the retailer uses the sales revenue to earn the interest rate during trade credit at the rate of 'I_{er}'. Hence interest earned by the retailer during trade credit per unit time is

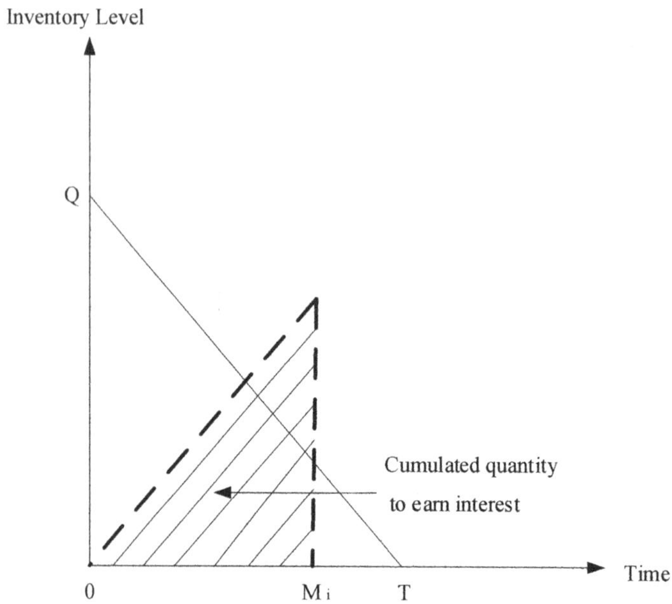

Fig. 3 Inventory level variation and loss of interest in scenario 2 (Ho et al., 2008)

$$\mathrm{IE}_{\mathrm{r}2i1} = \frac{\mathrm{I}_{\mathrm{er}}p}{T}\left[\int_{0}^{M_i} D_1(p,t)t\,\mathrm{d}t\right], \quad \text{where } i = 1, 2.$$

Moreover, after the trade credit M_i with some inventory on hand the retailer pays an interest charged at a rate of 'I_{cr}'. Therefore, the interest charged for the retailer per unit time is

$$\mathrm{IC}_{\mathrm{r}2i1} = \frac{I_{\mathrm{cr}}P_{\mathrm{s}}(1-k_i\alpha)}{T}\left[\int_{M_i}^{t_1} I_1(t)\mathrm{d}t + \int_{t_1}^{t_2} I_2(t)\mathrm{d}t + \int_{t_2}^{T} I_3(t)\mathrm{d}t\right].$$

Thus, the total profit achieved by the retailer per unit time is

$$\pi_{\mathrm{r}2i1}(p,T) = \mathrm{SR}_{\mathrm{r}} - \mathrm{OC}_{\mathrm{r}} - \mathrm{HC}_{\mathrm{r}} - \mathrm{PC}_{\mathrm{r}} + \mathrm{IE}_{\mathrm{r}2i1} - \mathrm{IC}_{\mathrm{r}2i1}$$

Case 2R.2: $t_1 \le M_i \le t_2 \le T$

This case indicates that the retailer can earn interest up to trade credit when the demand for the product is constant. Hence interest earned by the retailer during trade credit per unit time is

$$\mathrm{IE}_{\mathrm{r}2i2} = \frac{I_{\mathrm{er}} p}{T}\left[\int_0^{u_1} D_1(p,t)t\,\mathrm{d}t + \int_{u_1}^{M_i} D_2(p,t)t\,\mathrm{d}t\right].$$

Moreover, after the trade credit M_i with some inventory on hand the retailer pays an opportunity cost at a rate of 'I_{cr}'. Therefore, the interest charged for the retailer per unit time is

$$\mathrm{IC}_{\mathrm{r}2i2} = \frac{I_{\mathrm{cr}} P_{\mathrm{s}}(1-k_i\alpha)}{T}\left[\int_{M_i}^{t_2} I_2(t)\mathrm{d}t + \int_{t_2}^{T} I_3(t)\mathrm{d}t\right].$$

Therefore, total profit achieved by retailer per unit time is

$$\pi_{\mathrm{r}2i2}(p,T) = \mathrm{SR}_{\mathrm{r}} - \mathrm{OC}_{\mathrm{r}} - \mathrm{HC}_{\mathrm{r}} - \mathrm{PC}_{\mathrm{r}} + \mathrm{IE}_{\mathrm{r}22} - \mathrm{IC}_{\mathrm{r}22}.$$

Case 2R.3: $t_1 \le t_2 \le M_i \le T$

This case indicates that retailer can earn interest up to trade credit when demand decreases exponentially. Hence interest earned by the retailer during trade credit per unit time is

$$\mathrm{IE}_{\mathrm{r}2i3} = \frac{I_{\mathrm{e}_1} p}{T}\left[\int_0^{t_1} D_1(p,t)t\,\mathrm{d}t + \int_{t_1}^{t_2} D_2(p,t)t\,\mathrm{d}t + \int_{t_2}^{M_i} D_3(p,t)t\,\mathrm{d}t\right].$$

Moreover, after the trade credit M_i with some inventory on hand the retailer pays an interest charged at a rate of 'I_{cr}'. Therefore, the interest charged for the retailer per unit time is

$$\mathrm{IC}_{\mathrm{r}2i3} = \frac{I_{\mathrm{c}_1} P_{\mathrm{s}}(1-k_i\alpha)}{T}\left[\int_{M_i}^{T} I_3(t)\mathrm{d}t\right].$$

Hence, total profit achieved by retailer per unit time is

$$\pi_{\mathrm{r}2i3}(p,T) = \mathrm{SR}_{\mathrm{r}} - \mathrm{OC}_{\mathrm{r}} - \mathrm{HC}_{\mathrm{r}} - \mathrm{PC}_{\mathrm{r}} + \mathrm{IE}_{\mathrm{r}2i3} - \mathrm{IC}_{\mathrm{r}2i3}.$$

The whole scenario of the retailer's profit is summarized as follows:
The total profit earned by the retailer per unit time is

$$\pi_{\mathrm{r}}(p,T) = \begin{cases} \pi_{\mathrm{r}1i}(p,T), & T \le M_i \\ \pi_{\mathrm{r}2i}(p,T), & M_i \le T \end{cases}$$

where $\pi_{r2i}(p, T) = \begin{cases} \pi_{r2i1}, & M_i \leq t_1 \leq t_2 \leq T \\ \pi_{r2i2}, & t_1 \leq M_i \leq t_2 \leq T \\ \pi_{r2i3}, & t_1 \leq t_2 \leq M_i \leq T \end{cases}$.

3 Joint and Independent Decision

3.1 Joint Decision

Decisions made in the centralized decision-making structure are optimized from the whole supply chain standpoint where both players' aim is to maximize the whole supply chain profit.

$$\pi_J(p, T) = \pi_s(p, T) + \pi_r(p, T)$$

3.2 Independent Decision

In the decentralized option, each member of the supply chain attempts to optimize their own profit. Retailer optimizes his profit function and determines the optimal values of his decision variables, based on which the supplier optimizes his decision variables and optimizes his profit. Retailer's problem can be formulated as follows.

Objective function

$$\text{Max } \pi_r(p, T) = SR_r - OC_r - HC_r - PC_r + IE_{rjk} - IC_{rjk}$$

where $j = 1, 2$ and $k = 1, 2, 3$.

Thus, the retailer's decision variables can be optimized after which using the decision variables of a retailer, the supplier can optimize his total profit.

4 Numerical Examples

Example 5.1 (Joint and Independent Decision for Scenario 1 ($T \leq M_i$)**: for case 1.1** ($T \leq M_1$)**)**

The scale demand for the product is $a = 10{,}000$ units, the linear rate of change of demand for the product is $b_1 = 11\%$, the exponential rate of change of demand for the product is $b_2 = 9\%$, a time point when the increasing demand function changes to constant demand is $t_1 = 18.25 \approx 18$ days, the time point from where constant demand starts to decrease exponentially is $t_2 = 29.2 \approx 29$ days, purchasing cost for the retailer is $P_s = \$4.5$ per unit, the rate of interest earned by the retailer is $I_{er} = 18\%$, the rate of interest charged for the retailer is $I_{cr} = 16\%$, flexibility cost rate is $F_{cs} = 17\%$, Ordering cost per order incurred by the supplier is $A_s = \$1000$ per lot, ordering cost per order incurred by the retailer is $A_r = \$300$ per lot, the rate of interest charged by the supplier is $I_{cs} = 9\%$, holding cost for the retailer is $h = \$0.08$/unit/unit time, $k_1 = 1$, $k_2 = 0$, discount on the purchasing cost which is offered by the supplier to the retailer is $\alpha = 2\%$, first credit period offered by supplier to the retailer is $M_1 = 0.92 \approx 336$ days, second credit period offered by supplier to the retailer is $M_2 = 0.95 \approx 347$ days, purchasing cost for the supplier is $C = \$2$ per unit, price mark-up is $\eta = 1.2$, constant deterioration rate is $\theta = 10\%$.

With discount

Using Maple 13, the optimal values of the decision variables are obtained for the joint decision policy, i.e., cycle time $T = 0.9 \approx 328$ days, selling price of the product $p = \$13.53$ per unit, $Q = 692$ units and the optimal solution for the joint decision is $\pi_r(p, T) = \$2277.05$, $\pi_s(p, T) = \$1694.22$, $\pi_J(p, T) = \$3971.27$. Also, the optimal values of the decision variables are obtained for the independent decision policy, i.e., cycle time $T = 0.99 \approx 361$ days, selling price of the product $p = \$21.57$ per unit, $Q = 520$ units and the optimal solution for the independent decision is $\pi_r(p, T) = \$2192.35$, $\pi_s(p, T) = \$1218.16$, $\pi_I(p, T) = \$3410.51$.

Example 5.2 (Joint and Independent Decision for Scenario 1 ($T \le M_i$): for case 1.2 ($T \le M_2$))

Without a discount

Taking same data as given in Example 5.1 except $M_1 = 0.93 \approx 339$ days, the optimal value of decision variable for joint decision policy is, cycle time $T = 0.85 \approx 310$ days, selling price of the product $p = \$14.53$ per unit, $Q = 642$ units and the optimal solution for the joint decision is $\pi_r(p, T) = \$2311.50$, $\pi_s(p, T) = \$1687.21$, $\pi_J(p, T) = \$3998.71$. Also, the optimal values of the decision variables are derived in the independent decision policy is, cycle time $T = 0.925 \approx 337$ days, $p = \$24.48$ per unit, $Q = 490$ units and the optimal solution for the independent decision policy is $\pi_r(p, T) = \$2360.54$, $\pi_s(p, T) = \$1218.71$, $\pi_I(p, T) = \$3599.26$.

Example 5.3 (Joint and Independent Decision for Scenario 2 ($M_i \le T$): For case 2.1 ($M_1 \le t_1 \le t_2 \le T$))

With discount

Taking same data as given in Example 5.1 except $M_1 = 0.01 \approx 4$ days and $M_2 = 0.03 \approx 11$ days, the optimal value of decision variable for joint decision policy is, cycle time $T = 3.54$ years, selling price of the product $p = \$14.99$ per unit, $Q = 1710$ units and the optimal solution for the joint decision is $\pi_r(p, T) = \$1690.65$, $\pi_s(p, T) = \$1584.81$, $\pi_J(p, T) = \$3275.46$. Also, the optimal values of the decision variables are obtained in the independent decision is, cycle time $T = 4.44$ years, $p =$

\$43.52 per unit, $Q = 798$ units and the optimal solution for the independent decision policy is $\pi_r(p, T) = \$2365.24$, $\pi_s(p, T) = \$572.52$, $\pi_I(p, T) = \$2937.77$.

Example 5.4 (Joint and Independent Decision for Scenario 2 ($M_i \leq T$): For case 2.2 ($M_2 \leq t_1 \leq t_2 \leq T$)**)**

Without a discount

Taking same data as given in Example 5.1 except $M_1 = 0.01 \approx 4$ days and $M_2 = 0.03 \approx 11$ days, the optimal value of decision variable for joint decision is, cycle time $T = 3.56$ years, selling price of the product $p = \$14.94$ per unit, $Q = 1724$ units and the optimal solution for the joint decision is $\pi_r(p, T) = \$1625.87$, $\pi_s(p, T) = \$1643.41$, $\pi_J(p, T) = \$3269.28$. Also, we obtain the optimal values of the decision variables in the independent decision is, cycle time $T = 4.50$ years, $p = \$44.53$ per unit, $Q = 790$ units and the optimal solution for the independent decision is $\pi_r(p, T) = \$2339.15$, $\pi_s(p, T) = \$579.15$, $\pi_I(p, T) = \$2918.30$.

Example 5.5 (Joint and Independent Decision for Scenario 2 ($M_i \leq T$): For case 2.3 ($t_1 \leq M_1 \leq t_2 \leq T$)**)**

With discount

Taking same data as given in Example 5.1 except $M_1 = 0.07 \approx 25$ days and $M_2 = 0.075 \approx 28$ days, the optimal value of decision variable for joint decision policy is, cycle time $T = 2.60$ years, selling price of the product $p = \$13.79$ per unit, $Q = 1437$ units and the optimal solution for the joint decision is $\pi_r(p, T) = \$2049.13$, $\pi_s(p, T) = \$1688.40$, $\pi_J(p, T) = \$3737.54$. Also, the optimal values of the decision variables are obtained in the independent decision is, cycle time $T = 3.38$ years, $p = \$38.90$ per unit, $Q = 731$ units and the optimal solution for the independent decision policy is $\pi_r(p, T) = \$2732.97$, $\pi_s(p, T) = \$649.18$, $\pi_I(p, T) = \$3382.15$.

Example 5.6 (Joint and Independent Decision for Scenario 2 ($M_i \leq T$): For case 2.4 ($t_1 \leq M_2 \leq t_2 \leq T$)**)**

Without a discount

Taking same data as given in Example 5.1 except $M_1 = 0.07 \approx 25$ days and $M_2 = 0.075 \approx 28$ days, the optimal value of decision variable for joint decision policy is, cycle time $T = 3.55$ years, selling price of the product $p = \$14.73$ per unit, $Q = 1743$ units and the optimal solution for the joint decision is $\pi_r(p, T) = \$1618.77$, $\pi_s(p, T) = \$1664.50$, $\pi_J(p, T) = \$3283.27$. Also, we obtain the optimal values of the decision variables in the independent decision is, cycle time $T = 4.49$ years, $p = \$44.23$ per unit, $Q = 793$ units and the optimal solution for the independent decision policy is $\pi_r(p, T) = \$2345.23$, $\pi_s(p, T) = \$582.24$, $\pi_I(p, T) = \$2927.47$.

Example 5.7 (Joint and Independent Decision for Scenario 2 ($M_i \leq T$): For case 2.5 ($t_1 \leq t_2 \leq M_1 \leq T$)**)**

With discount

Taking same data as given in Example 5.1 except $M_1 = 0.12 \approx 44$ days and $M_2 = 0.20 \approx 73$ days, the optimal value of decision variables for joint decision policy is, cycle time $T = 2.05$ years, selling price of the product $p = \$13.19$ per unit, $Q = 1239$ units and the optimal solution for the joint decision is $\pi_r(p, T) = \$2278.75$, $\pi_s(p, T) = \$1756.89$, $\pi_J(p, T) = \$4035.64$. Also, the optimal values of the decision variables are obtained in the independent decision policy is, cycle time $T = 2.81$ years, $p = \$36.41$ per unit, $Q = 685.60$ units and the optimal solution for the independent decision policy is $\pi_r(p, T) = \$2961.19$, $\pi_s(p, T) = \$706.45$, $\pi_I(p, T) = \$3667.65$.

Example 5.8 (Joint and Independent Decision for Scenario 2 ($M_i \le T$): For case 2.6 ($t_1 \le t_2 \le M_2 \le T$))

Without a discount

Taking same data as given in Example 5.1 except $M_1 = 0.12 \approx 44$ days and $M_2 = 0.20 \approx 73$ days, the optimal value of decision variables for joint decision policy is, cycle time $T = 3.52$ years, selling price of the product $p = \$14.19$ per unit, $Q = 1794$ units and the optimal solution for the joint decision policy is $\pi_r(p, T) = \$1602.32$, $\pi_s(p, T) = \$1721.82$, $\pi_J(p, T) = \$3324.14$. Also, the optimal values of the decision variables are obtained in the independent decision policy is, cycle time $T = 4.44$ years, $p = \$43.36$ per unit, $Q = 799.64$ units and the optimal solution for the independent decision policy is $\pi_r(p, T) = \$2364.07$, $\pi_s(p, T) = \$591.24$, $\pi_I(p, T) = \$2955.31$.

From Table 1, players gain more profit when they take a joint decision and with discount strategy. Case 5.7 ($t_1 \le t_2 \le M_1 \le T$) is the best case of all.

Optimality of the total profit of the supply chain in a joint decision is described by two methods, i.e., by the graph, and by hessian matrix. As shown in Fig. 4, the unit total profit of the joint decision for the supply chain is concave up.

The proof of global optimality using the well-known Hessian matrix is shown as follows:

Let $|H(p^*, T^*)|$ be the determinant of the Hessian matrix $H(p^*, T^*) = \begin{pmatrix} \frac{\partial^2 \pi_J(p^*,T^*)}{\partial p^2} & \frac{\partial^2 \pi_J(p^*,T^*)}{\partial p \partial T} \\ \frac{\partial^2 \pi_J(p^*,T^*)}{\partial p \partial T} & \frac{\partial^2 \pi_J(p^*,T^*)}{\partial T^2} \end{pmatrix}$ of the objective function $\pi_J(p, T)$ (profit function) at the optimal point (p^*, T^*).

For the function to be concave, the following sufficient condition must be satisfied.

$\det(H(p^*, T^*)) < 0$, provided that, $\left(\frac{\partial^2 \pi_J(p^*,T^*)}{\partial p^2}\right)\left(\frac{\partial^2 \pi_J(p^*,T^*)}{\partial T^2}\right) - \left(\frac{\partial^2 \pi_J(p^*,T^*)}{\partial p \partial T}\right)^2 > 0$ additionally, $\left(\frac{\partial \pi_J(p^*,T^*)}{\partial p}\right) < 0$ and $\left(\frac{\partial \pi_J(p^*,T^*)}{\partial T}\right) < 0$ (Yu, 2018).

For the optimal case $t_1 \le t_2 \le M_1 \le T$,

$\left(\frac{\partial^2 \pi_J(p^*,T^*)}{\partial p^2}\right)\left(\frac{\partial^2 \pi_J(p^*,T^*)}{\partial T^2}\right) - \left(\frac{\partial^2 \pi_J(p^*,T^*)}{\partial p \partial T}\right)^2 = 1607.98 > 0$, $\frac{\partial^2 \pi_J(p^*,T^*)}{\partial p^2} = -6.34 < 0$ and $\frac{\partial^2 \pi_J(p^*,T^*)}{\partial T^2} = -260.87 < 0$. Hence, the said solution is a unique optimal solution.

Table 1 Optimal solutions

Scenarios	With discount/without discount	Cases	Joint decision			Independent decision		
			$\pi_r(p, T)$	$\pi_s(p, T)$	$\pi_J(p, T)$	$\pi_r(p, T)$	$\pi_s(p, T)$	$\pi_I(p, T)$
$T \le M_i$	With discount	$T \le M_1$	2277.05	1694.22	3971.27	2192.35	1218.16	3410.51
	Without discount	$T \le M_2$	2311.50	1687.21	3998.71	2360.54	1238.71	3599.26
$M_i \le T$	With discount	$0 \le M_1 \le t_1 \le t_2 \le T$	1690.65	1584.81	3275.46	2365.25	572.52	2937.77
		$0 \le t_1 \le M_1 \le t_2 \le T$	2049.14	1688.40	3737.54	2732.97	649.18	3382.15
		$0 \le t_1 \le t_2 \le M_1 \le T$	**2278.75**	**1756.89**	**4035.64**	2961.19	706.45	3667.65
	Without discount	$0 \le M_2 \le t_1 \le t_2 \le T$	1625.87	1643.41	3269.28	2339.15	579.15	2918.30
		$0 \le t_1 \le M_2 \le t_2 \le T$	1618.77	1664.50	3283.27	2345.23	582.14	2927.47
		$0 \le t_1 \le t_2 \le M_2 \le T$	1602.32	1721.82	3324.14	2364.07	591.24	2955.31

Bold values are optimum values of decision parameters

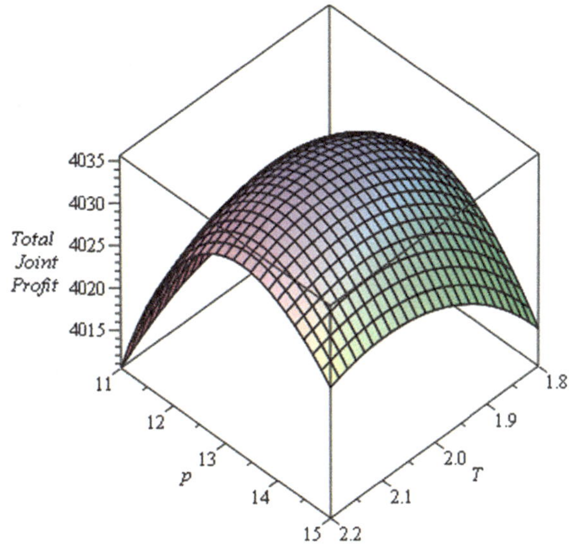

Fig. 4 Concavity of the profit function

Special case: To explore the impact of trade credit when choosing between an independent or joint decision on the supply chain performance, using the same data as in Example 5.1, the optimal solutions of 'cash on delivery' (i.e., $M_1 = M_2 = 0$) and '2/44 net 73' for each case are listed in Table 2.

Table 2 shows that the total profit for both the players and the whole supply chain for the two different type of credit limit strategy is greater than the total profit for the cash on delivery strategy. Therefore, the two different types of trade credits are beneficial to the supply chain as a whole. However, the profit gains in percentage are not always positive for the supplier. Under second credit limit 1.7 years or as the supplier extends the due date to second trade credit 2 years after delivery the supplier's profit gains in percentage are negative. To analyze the effect of trade credit using the same data of Example 5.1, computational result about M_1 and M_2 are obtained. From Table 2 it is analyzed that after 2 years of trade credit there is no effect of M_1 trade credit. In addition, after $M_2 = 2$ years discount in purchasing cost strategy is no longer beneficial for the players as well as supply chain. The positive and negative impact of total profit in % is described in the last three columns of Table 2.

From Table 3, it is examined that if the supply chain adopts joint decision with two different trade credits strategy than supply chain earns more profit compare to other strategies. Table 3 shows that under the joint and independent decision policies if the supplier offers trade credit to the retailer than it results in a lower selling price and therefore a greater market demand and supply chain profit. However, when the players opt independent policy, nevertheless of whether or not the supplier offers trade credit to the retailer, the selling price set in order to maximize the retailer's profit is two times more than that associated with a joint policy. The increasing price in turn shrinks market demand affecting the retailer's order quantity to drip for each

Table 2 Effect of the various credit limit on the total profit of the supply chain

M_1 (in a year)	M_2 (in a year)	The optimal time for payment (in a year)	p^* (in \$)	Q^* (units)	T^* (in a year)	Profit			Profit gain %		
						$\pi_r(p, T)$ (in \$)	$\pi_s(p, T)$ (in \$)	$\pi(p, T)$ (in \$)	$\pi_r(p, T)$ (in \$)	$\pi_s(p, T)$ (in \$)	$\pi(p, T)$ (in \$)
0	0	–	13.53	1201	2.027	2286.55	1727.30	4013.86	–	–	–
0	0.2	0	13.53	1201	2.027	2286.55	1727.30	4013.86	+0.00	+0.00	+0.00
0.06	0.2	0.06	13.34	1219	2.035	2282.22	1743.98	4026.20	−0.19	+0.97	+0.31
0.12	0.2	0.12	13.19	1239	2.050	2278.75	1756.89	4035.64	−0.34	+1.71	+0.54
0.18	0.2	0.18	13.06	1260	2.071	2276.01	1766.22	4042.23	−0.46	+2.25	+0.71
0	1.7	1.7	11.34	1958	2.998	2191.19	1860.46	4051.64	−4.17	+7.71	+0.94
0.06	1.7	1.7	11.34	1958	2.998	2191.19	1860.46	4051.64	−4.17	+7.71	+0.94
0.12	1.7	1.7	11.34	1958	2.998	2191.19	1860.46	4051.64	−4.17	+7.71	+0.94
0.18	1.7	1.7	11.34	1958	2.998	2191.19	1860.46	4051.64	−4.17	+7.71	+0.94
0	2	2	11.71	1778	2.781369	2586.42	1675.97	4262.39	+13.11	−2.97	+6.19
0.06	2	2	11.71	1778	2.781369	2586.42	1675.97	4262.39	13.11	−2.97	6.19
0.12	2	2	11.71	1778	2.781369	2586.42	1675.97	4262.39	13.11	−2.97	6.19
0.18	2	2	11.71	1778	2.781369	2586.42	1675.97	4262.39	13.11	−2.97	6.19

Profit gain = [(profit with trade credit − profit without trade credit)/profit without trade credit] * 100% (Ho et al., 2008)

Table 3 Optimal profit of the whole supply chain under different strategies

Decision making	Credit term(s)	Time for payment (in days)	Q (units)	p (in \$)	T (in year)	$\pi_r(p, T)$ (in \$)	$\pi_s(p, T)$ (in \$)	$\pi(p, T)$ (in \$)
Independent	Cash on delivery	0	679	36.97	2.81	2952.23	700.59	3652.82
	Trade credit 2/44, net 73	44	685	36.41	2.81	2961.19	706.45	3667.65
Joint	Cash on delivery	0	1201	13.52	2.03	2286.55	1727.3	4013.85
	Trade credit 2/44, net 73	44	1239	**13.19**	**2.05**	**2278.75**	**1756.89**	**4035.64**
Allocated						3258.30	777.33	4035.63

Bold values are optimum values of decision parameters

order. If the order quantity is reduced than the profit of the supplier and supply chain decrease remarkably. Additionally, from the supplier's point of view, a joint decision is more profitable than an independent policy even though the reverse is true for the retailer. Hence, in order to benefit both the players, a compensation method suggested by Goyal (1976) is applied to sustain long term business between both the players. The profit of the players is reallocated as follows:

$$\begin{aligned}\text{Retailer's profit} &= \pi_J\left(p^*, T^*\right) \times \frac{\pi_r(p^*, T^*)}{[\pi_r(p^*, T^*) + \pi_s(p^*, T^*)]}\\ &= 4035.64 \times \frac{2961.19}{3667.65}\\ &= 3258.30\end{aligned}$$

$$\begin{aligned}\text{Supplier's profit} &= \pi_J\left(p^*, T^*\right) \times \frac{\pi_s(p^*, T^*)}{[\pi_r(p^*, T^*) + \pi_s(p^*, T^*)]}\\ &= 4035.64 \times \frac{706.45}{3667.65}\\ &= 777.33\end{aligned}$$

The allocated results are also listed at the bottom of Table 3.

In Table 4, to illustrate the benefit of a coordinated lot size trade credit policy more clearly, a Summary of the profit of the supply chain under different strategies is listed in Table 4. This shows that the profit increase of a joint supply chain system is \$361.03 (= \$4013.85 − \$3652.82) for the 'cash on delivery' scenario and \$367.99

Table 4 Summary of the profit of the supply chain under different strategies

Credit term(s)	Independent decision	Joint decision	Improvement
Cash on delivery	\$3652.82	\$4013.85	\$361.03 (9.88%)
Trade credit 2/44, net 73	\$3667.65	\$4035.64	\$367.99 (10%)
Improvement	\$14.83 (0.4%)	\$21.79 (0.54%)	\$382.82 (10.48%)

(= \$4035.64 − \$3667.65) for the trade credit scenario. The percentage increase is approximate 10% in both the examples. Moreover, profit increase in the independent decision is \$14.83 (= \$3667.65 − \$3652.82) approximately 0.4% compared to cash on delivery strategy. Profit increase in the joint decision is \$21.79 (= \$4035.64 − \$4013.85) approximately 0.54% compared to cash on delivery strategy. In conclusion, the joint procedure of optimizing supply chain's total profit and trade credit policies is beneficial for the whole supply chain performance.

5 Sensitivity Analysis

Table 5 depicts the sensitivity analysis of example for centralized option carried out by varying one variable at a time as −20, −10, 10, and 20%.

To observe the sensitivity of the inventory parameters on the optimal solution, the data provided in the numerical example are considered. Optimal solutions for different values of a, b_2, t_1, t_2, I_{cr}, f_{cs}, A_r, h, η and C are presented in Table 5. The following observations could be made from Table 5.

1. Scale demand of the product, the exponential rate of change of demand for the product, time point t_1 and flexibility cash rate of the supplier decreases selling price of the product slowly however time point t_2, rate of interest earned for the retailer, ordering cost for the retailer and holding cost rate increases selling price of the product slowly. Moreover, the mark-up for selling price increases selling price of the product rapidly whereas the purchasing cost of the product increases the selling price of the product rapidly.
2. Rate of interest earned for the retailer, scale demand of the product, the exponential rate of change of demand for the product and time point t_1 decreases cycle time slowly whereas flexibility cash rate of the supplier, time point t_2, ordering cost for the retailer and holding cost rate increases cycle time slowly. In addition, the mark-up for selling price and purchasing cost of the product increase cycle time rapidly.
3. The exponential rate of change of demand for the product, time point t_2, rate of interest earned for the retailer, ordering cost for the retailer and holding cost rate decreases the total joint profit of the supply chain slowly however scale demand

Table 5 Sensitivity analysis of inventory parameters

Inventory parameter	Change (in %)	p	T	$\pi_J(p, T)$
a	8000	13.26	2.12	3199.73
	9000	13.22	2.08	3617.55
	10,000	**13.19**	**2.05**	**4035.64**
	11,000	13.16	2.02	4453.94
	12,000	13.14	2.00	4872.39
b_2	0.072	13.36	2.20	4113.76
	0.081	13.27	2.12	4073.85
	0.09	**13.19**	**2.05**	**4035.64**
	0.099	13.11	1.99	3998.98
	0.108	13.05	1.93	3963.70
t_1	0.04	13.37	2.29	3906.79
	0.045	13.28	2.17	3969.46
	0.05	**13.19**	**2.05**	**4035.64**
	0.055	13.10	1.92	4105.95
	0.06	13.01	1.78	4181.24
t_2	0.064	12.90	1.61	4266.28
	0.072	13.04	1.84	4143.88
	0.08	**13.19**	**2.05**	**4035.64**
	0.088	13.33	2.24	3937.71
	0.096	13.48	2.42	3847.71
I_{cr}	0.128	12.46	2.16	4094.31
	0.144	12.83	2.10	4064.08
	0.16	**13.19**	**2.05**	**4035.64**
	0.176	13.53	2.01	4008.75
	0.192	13.86	1.97	3983.21
f_{cs}	0.136	13.97	1.98	3976.64
	0.153	13.58	2.01	4005.40
	0.17	**13.19**	**2.05**	**4035.64**
	0.187	12.78	2.09	4067.58
	0.204	12.36	2.14	4101.44
A_r	240	13.13	1.99	4065.33
	270	13.16	2.02	4050.38
	300	**13.19**	**2.05**	**4035.64**
	330	13.22	2.08	4021.11
	360	13.25	2.11	4006.76
h	0.064	13.07	2.02	4065.56

(continued)

Table 5 (continued)

Inventory parameter	Change (in %)	p	T	$\pi_J(p, T)$
	0.072	13.13	2.03	4050.56
	0.08	**13.19**	**2.05**	**4035.64**
	0.088	13.25	2.07	4020.81
	0.096	13.31	2.08	4006.05
η	1.08	29.25	1.87	5966.68
	1.2	**13.19**	**2.05**	**4035.64**
	1.32	9.18	2.20	2898.40
	1.44	7.37	2.34	2140.22
C	1.6	10.40	1.87	4307.48
	1.8	11.79	1.96	4163.46
	2	**13.19**	**2.05**	**4035.64**
	2.2	14.60	2.14	3920.73
	2.4	16.02	2.22	3816.34

Bold values are optimum values of decision parameters

of the product, time point t_1 and flexibility cash rate of the supplier increases the total joint profit of the supply chain slowly. Moreover, the mark-up for selling price and purchasing cost of the product decreases cycle time rapidly.

The model examines that mark-up for selling price and purchasing cost of the product is a highly impactful parameter for the model.

6 Conclusions

The paper contained two-layered supply chain inventory model of the constant deteriorating item. This model considered time- and price-dependent trapezoidal demand which is a very realistic approach for electronics and fashion industries. In this paper, supplier gave two different types of trade credit options that if retailer pay at first trade credit then the retailer can be entitled to get a discount in purchasing cost. However, if the player failed to pay at first and paid all the payment at the second trade credit then the player will not be entitled to the same. Furthermore, the player also discussed two different decisions, one is joint, and other is an independent decision. Paper concluded that if the retailer pays at the first trade credit and takes benefit of discount and also supply chain worked together then the whole supply chain gets more profit than other decisions. Moreover, this discount policy is not useful for a long period of the business. As a result, the paper concluded from Table 4 that if the supplier sets the long period of trade credit means nearer to cycle time then discount policy is not worked.

The current study can have numerous likely extensions, for example, the model can be further generalized by finite production rate, time-varying deterioration product, partial or full backlogging credit limit related with order amount at the receipt in the inventory system. One can also analyze and apply a multi-echelon supply chain. One can allow shortages in this model.

References

Aggarwal, S. P., & Jaggi, C. K. (1995). Ordering policies of deteriorating items under permissible delay in payments. *The Journal of the Operational Research Society, 46*(5), 658–662.

Bakker, M., Riezebos, J., & Teunter, R. H. (2012). Review of inventory system with a deterioration since 2001. *European Journal of Operation Research, 221*(2), 275–284.

Bykadorov, I., Ellero, A., Moretti, E., & Vianello, S. (2009). The role of a retailer's performance in optimal wholesale price discount policies. *European Journal of Operational Research, 194*(2009), 538–550.

Cai, X., Feng, Y., Li, Y., & Shi, D. (2013). Optimal pricing policy for a deteriorating product by dynamic tracking control. *International Journal of Production Research, 51*(8), 2491–2504.

Chang, C. T., Cheng, M. C., & Ouyang, L. Y. (2015). Optimal pricing and ordering policies for non-instantaneously deteriorating items under order-size-dependent delay in payments. *Applied Mathematical Modelling, 39*(1), 747–763.

Chang, H. (2013). A note on an economic lot size model for price-dependent demand under quantity and freight discounts. *International Journal of Production Economics, 144*(2013), 175–179.

Chen, S. C., Cárdenas-Barrón, L. E., & Teng, J. T. (2014). Retailer's economic order quantity when the supplier offers conditionally permissible delay in payments link to order quantity. *International Journal of Production Economics, 155*(2014), 284–291.

Cheng, M., Zhang, B., & Wang, G. (2011). Optimal policy for deteriorating items with trapezoidal type demand and partial backlogging. *Applied Mathematical Modelling, 35*, 3552–3560.

Chua, G. A., Mokhlesi, R., & Sainathan, A. (2016). Optimal discounting and replenishment policies for perishable products. *International Journal of Production Economics, 186*(2017), 8–20.

Drezner, Z., & Wesolowsky, G. O. (1989). Multi-buyer discount pricing. *European Journal of Operational Research, 40*(1989), 38–42.

Feng, L., Chan, Y. L., & Cárdenas-Barrón, L. E. (2017). Pricing and lot-sizing polices for perishable goods when the demand depends on selling price, displayed stocks, and expiration date. *International Journal of Production Economics, 185*, 11–20.

Goyal, S. K. (1976). An integrated inventory model for a single supplier–single customer problem. *International Journal of Production Research, 15*(1), 107–111.

Goyal, S. K., & Giri, B. C. (2001). Recent trend in modeling of deteriorating inventory. *European Journal of Operational Research, 134*(1), 1–16.

Goyal, S. K., & Nebebe, F. (2000). Deterioration of economic production-shipment policy for a single vendor single buyer system. *European Journal of the Operation Research, 121*(1), 175–178.

Ho, C. H., Ouyang, L. Y., & Su, C. H. (2008). Optimal pricing, shipment and payment policy for an integrated supplier–buyer inventory model with two-part trade credit. *European Journal of Operational Research, 187*(2008), 496–510.

Khouja, M., Ajjan, H., & Liu, X. (2019). The effect of return and price adjustment policies on a retailer's performance. *European Journal of Operational Research*. https://doi.org/10.1016/j.ejor.2019.01.021

Lio, C., Leng, M., Huang, J., & Liang, L. (2014). Supply chain analysis under a price-discount incentive scheme for electric vehicles. *European Journal of Operational Research, 235*(2014), 329–333.

Motlagh, S. M. H., Nematollahi, M., Johari, M., & Sarker, B. R. (2018). A collaborative model for coordination of monopolistic manufacturer's promotional efforts and competing duopolistic retailers' trade credits. *International Journal of Production Economic*. https://doi.org/10.1016/j.ijpe.2018.07.027

Moussawi-Haidar, L., Salameh, M., & Nasr, W. (2014). Effect of deterioration on the instantaneous replenishment model with imperfect quality items. *Applied Mathematical Modelling, 38*(24), 5956–5966.

Nie, T., & Du, S. (2016). Dual-fairness supply chain with quantity discount contracts. *European Journal of Operational Research, 258*(2), 491–500.

Niu, B., Chen, L., Liu, Y., & Jin, Y. (2019). Joint price and quality decisions considering Chinese customers' variety seeking behavior. *International Journal of Production Economics*. https://doi.org/10.1016/j.ijpe.2019.02.022

Qin, Y., Tang, H., & Guo, C. (2007). Channel coordination and volume discounts with price-sensitive demand. *International Journal of Production Economics, 105*(2007), 43–53.

Raafat, F. (1991). Survey of literature on continuously deteriorating inventory models. *The Journal of the Operational Research Society, 42*(1), 27–37.

Rabbani, M., Zia, N. P., & Rafiei, H. (2015). Coordinated replenishment and marketing policies for non-instantaneous stock deterioration problem. *Computers & Industrial Engineering, 88*, 49–62.

Rameswari, M., & Uthayakumar, R. (2017). An integrated inventory model for deteriorating items with price-dependent demand under two-level trade credit policy. *International Journal of Systems Science: Operations & Logistics*. https://doi.org/10.1080/23302674.2017.1292432

Rau, H., Wu, M. Y., & Wee, H. M. (2003). Integrated inventory model for deteriorating items under a multi-echelon supply chain environment. *International Journal of Production Economics, 86*(1), 155–168.

Sarkar, B. (2012). An EOQ model with delay in payments and time varying deterioration rate. *Mathematical and Computer Modelling, 55*(3–4), 367–377.

Sarkar, B., & Mahapatra, A. S. (2017). Periodic review fuzzy inventory model with variable lead time and fuzzy demand. *International Transactions in Operational Research, 24*(5), 1197–1227.

Sarkar, B., & Saren, S. (2017). Ordering and transfer policy and variable deterioration for a warehouse model. *Hacettepe Journal of Mathematics and Statistics, 46*(5), 985–1014.

Sarkar, B., Saren, S., & Cárdenas-Barrón, L. E. (2015). An inventory model with trade-credit policy and variable deterioration for fixed lifetime products. *Annals of Operations Research, 229*(1), 677–702.

Sarkar, M., & Sarkar, B. (2013). An economic manufacturing quantity model with probabilistic deterioration in a production system. *Economic Modelling, 31*, 245–252.

Shah, N. H., Chaudhari, U., & Jani, M. Y. (2016a). An integrated production-inventory model with preservation technology investment for time-varying deteriorating item under time and price sensitive demand. *International Journal of Inventory Research, 3*(1), 81–98.

Shah, N. H., Chaudhari, U., & Jani, M. Y. (2016b). Optimal policies for time-varying deteriorating item with preservation technology under selling price and trade credit dependent quadratic demand in a supply chain. *International Journal of Applied and Computational Mathematics, 3*(2), 363–379.

Shah, N. H., Chaudhari, U., & Jani, M. Y. (2019). Effect of manufacturer's innovation and retailer's promotion under trapezoidal demand with centralized and decentralized options. *TOP, 27*(1), 55–69.

Shah, N. H., Gor, A. S., & Jhaveri, C. A. (2011). Determination of optimal ordering and transfer policy for deteriorating inventory system when demand is quadratic. *International Journal of Management Science and Engineering Management, 6*(4), 278–283.

Shah, N. H., & Jani, M. Y. (2016). Economic order quantity model for non-instantaneously deteriorating item under order size dependent trade credit for prize sensitive quadratic demand. *AMSE Journals—2016 Series, 37*(1), 1–19.

Shah, N. H., Jani, M. Y., & Chaudhari, U. (2017). Retailer's optimal policies for price-credit dependent trapezoidal demand under two-level trade credit. *International Journal of Operations and Quantitative Management, 23*(2), 115–130.
Shao, L., Yang, J., & Zhang, M. (2017). Subsidy scheme or price discount scheme? Mass adoption of electric vehicles under different market structures. *European Journal of Operational Research.* https://doi.org/10.1016/j.ejor.2017.04.030
Sobhani, A., Wahab, M. I. M., & Jaber, M. Y. (2019). The effect of working environment aspects on a vendor–buyer inventory model. *International Journal of Production Economics.* https://doi.org/10.1016/j.ijpe.2018.11.017
Tai, A. H., Xie, Y., He, W., & Ching, W. K. (2019). Joint inspection and inventory control for deteriorating items with random maximum lifetime. *International Journal of Production Economics.* https://doi.org/10.1016/j.ijpe.2018.03.020
Taleizadeh, A. A., & Pentico, D. W. (2014). An economic order quantity model with partial backordering and all-units discount. *International Journal of Production Economics, 155*(2014), 172–184.
Tiwari, S., Cárdenas-Barrón, L. E., Goh, M., & Shaikh, A. A. (2018). Joint pricing and inventory model for deteriorating items with expiration dates and partial backlogging under two-level partial trade credits in supply chain. *International Journal of Production Economics.* https://doi.org/10.1016/j.ijpe.2018.03.006
Venegas, B. B., & Ventura, J. A. (2017). A two-stage supply chain co-ordination mechanism considering price sensitive demand and quantity discounts. *European Journal of Operational Research.* https://doi.org/10.1016/j.ejor.2017.06.030
Viswanathan, S., & Wang, Q. (2003). Discount pricing decisions in distribution channels with price-sensitive demand. *European Journal of Operational Research, 149*(2003), 571–587.
Wang, H., Yu, Y., Zhang, W., & Hua, Z. (2018). Procurement strategies for lost-sales inventory systems with all-units discounts. *European Journal of Operational Research.* https://doi.org/10.1016/j.ejor.2018.06.053
Wee, H. M., & Yu, J. (1997). A deteriorating inventory model with a temporary price discount. *International Journal of Production Economics, 53*(1997), 81–90.
Wu, J., Al-Khateeb, F. B., Teng, J. T., & Cárdenas-Barrón, L. E. (2016). Inventory models for deteriorating items with maximum lifetime under downstream partial trade credits to credit-risk customers by discounted cash-flow analysis. *International Journal of Production Economics, 171*(1), 105–115.
Yang, H. L. (2020). Retailer's ordering policy for demand depending on the expiration date with limited storage capacity under supplier credits linked to order quantity and discounted cash flow. *International Journal of Systems Science: Operations & Logistics.* https://doi.org/10.1080/23302674.2019.1701727
Yang, P. C. (2004). Pricing strategy for deteriorating items using quantity discount when demand is price sensitive. *European Journal of Operational Research, 157*(2004), 389–397.
Yu, J. C. P. (2018). Optimizing a two-warehouse system under shortage backordering, trade credit, and decreasing rental conditions. *International Journal of Production Economics.* https://doi.org/10.1016/j.ijpe.2018.06.003

A Coordinated Single-Vendor Single-Buyer Inventory System with Deterioration and Freight Discounts

Monika K. Naik and Nita H. Shah

Abstract This chapter deals with a coordinated inventory model by considering supply chain of two stage, single-vendor and single-buyer. An equally sized shipment from vendor to buyer is conducted, and the buyer's rate of market demand is taken as a constant. Also, in the model, the concept of cost associated with freight discount is undertaken, and formulations are done on the basis of all-weight freight discount model and incremental freight discount model. In this chapter, an estimation of the optimal values of replenishment cycle length, lot size by minimizing the buyer's total cost, vendor's total cost as well as total cost of the supply chain inventory system dealing deteriorating items are considered. The increase in the number of production batch lot size factor and number of shipments from the vendor to the buyer will lead to decrease the total cost. Numerical examples are provided to illustrate the theoretical results and convexity of total cost is established. Managerial observations are outlined using sensitivity analysis. The result analysis demonstrates that on imposing freight discount into inventory model results in significant reduction on total cost. Finally, it can be concluded that freight discount model associated with incremental concept gives substantial effects on minimizing the objective of system's aggregate inventory cost.

Keywords Inventory models · Single-vendor and single-buyer · Freight cost · Deterioration · All-weight freight discount · Incremental freight discount

1 Introduction

The inventory models related to system dealing with two-step supply chain having a buyer and a vendor are considered as a major research area which is joint economic lot sizing model (JELS). Model focuses majorly on combining manufacturing result in vendor direction as well as shipment plan in buyer direction to minimize aggregate

M. K. Naik (✉)
Vadodara, Gujarat, India

N. H. Shah
Department of Mathematics, Gujarat University, Ahmedabad, Gujarat, India

N. H. Shah and M. Mittal (eds.), *Soft Computing in Inventory Management*, Inventory Optimization, https://doi.org/10.1007/978-981-16-2156-7_11

cost. Though, generally JELS included cost associated with freight discount as a portion of ordering cost (OC) by disregarding its association with size of shipments. In real situations, the cost associated with freight discount is the key element of aggregate cost associated with logistic. The authors Swenseth and Godfrey (2002) claimed that uplifting of fifty percentage of the aggregate cost associated with total logistic is due to carriage action. So, linking cost associated with freight discount in manufacturing and inventory choices is necessary to add in order to have a well concluding scheduling choice.

Baumol and Vinod (1970) were the first authors who have introduced the inventory–theoretic models including transportation and inventory costs. By using enumeration technique, Langley (1980) considered actual carrier freight rates function into lot sizing decision. Abad and Aggarwal (2005) developed a model for determining the buyer's lot sizing and pricing that there are freight and all-unit quantity discount. Ertogral et al. (2007) introduced a production-inventory model including freight cost by considering cost associated with discounts of freight structures in all unit. Toptal (2009) included cost associated with freight discounts and all-unit quantity discounts in cost function of inventory. Mendoza and Ventura (2008) proposed an algorithm depending on a grossly simplified freight rate structure. He et al. (2010) explained an algorithm for finding the optimal purchase quantity utilizing actual freight rates. Darwish (2008) extended the model by including freight rate discount. Juhari et al. (2016) introduced an integrated inventory model for single-vendor single-buyer system with freight rate discount and stochastic demand. An inventory model dealing with modeling and analyzing incremental quantity discounts in transportation costs for a joint economic lot sizing problem was derived by Rasay et al. (2019). An integrated inventory system with freight costs and two types of quantity discounts was proposed by Darma and Wangsa (2020).

As such, deterioration is a process of becoming gradually worse, damage, decay, spoilage, loss of utility resulting in a declination of the usefulness of the original one. Deterioration reduces the quality and physical quantity of inventory. The product's selling price is one of the key factors in uplifting customer's demand of a product which is directly influenced by customer's satisfaction level. Recent studies include selling price-based rate of market demand and much weightage on deterioration is drawn to highlight the shorter life cycles of goods. Therefore, appropriate inventory control of deterioration of items is considered to be a crucial matter to elaborate.

Datta and Pal (2001) proposed an inventory model with stock-dependent and price-based demand rate. Further, joint pricing inventory model for deteriorating items with quantity discount and time-dependent partial backlogging by applying Weibull distribution was derived by Papachristos and Skouri (2003). Singh (2006) studied an inventory model for deteriorating items with price-based demand. Chang et al. (2010) proposed an optimal replenishment policy for non-instantaneous deteriorating items with stock dependent demand. Under progressive payment scheme, for price-stock-based demand for obtaining an optimal ordering and pricing policy a model was proposed by Shah et al. (2011).

Hou et al. (2011) derived an inventory model for perishable products under partial backlogging, inflation having stock-based selling rate. Two warehouses inventory model for non-instantaneous perishable products for stock-dependent demand were proposed by Singh and Malik (2011).

On considering a joint pricing policy, partial backlogging and time–price-based market demand rate for a non-instantaneous deteriorating item was proposed by Maihami and Kamalabadi (2012). Panda et al. (2013) explained an inventory model for deteriorating products by utilizing ramp-type demand. An inventory model by Qin et al. (2014) estimates an optimal solution by formulating an algorithm for calculating selling price, where deterioration is considered as quality and physical quantity dependent.

An inventory model by Rabbani et al. (2016) was proposed dealing with immediate deterioration for quality and delayed deterioration for physical quantity for estimating optimal dynamic pricing and replenishment policies. An inventory model under price- and stock-dependent demand for controllable deterioration rate with shortages and preservation technology investment was represented by Mishra et al. (2017). An integrated inventory model for deteriorating items with price-dependent demand under two-level trade credit policy was derived by Rameswari and Uthayakumar (2018). An inventory control problem by considering joint pricing of duopoly retailers with deteriorating items and linear demand was considered by Mahmoodi (2019). An economic order quantity model under two-level partial trade credit for time varying deteriorating items was described by Mahata et al. (2020).

The uniqueness of this chapter is it consists of constant demand rate where an estimation of the optimal values of replenishment cycle length, lot size by minimizing the buyer's aggregate cost, vendor's aggregate cost as well as total cost of the supply chain inventory system dealing deteriorating items are considered. Finally, the model is validated through hypothetical data.

The chapter contains five sections. In Sect. 2, notations and assumptions are explained. Section 3 deals with the development of mathematical model. Numerical examples and sensitivity analysis are given in Sect. 4. Section 5 consists of conclusion part.

2 Notations and Assumptions

2.1 Notations

Inventory parameters	
D	Rate of market demand/unit time (in units)
P	Rate of production/unit time (in units)
K	Setup cost of production (in dollars)
A	Cost of order by buyer/order with size (in dollars)
v	Cost of purchase/unit product (in dollars)

(continued)

(continued)

Inventory parameters	
FC_j	Cost of freight discount by buyer at discount level *j*/unit product (in dollars)
PF_j	Addition of cost of purchase and cost of freight discount at level of discount *j* (in dollars)
PC	Cost of production by vendor/unit product (in dollars)
t_1	Time for in-transit (in years)
Q_j	Breakpoint of quantity at level of discount *j* (in units)
OC	Cost of ordering/unit time (in dollars)
SC_j	Cost of shipping at level of discount level *j*/unit time (in dollars)
HCB	Aggregate cost of holding by buyer/unit time (in dollars)
HCT	Cost of holding related to in-transit by buyer/unit time (in dollars)
HCH	Cost of holding related to in-house by buyer/unit time (in dollars)
SCV	Cost of Setup by vendor/unit time (in dollars)
HCV	Cost of holding by vendor/unit time (in dollars)
TCB_j	Projected cost for buyer/unit time at level of discount *j* (in dollars)
TCV	Projected cost for vendor/unit time (in dollars)
TC_j	Projected aggregate cost/unit time at level of discount *j* (in dollars)
ICH	Charge of inventory carrying related to in-transit by buyer (in dollars)
ICT	Charge of inventory carrying related to in-house by buyer (in dollars)
ICV	Charge of inventory carrying by vendor (in dollars)
n	Count of shipments from vendor to buyer (an integer which is positive)
m	Lot size factor of batch of production (in a positive integer)
Q	Equal shipment size from vendor to buyer (in units)
T	Replenishment cycle length (in years)
θ_1	Deterioration rate from buyer to vendor
θ_2	Deterioration rate from vendor to customer

2.2 Assumptions

1. A single-vendor single-buyer integrated inventory system for single item is considered.
2. The market demand is taken constant.
3. The product is sold to buyer by vendor then customer purchases the product from buyer.
4. The buyer orders the product to the vendor in a constant lot of size nq.
5. The buyer's order is considered in nq/D interval.

Table 1 The fright cost offered by the shipper

K	Weight of shipment P	Freight cost N_k
0	$0 < P < M_1$	N_0
1	$M_1 \leq P < M_2$	N_1
$\vdots$	$\vdots$	$\vdots$
K	$P \geq K$	N_K

Source Juhari et al. (2016)

6. The batch size of vendor production is mq with finite rate of production $P(P > D)$.
7. Let the deterioration rates be θ_1 and θ_2 be constants where $0 \leq \theta_1, \theta_2 \leq 1$.
8. The freight cost is considered and charged to the buyer.

In this problem, the buyer pays freight cost $\left(Y_j\right)$ to the shipper for each shipment weight of W, scheduled by the shipper assuming that the weight of a shipment is proportional to its lot size. The shipper provides two discount policies, namely all-weight freight discount and incremental freight discount. The fright cost offered by the shipper as shown in Table 1 as in Juhari et al. (2016). Here, M_K is the weight of freight where rate of freight breakpoint comes. The fright-rate breakpoint occurs at the sequence $M_1 < M_2 < M_3 < \ldots < M_K$. Each weight's fright cost (N_k) is incurred at a shipment for weight W that lies on interval M_K and M_{K+1} with $N_0 > N_1 > N_2 > \ldots > N_K$.

In case of implementing the discount associated with incremental policy, cost associated with freight discount in the scheduled table is applicable to weight lying in the discount category range. However, considering the policy of discount as all-weight which is applicable to all weight shipping as elongated as the weight of shipping is upgrowing the rate of freight breakpoint. This plan of discount is dependent on weight of freight which can be changed by $q_k = M_k/p$. where q_k represents the lot size if breakpoint of freight rate arises and p is the weight for freight per unit product. Therefore, cost of freight occurring at cut-off point k is calculated as $F_k = pN_k$.

Assume that the payment is received by the vendor which is previously delivered and the shipper accumulates sum later the items reach at the place of buyer. Therefore, consider the categories of cost of holding by buyer as cost associated with in-transit and cost associated with in-house. The cost of holding by buyer is associated per item to buyer from vendor throughout in-transit duration (t). The cost of holding associated with in-transit sum is based on cost of purchasing as buyer have yet to recompense the cost associated with freight discount in case items yet on the journey. While cost of holding associated with in-house sum is based on cost of purchasing and cost associated with freight discount, as once the arrival of shipment at buyer's place, the freight cost has been paid.

3 Mathematical Model Formulation

Let $\theta_1 = \theta_{01},\ 0 \le \theta_{01} \le 1, \theta_2 = \theta_{02},\ 0 \le \theta_{02} \le 1$ be the constant deterioration rates from buyer to vendor and vendor to customers. The inventory level $I_i(t)$ for $i = 1, 2$ at any time instant t, at buyer and at vendor, respectively, declines due to the combined effect of rate of demand and deterioration. Also, increases due to production rate per unit time P are governed by the following differential equations for each time periods.

$$\frac{\mathrm{d}I_1(t)}{\mathrm{d}t} = P - D - \theta_1 I_1(t); \quad 0 \le t \le t_1 \tag{1}$$

$$\frac{\mathrm{d}I_2(t)}{\mathrm{d}t} = D - \theta_2 I_2(t); \quad t_1 \le t \le T \tag{2}$$

with boundary conditions;

$$I_1(0) = I_2(T) = 0. \tag{3}$$

On applying the boundary conditions to Eqs. (1) and (2), we get the respective inventory levels of buyer and vendor

$$I_1(t) = \frac{(P - D)}{\theta_1} + \frac{(D - P)}{\theta_1 \mathrm{e}^{\theta_1 t}} \tag{4}$$

$$I_2(t) = \frac{D\left(-1 + \mathrm{e}^{\theta_2 (T-t)}\right)}{\theta_2} \tag{5}$$

This section consists of proposing two inventory models containing the freight discount policy stated as freight discount model associated with all-weight policy and freight discount model associated with incremental policy.

1. Freight discount model associated with all-weight policy

The model's main aim is to minimize the projected aggregate cost per unit time $\left(\mathrm{TC}_j\right)$ of inventory system consisting of the projected buyer cost $\left(\mathrm{TCB}_j\right)$ at level j and the projected cost to vendor (TCV). The projected cost associated with buyer contains ordering cost/unit time (OC), cost associated with shipping at level of discount j/unit time $\left(\mathrm{SC}_j\right)$, cost of holding to buyer/unit time (HCB). For buyer, ordering cost (OC) for each order (A) is acquired by buyer per order having size (nQ) and amount of order/unit time (D/nQ). Therefore, below costs are calculated as

The ordering cost (OC) per unit time:

$$\text{The ordering cost (OC) per unit time: OC} = \frac{DA}{nQ} \tag{6}$$

The (SC_j) is incurred by the buyer to the shipper on each shipment with size of Q at the level j. The cost associated with level j of freight discount policy (FC_j) and the cost of freight discount for batch size Q are calculated as QF_j. Therefore, (SC_j) per unit time is defined by taking the product of number of shipments per unit time (D/Q), and hence, shipment cost is given as follows:

$$\mathrm{SC}_j = \frac{D(\mathrm{FC}_j)Q}{Q}; \quad j = 0, 1, \ldots J \tag{7}$$

The HCB contains two types of cost associated with holding, namely cost associated with holding in in-transit policy HCT and cost associated with holding in-house policy HCH. The cost associated with holding in in-transit policy is calculated using Eq. (4):

$$\mathrm{HCT} = v\mathrm{ICT}\int_0^{t_1} I_1(t)\mathrm{d}t \tag{8}$$

The charge associated in carrying inventory by in-house policy ICH, the aggregate of cost of purchasing, cost of freight discount FC_j and average of level of inventory of buyer in duration, cost associated in holding inventory with in-house policy for buyer are derived as

$$\mathrm{HCH} = \mathrm{ICH}(v + \mathrm{FC}_j)\frac{Q}{2} \tag{9}$$

Therefore, the calculation of aggregate cost of holding by buyer is the total of Eqs. (8) and (9)

$$\mathrm{HCB} = \mathrm{HCT} + \mathrm{HCH} = v\mathrm{ICT}\int_0^{t_1} I_1(t)\mathrm{d}t + \mathrm{ICH}(v + \mathrm{FC}_j)\frac{Q}{2} \tag{10}$$

Lastly, the projected cost for buyer/unit time TCB_j can be derived using Eqs. (6), (7) and (10)

$$\mathrm{TCB}_j = \mathrm{OC} + \mathrm{HCB} + \mathrm{SC}_j, \quad \text{for } j = 0, 1, 2 \ldots J \tag{11}$$

2. Freight discount model associated with incremental policy

The projected aggregate cost/unit time TC_j for freight discount model associated with incremental policy consists of the projected buyer cost TCB_j and the projected vendor cost TCV. The projected cost for the buyer consists of OC, SC_j and cost of holding of the buyer HCB. In derivation of aggregate projected cost/unit time for incremental freight discount model, we utilize buyer's shipping cost and buyer's cost of holding associated with in-house policy that utilizes freight discount model of incremental policy depending on incremental quantity discount model developed by Muckstadt and Sapra (2010).

On the basis of the calculation of SC_j in (7), deriving the updated SC_j which utilizes freight discount model associated with incremental policy. Derived model consists of cost associated with aggregate of cost associated with freight discount for a shipment size of Q lying on discount interval FC_j, and FC_{j+1} is given by:

$$\begin{aligned}\mathrm{FC}(Q) &= \mathrm{FC}_0(Q_1 - Q_0) + \mathrm{FC}_1(Q_2 - Q_1) + \cdots + \mathrm{FC}_{j-1}(Q_j - Q_{j-1})\\ &\quad + \mathrm{FC}_j(Q - Q_j),\\ &\text{where, } j = 1, 2, \ldots J\end{aligned} \tag{12}$$

As stated in Juhari et al. (2016), we can derive the shipping cost in the similar manner as

$$\begin{aligned}\mathrm{SC}_j &= \frac{D(\mathrm{FC}_j)Q}{Q}; \quad j = 0, 1, \ldots J\\ &= D\big((R_j + \mathrm{FC}_j Q - \mathrm{FC}_j Q)/Q\big)\end{aligned} \tag{13}$$

where $R_j = (\mathrm{FC}_0)(Q(1) - Q(0)) + (\mathrm{FC}_1)(Q(2) - Q(1)) + \cdots + (\mathrm{FC}_{j-1})(Q(j) - Q(j-1))$ and taking $R_0 = 0$.

In order to derive the cost associated with in-house holding policy based on freight discount model with incremental policy, using Eq. (8) as the elementary equation. In case of freight discount model with incremental policy, the aggregate of cost of purchasing and cost of freight discount at discount level j and SC_j is derived as $\mathrm{SC}_j = v + \mathrm{FC}_j$. Therefore, Eq. (8) is

$$\mathrm{HCT} = (v + \mathrm{FC}_j)\mathrm{ICT}\int_0^{t_1} I_1(t)\mathrm{d}t \tag{14}$$

Therefore, fright cost associated with holding in-house inventory by incremental policy is

$$\mathrm{HCH} = \mathrm{ICH}(v + \mathrm{FC}_j)\frac{Q}{2} \tag{15}$$

Therefore, the buyer's total holding cost is given by

$$\mathrm{HCB} = \mathrm{HCT} + \mathrm{HCH} = (v + \mathrm{FC}_j)\mathrm{ICT}\int_0^{t_1} I_1(t)\mathrm{d}t + \mathrm{ICH}(v + \mathrm{FC}_j)\frac{Q}{2} \tag{16}$$

Lastly, the projected cost for buyer/unit time in incremental freight model TCB_j can be calculated by considering Eqs. (6), (12) and (16)

$$\mathrm{TCB}_j = \mathrm{OC} + \mathrm{HCB} + \mathrm{SC}_j, \quad \text{for } j = 0, 1, 2 \ldots J \tag{17}$$

The projected cost by vendor contains cost of setup (SCV) as well as cost of holding by vendor (HCV). As the cost associated with setup of vendor for individual production run as K and the quantity of setup of production/unit time is $\frac{D}{mQ}$, cost associated with setup/unit time can be computed by

$$\text{Setup cost of vendor: SCV} = \frac{DK}{mQ} \tag{18}$$

The cost of holding by vendor is computed by charge of carrying inventory ICV, cost of production PC and the average of level of inventory of vendor. Therefore, the

$$\text{Holding cost of vendor: HCV} = \frac{mQ\,\mathrm{ICV}\,\mathrm{PC}\int_{t_1}^{T} I_2(t)\mathrm{d}t}{2P} \tag{19}$$

Therefore, the total vendor cost can be calculated as

$$\mathrm{TCV} = \mathrm{SCV} + \mathrm{HCV} = \frac{DK}{mQ} + \frac{mQ\,\mathrm{ICV}\,\mathrm{PC}\int_{t_1}^{T} I_2(t)\mathrm{d}t}{2P} \tag{20}$$

Therefore, the total cost of inventory system can be calculated as

$$\mathrm{TC}_j = \mathrm{TCB}_j + \mathrm{TCV}, \quad \text{where } j = 1, 2, \ldots J \tag{21}$$

Solution Methodology

The procedure for finding the optimal solution can be computed by using the following algorithm, in both cases with respective formulae for computing the optimality.

Solution Algorithm for Both Cases

1. Start.
2. For fixed n and m, computing the sum of ordering cost and freight cost per unit.
3. Computing production lot size Q_j, for each $j = 0, 1, 2 \ldots, J$ and replenishment cycle length T.
4. Computing total cost TC_j, for each $j = 0, 1, 2 \ldots, J$.
5. Is $Q_j^* \leq Q_j, j = 0, 1, 2 \ldots, J$. If yes, go to step 6; otherwise, go to step 7.
6. Q_j^* is the feasible solution then, computing total cost TC_j at Q_j^*, where $\mathrm{TC}\left(Q_j^*\right) = \mathrm{TC}_j^*$. Then, go to step 8.
7. Q_j^* is not a feasible solution then, computing production lot size Q_j, for another j value and replenishment cycle length T. Then, go to step 4.

8. Is $TC_j^* \le TC_j$, for each j as 0, 1, 2 ..., J and for all m as $m - 1$. If yes, set m as $m + 1$ and switch to step 9; otherwise, repeat steps 1–5.
9. Is $TC_j^* \le TC_j$, for each $j = 0, 1, 2 \ldots, J$. Then, go to step 10 otherwise go to step 5.
10. TC_j^* is final optimal solution.
11. Stop.

Now, by classical optimization technique to minimize the total cost stated in Eq. (22), we apply the necessary and sufficient condition:

$$\frac{\partial TC_j}{\partial T} = 0, \quad \frac{\partial TC_j}{\partial Q} = 0 \tag{22}$$

To check the convexity of the total cost function of obtained solution, we adopt the below stated algorithm,

Step 1: Assigning the inventory parameters some specific hypothetical values.
Step 2: Obtaining the solutions by solving simultaneous equations stated in Eq. (22), utilizing the mathematical software Maple XVIII.
Step 3: For convexity of total cost function with respect to optimal replenishment cycle and ordered quantity, computing all the eigen values of below stated Hessian matrix H for the optimal values obtained from Eq. (22), $H = \begin{bmatrix} \frac{\partial^2 TC_j}{\partial T^2} & \frac{\partial^2 TC_j}{\partial TQ} \\ \frac{\partial^2 TC_j}{\partial QT} & \frac{\partial^2 TC_j}{\partial Q^2} \end{bmatrix}$.

If all of the eigenvalues are positive, the total cost is minimum at the optimal values. Then, we can conclude that total cost function is convex in nature with respect to replenishment cycle lengths as well as ordered quantity both.

4 Numerical Example and Sensitivity Analysis

4.1 Numerical Analysis

Consider the specified value of the variables in all-units freight discount model and incremental freight discount model for different freight discount policies with cases with $n = 1$–2 and $m = 1$–4 as in Tables 2 and 3, respectively.

Consider the specified value of the variables in incremental freight discount model for different freight discount policies with cases with $n = 1$–2 and $m = 1$–4.

Table 2 All-units freight discount model with n = 1–2 and m = 1–4

D units	*P* units	*K* \$	*A* \$	ICT \$	ICH \$	ICV \$	*m*	*n*	t_1 years	PC \$	θ_1 %	θ_2 %
10,000	50,000	10	10	0.01	0.8	0.2	1	1	1	2	10	10
					0.6		2				30	20
				0.67	0.45	0.3	3				30	25
				0.92	0.451		4					
				0.01	0.8	0.2	1				10	10
					0.6		2					
				0.1	0.54		3					
				0.7	0.552	0.1	4					
				0.01	0.6	0.1	1				10	10
					0.45		2					
				0.88	0.451		3					
				0.455	0.147		4					
				0.2	0.7	0.1	1				10	10
				0.09	0.52		2					
				0.48	0.49		3					
				0.75	0.325		4					
10,000	50,000	10	10	0.01	0.6	0.2	1	2	1	2	10	10
					0.4		2					
					0.334		3					
				0.9	0.314		4					
				0.99	0.675		1					
				0.99	0.475		2					
				0.99	0.334		3					
				0.89	0.265		4					
				0.8	0.496	0.1	1					
				0.87	0.35		2					
				0.87	0.3		3					
				0.81	0.178		4					
				0.68	0.56		1					
				0.9	0.403		2					
				0.8	0.198		3					
				0.89	0.172		4					

Source Own

Table 3 Incremental freight discount model with n = 1–2 and m = 1–4

D units	P units	K \$	A \$	ICT \$	ICH \$	ICV \$	m	n	t_1 years	PC \$	θ_1 %	θ_2 %
10,000	50,000	10	10	0.93	0.751	0.1	1	1	1	2	10	10
				0.9	0.603		2					
				0.83	0.54		3					
				0.98	0.399		4			1		
				0.89	0.6		1	2		2		
				0.959	0.471		2					
				0.95	0.421		3			3		
				0.9	0.34		4			2		
				0.93	0.86		1	1		2		
				0.91	0.68		2			2		
				0.863	0.41		3			2	1	1
				0.85	0.282	0.6	4			3	90	90
				0.9	0.68	0.1	1	2		2	10	10
				0.9	0.504		2		2	2		
				0.9	0.315		3					
10,000	50,000	10	10	0.9	0.2719		4					
				0.480	0.379	0.1	1	1	1	2	10	10
				0.5	0.299		2					
				0.752	0.3		3					
				0.65	0.23		4					
				0.53	0.37		1	2	1			
				0.041	0.24		2					
				0.385	0.25		3					
				0.69	0.22		4					

Source Own

Solution: All units freight discount model [For $n = 1$]

Case with freight discount rate	Freight discount rate FC_j	Production batch lot size m	Production lot size Q_j	Buyer cost TCB_j	Vendor cost TCV	Total cost TC_j
$0 < w < 450$	1.5	1	447	15,671.361	223.498	15,894.859
		2	**447**	**15,559.490**	**111.735**	**15,671.225**
		3	447	15,630.178	74.501	15,704.680
		4	447	15,651.303	55.808	15,707.111
$450 \leq w < 550$	1.2	1	476	12,629.792	209.660	12,839.452
		2	477	12,524.877	104.813	12,629.691
		3	**477**	**12,497.068**	**69.851**	**12,566.919**

(continued)

(continued)

Case with freight discount rate	Freight discount rate FC_j	Production batch lot size m	Production lot size Q_j	Buyer cost TCB_j	Vendor cost TCV	Total cost TC_j
		4	477	12,527.746	52.337	12,580.084
$550 \leq w < 600$	0.9	1	592	9506.866	168.737	9675.604
		2	**592**	**9422.429**	**84.355**	**9506.784**
		3	592	9451.362	56.267	9507.630
		4	592	9558.392	42.219	9600.612
$w \geq 600$	0.6	1	603	6506.029	166.528	6675.772
		2	603	6491.698	95.386	6502.491
		3	**603**	**6415.595**	**58.497**	**6472.895**
		4	603	6468.791	41.405	6510.197

All units freight discount model [For $n = 2$]

Case with freight discount rate	Freight discount rate FC_j	Production batch lot size m	Production lot size Q_j	Buyer cost TCB_j	Vendor cost TCV	Total cost TC_j
$0 < w < 450$	1.5	1	447	15,447.790	223.462	15,671.252
		2	447	15,335.950	111.695	15,447.646
		3	**447**	**15,298.959**	**74.523**	**15,373.483**
		4	447	15,435.410	55.919	15,491.329
$450 \leq w < 550$	1.2	1	477	12,499.287	209.509	12,708.797
		2	**477**	**12,394.333**	**104.701**	**12,499.035**
		3	477	12,440.065	69.865	12,509.931
		4	477	12,478.590	52.401	12,530.992
$550 \leq w < 600$	0.9	1	592	9389.731	168.744	9558.476
		2	592	9309.845	84.349	9394.194
		3	**592**	**9281.695**	**56.226**	**9337.921**
		4	592	9369.432	42.165	9411.597
$w \geq 600$	0.6	1	603	6375.015	165.704	6540.720
		2	**603**	**6306.272**	**82.852**	**6389.124**
		3	603	6374.880	55.240	6430.120
		4	603	6435.708	41.453	6477.161

Freight discount model associated with incremental policy [For $n = 1$]

Case with freight discount rate	Freight discount rate FC_j	Production batch lot size m	Production lot size Q_j	Buyer cost TCB_j	Vendor cost TCV	Total cost TC_j
$0 < w < 450$	1.5	1	447	15,952.248	223.550	16,175.798
		2	**447**	**15,831.794**	**111.829**	**15,943.623**
		3	447	15,772.021	74.428	15,846.449
		4	447	15,948.493	54.688	16,003.182
$450 \leq w < 550$	1.2	1	476	15,629.970	209.474	15,839.445
		2	477	15,519.314	104.653	15,623.968
		3	**477**	**15,624.065**	**69.740**	**15,693.805**
		4	477	15,642.360	52.396	15,694.756
$550 \leq w < 600$	0.9	1	592	3135.090	168.896	3303.987
		2	**592**	**3090.807**	**84.348**	**3175.156**
		3	592	3111.631	56.265	3167.897
		4	592	3143.771	42.202	3185.974
$w \geq 600$	0.6	1	603	1223.081	165.676	1388.758
		2	603	1096.758	82.902	1179.660
		3	**603**	**1136.054**	**55.222**	**1191.276**
		4	603	1212.691	41.5055	1254.197

Freight discount model associated with incremental policy [For $n = 2$]

Case with freight discount rate	Freight discount rate FC_j	Production batch lot size m	Production lot size Q_j	Buyer cost TCB_j	Vendor cost TCV	Total cost TC_j
$0 < w < 450$	1.5	1	447	15,716.300	223.460	15,939.761
		2	447	15,625.678	111.770	15,737.448
		3	**447**	**15,585.232**	**74.454**	**15,659.686**
		4	447	15,629.220	55.834	15,685.055
$450 \leq w < 550$	1.2	1	476	15,417.084	209.569	15,626.653
		2	**477**	**15,311.944**	**104.751**	**15,416.695**
		3	477	15,421.385	69.786	15,491.171
		4	477	15,475.096	52.310	15,527.407
$550 \leq w < 600$	0.9	1	592	3074.397	168.684	3243.081
		2	592	3027.813	84.418	3112.232
		3	**592**	**3058.238**	**56.257**	**3114.495**
		4	592	3133.109	42.166	3175.275
$w \geq 600$	0.6	1	603	1143.678	165.723	1309.401

(continued)

(continued)

Case with freight discount rate	Freight discount rate FC_j	Production batch lot size m	Production lot size Q_j	Buyer cost TCB_j	Vendor cost TCV	Total cost TC_j
		2	**603**	**1076.325**	**82.889**	**1159.214**
		3	603	1040.415	55.259	1095.675
		4	603	1142.980	41.408	1184.388

As such in the incremental freight discount policy, with number of shipments from vendor to buyer as 2 and production batch lot size as 3 gives the minimum total cost with 1095.67 dollars with the optimal values as shown in Table 4. The eigen values of Hessian matrix at the optimal values for incremental freight discount are given by

$$H = \begin{bmatrix} \frac{\partial^2 TC_4}{\partial T^2} & \frac{\partial^2 TC_4}{\partial TQ} \\ \frac{\partial^2 TC_4}{\partial QT} & \frac{\partial^2 TC_4}{\partial Q^2} \end{bmatrix} = \begin{bmatrix} 0.001181 & 0 \\ 0 & 36.2054 \end{bmatrix} \text{ and } \lambda_1 = 0.001810 > 0,\ \lambda_2 = 36.2054 > 0.$$

Both the eigenvalues of Hessian matrix are positive. Therefore, the cost function is convex in nature. So, it is a positive definite matrix, and hence, total cost function is convex in nature.

5 Sensitivity Analysis and Conclusion

- By using Table 5, on varying the inventory parameters like the in-transit inventory carrying charge incurred by buyer and purchasing cost plays a vital role in declination of the total cost of the coordinated system, which is desirable. Incremental freight discount model gives the minimum total cost of the system. By increasing the m, n values, the total cost of the system decreases.
- The result analysis demonstrates that on imposing freight discount into inventory model results in significant reduction on total cost. Finally, it can be concluded that freight discount model associated with incremental policy gives important effects on minimizing the objective of system's total inventory cost.
- Some possible future directions for research are:

1. To uplift the demand of the firm, efforts for advertising and/or service investment can be utilized. 2. Learning effects could be considered. 3. Shortages can be considered. 4. Demand can be considered as one or combination of time, price, reliability or trade credit dependent. 5. Preservation technology investment can be utilized.

Table 4 Optimal values and total cost function in both cases

Case with freight discount rate	Case	No. of shipments from vendor to buyer	Replenishment cycle length T	Production batch lot size	Production lot size Q_j	Buyer cost TCB_j	Vendor cost TCV	Total cost TC_j
$0 < w < 450$	All unit freight discount	2	0.0603	2	603	6306.72	82.852	6389.12
\$0.6	Incremental freight discount	2	0.0603	3	603	1040.41	55.259	1095.67

Source Own

Table 5 Sensitivity analysis of decision variables along various inventory parameters

Inventory parameters	Decision variables	Percentage variation of decision variables				
		−20%	−10%	0	10%	20%
D	TCB	609.837	815.6	1040.415	1282.097	1538.822
	TCV	46.954	51.208	55.259	59.129	62.838
	TC	656.792	866.809	1095.675	1341.226	1601.661
	Q	567	585	603	620	636
	T	0.0709	0.065	0.060	0.056	0.053
P	TCB	784.255	916.517	1040.415	1156.818	1266.472
	TCV	57.813	56.493	55.259	54.103	53,016
	TC	842.068	973.011	1095.675	1210.921	1319.488
	Q	576	590	603	616	628
	T	0.057	0.059	0.060	0.061	0.062
K	TCB	897.699	970.468	1040.415	1107.722	1172.552
	TCV	45.412	50.397	55.259	60.005	64.641
	TC	943.112	1020.865	1095.675	1167.727	1237.193
	Q	587	595	603	611	618
	T	0.058	0.059	0.060	0.061	0.061
A	TCB	804.642	925.992	1040.415	1148.568	1251.020
	TCV	57.565	56.377	55.259	54.205	53.209
	TC	862.208	982.369	1095.675	1202.773	1304.230
	Q	579	591	603	614	626
	T	0.057	0.059	0.060	0.061	0.062
PC	TCB	1040.415	104.415	1040.415	1040.415	1040.415
	TCV	55.259	55.259	55.259	55.259	55.259
	TC	1095.675	1095.675	1095.675	1095.675	1095.675
	Q	603	603	603	603	603
	T	0.0603	0.0603	0.0603	0.0603	0.0603
v	TCB	2128.251	2111.160	2094.241	2077.491	2060.907
	TCV	42.070	42.271	42.471	42.669	42.865
	TC	2170.321	2153.432	2136.713	2120.161	2103.772
	Q	792	788	784	781	777
	T	0.079	0.078	0.078	0.078	0.077
ICT	TCB	2007.390	2051.481	2094.241	2135.738	2176.032
	TCV	43.366	42.912	42.471	42.044	41.630
	TC	2050.756	2094.393	2136.713	2177.782	2217.662
	Q	768.644	776	784	792	800
	T	0.076	0.077	0.078	0.079	0.080

(continued)

Table 5 (continued)

Inventory parameters	Decision variables	Percentage variation of decision variables				
		−20%	−10%	0	10%	20%
ICH	TCB	1566.987	1296.844	1040.415	796.731	563.754
	TCV	49.425	52.423	55.259	57.956	60.533
	TC	1616.413	1348.882	1095.675	854.688	624.288
	Q	674	635	603	575	550
	T	0.067	0.063	0.060	0.057	0.055
ICV	TCB	1040.415	1040.415	1040.415	1040.415	1040.415
	TCV	55.259	55.259	55.259	55.259	55.259
	TC	1095.675	1095.675	1095.675	1095.675	1095.675
	Q	603	603	603	603	603
	T	0.060	0.060	0.060	0.060	0.060
t_1	TCB	665.041	851.663	1040.415	−235.686	−231.526
	TCV	59.006	57.140	55.259	68.089	68.047
	TC	724.048	908.803	1095.675	−167.597	−163.479
	Q	564	583	603	489	489
	T	0.0706	0.064	0.060	0.445	0.408
θ_1	TCB	1046.731	1043.568	1040.415	1037.273	1034.141
	TCV	55.196	55.228	55.259	55.290	55.321
	TC	1101.928	1098.796	1095.675	1092.564	1089.463
	Q	603	603	603	602	602
	T	0.060	0.060	0.060	0.060	0.060
θ_2	TCB	1040.415	1040.415	1040.415	1040.415	1040.415
	TCV	55.259	55.259	55.259	55.259	55.259
	TC	1095.675	1095.675	1095.675	1095.675	1095.675
	Q	603	603	603	603	603
	T	0.060	0.060	0.060	0.060	0.060

Source Own

References

Abad, P. L., & Aggarwal, V. (2005). Incorporating transport cost in the lot size and pricing decisions with downward sloping demand. *International Journal of Production Economics, 95*(3), 297–305.

Baumol, W. J., & Vinod, H. D. (1970). An inventory theoretic model of freight transport demand. *Management Science, 16*(7), 413–421.

Chang, C. T., Teng, J. T., & Goyal, S. K. (2010). Optimal replenishment policies for non-instantaneous deteriorating items with stock-dependent demand. *International Journal of Production Economics, 123*(1), 62–68.

Wangsa, I. D., & Wee, H. M. (2020). Integrated inventory system with freight costs and two types of quantity discounts. *International Journal of Logistics Systems and Management, 35*(1), 119–147.

Darwish, M. A. (2008). Joint determination of order quantity and reorder point of continuous review model under quantity and freight rate discounts. *Computers and Operations Research, 35*(12), 3902–3917.

Datta, T. K., & Pal, A. K. (2001). An inventory system stock-dependent, price sensitive demand rate. *Production Planning and Control, 12*, 13–20.

Ertogral, K., Darwish, M., & Ben-Daya, M. (2007). Production and shipment lot sizing in a vendor-buyer supply chain with transportation cost. *European Journal of Operational Research, 176*(3), 1592–1606.

He, W. M., Hu, Y. H., & Guo, L. L. (2010). Model and algorithm of JIT purchase based on actual freight rate. *Applied Mechanics and Materials, 37–38*, 675–678.

Hou, K. L., Huang, Y. F., & Lin, L. C. (2011). An inventory model for deteriorating items with stock-dependent selling rate and partial backlogging under inflation. *African Journal of Business Management, 5*(10), 3834–3843.

Juhari, W. A., Fitriyani, A., & Aisyati, A. (2016). An integrated inventory model for single-vendor single-buyer system with freight rate discount and stochastic demand. *International Journal of Operational Research, 25*(3), 327–350.

Langley, J. C. (1980). The inclusion of transportation costs in inventory models: Some considerations. *Journal of Business Logistic, 2*(1), 106–125.

Mahata, P., Mahata, G. C., & De, S. K. (2020). An economic order quantity model under two-level partial trade credit for time varying deteriorating items. *International Journal of Systems Science: Operations & Logistics, 7*(1), 1–17. https://doi.org/10.1080/23302674.2018.1473526

Mahmoodi, A. (2019). Joint pricing and inventory control of duopoly retailers with deteriorating items and linear demand. *Computers & Industrial Engineering*. https://doi.org/10.1016/j.cie.2019.04.017

Maihami, R., & Kamalabadi, I. N. (2012). Joint pricing and inventory control for non-instantaneous deteriorating items with partial backlogging and time and price dependent demand. *International Journal of Production Economics, 136*(1), 116–122.

Mendoza, A., & Ventura, J. A. (2008). Incorporating quantity discounts to the EOQ model with transportation costs. *International Journal of Production Economics, 113*(2), 754–765.

Mishra, U., Barrón, L. E. C., Tiwari, S., Shaikh, A. A., & Garza, G. T. (2017). An inventory model under price and stock dependent demand for controllable deterioration rate with shortages and preservation technology investment. *Annals of Operations Research, 254*(1), 165–190.

Muckstadt, J. A., & Sapra, A. (2010). *Principles of inventory management: When you are down to four, order more*. Springer Series in Operations Research and Financial Engineering. Springer Science.

Panda, S., Saha, S., & Basu, M. (2013). Optimal pricing and lot-sizing for perishable inventory with price and time dependent ramp-type demand. *International Journal of Systems Science, 44*(1), 127–138.

Papachristos, S., & Skouri, K. (2003). An inventory model with deteriorating items, quantity discount, pricing and time-dependent partial backlogging. *International Journal of Production Economics, 83*(3), 247–256.

Qin, Y., Wang, J., & Wei, C. (2014). Joint pricing and inventory control for fresh produce and foods with quality and physical quantity deteriorating simultaneously. *International Journal of Production Economics, 152*, 42–48.

Rabbani, M., Zia, N. P., & Rafiei, H. (2016). Joint optimal dynamic pricing and replenishment policies for items with simultaneous quality and physical quantity deterioration. *Applied Mathematics and Computation, 287*, 149–160.

Rameswari, M., & Uthayakumar, R. (2018). An integrated inventory model for deteriorating items with price-dependent demand under two-level trade credit policy. *International Journal of Systems Science: Operations & Logistics, 5*(3), 253–267. https://doi.org/10.1080/23302674.2017.1292432

Rasay, H., & Golmohammadi A. M. (2019). Modeling and analyzing incremental quantity discounts in transportation costs for a joint economic lot-sizing problem. *Iranian Journal of Management Studies*. https://doi.org/10.22059/IJMS.2019.253476.673494

Shah, N. H., Patel, A. R., & Louc, K. R. (2011). Optimal ordering and pricing policy for price sensitive stock-dependent demand under progressive payment scheme. *International Journal of Industrial Engineering Computations, 2*, 523–532.

Singh, S. R. (2006). Production inventory model for perishable product with price dependent demand. *Reference Des ERA, 1*(1), 1–10.

Singh, S. R., & Malik, A. K. (2011). Two warehouses inventory model for non-instantaneous deteriorating items with stock dependent demand. *International Transactions in Applied Sciences, 3*(4), 911–920.

Swenseth, S. R., & Godfrey, M. R. (2002). Incorporating transportation costs into inventory replenishment decisions. *International Journal of Production Economics, 77*(3), 113–130.

Toptal, A. (2009). Replenishment decisions under an all-units discount schedule and stepwise freight cost. *European Journal of Operational Research, 198*(2), 504–510.

9789811621550